CROSSING *the Line*

NEW AMERICANISTS *A Series Edited by Donald E. Pease*

CROSSING *the Line*

Racial Passing in

Twentieth-Century

U.S. Literature

and Culture

GAYLE WALD

Duke University Press

Durham and London

2000

© 2000 Duke University Press
All rights reserved
Printed in the United States of
America on acid-free paper ⊗
Typeset in Janson by Tseng
Information Systems, Inc.
Library of Congress Cataloging-in-
Publication Data appear on the
last printed page of this book.

CONTENTS

Like race, one of the central concerns of this book, academic knowledge is a social product mediated by the very histories and cultures that it also translates and interprets. This study of U.S. cultural representations of racial passing is no exception. In the several years that I have been working on this book since its origin as a Ph.D. dissertation, "racial passing" has emerged as a site of knowledge-production within academic institutions, as measured by a proliferation of recent academic conferences, anthologies, and scholarly publications that touch on this theme. Moreover, many of the primary sources for this study—most of them previously obscure, hard to find, or out of print—have become so readily accessible and even familiar that it is easy to forget that their visibility is still quite novel.

Evidence of the rise of racial passing to prominence as an object of academic study is offered by the recent history of Nella Larsen's *Passing* (1929), a book whose reputation had languished prior to its 1986 republication (in a single-volume edition with Larsen's novella *Quicksand*) by Rutgers University Press as part of its American Women Writers series. *Quicksand and Passing* was introduced to readers by Deborah McDowell, whose re-reading of Larsen's work helped to broaden its appeal within feminist literary studies, American literary studies, and gay and lesbian studies. In the decade that followed, the book became the best-selling title in the history of the press. By 1997 it had sold a remarkable seventy thousand copies, generating enough revenue to finance the republication of other forgotten American women writers' texts.[1] That same year, in response to what was apparently a burgeoning market for Larsen's work, Penguin Books lent its Twentieth-Century Classics imprimatur to a new edition of *Passing*—this time notably published without *Quicksand* as a companion text.

If the "canon wars" of the last several decades have taught us anything, it is that texts acquire or lose status based on needs and interests extrinsic to their existence as aesthetic objects. In light of this observation, we can locate *Passing*'s rise to prominence at the crossroads of several trends: primarily, the efforts of black feminist scholars to counter the cultural amnesia that has affected the reputations of so many African American women writers, but also the rise to prominence of race theory as a field of scholarly production, the burgeoning of multiculturalism as a political and theoretical concern, the expansion of African American literary and cultural studies in higher education, and the training of an unprecedented number of scholars in the field who are not themselves African American. Each of these trends has a complicated history tied to distinct institutional, economic, political, and cultural factors. Yet their co-incidence suggests that the emergence of racial passing as an object of academic interest cannot be separated from the complex and multivalent institutional histories of American and African American literary and cultural studies.

Crossing the Line interrogates twentieth-century cultural representations of the fluidity of identities across the "line" of race, arguing that racial identities have been—and continue to be—important sites of negotiation and struggle in a society that vests enormous power in the fictions of race and in the notion of stable, embodied racial difference. In my analyses of racial passing narratives I establish the pliability and instrumentality of race, as it is lived through other, intersecting categories of identity. In particular, I highlight the enterprise of "crossing the line" as a strategic appropriation of race's power, emphasizing the stakes of such appropriation for racially defined subjects.

The findings of this study help to explain ongoing investments in "identity" at the turn of the twenty-first century. Indeed, for readers who bring to this book expectations shaped by a notion of the "free play" of individualized selves across socially produced lines of difference, *Crossing the Line* will inevitably prove disappointing. Such interest as this study has in issues of identity, moreover, cannot be separated from questions of my own position as a white female scholar working in the fields of African American literary and cultural studies. I was made particularly aware of this position several years ago, when after delivering a paper based on research that eventually became a part of this book, I was asked whether there was anything self-referential about my work on racial passing. Although there are a number of possible ways to interpret this question, as I understood it then, the questioner was asking me to clarify my personal stake in a project that seemed so intimately bound up with an experience of racial oppression that I presumably could not share. Implicit in this question were related questions about institutional practices, given that I was at a graduate student conference organized around the theme of African American studies.

My response to the questioner touched on the necessity of interrogating the work of identities, including "white" identities—an explanation that, in retrospect, strikes me as germane and yet also inadequate. The histories of whiteness and blackness as metaphors for different human "selves" are intricately and intimately interwoven, and I would hardly be the first to claim that in order to unpack these metaphors we need to understand "race" from the point of view of its beneficiaries, not merely those whom it defines. For me, part of the interest of narratives of racial passing lies precisely in their ability to demonstrate the failure of race to impose stable definitions of identity, or to manifest itself in a reliable, permanent, and/or visible manner. Yet in inquiring into how subjects have negotiated race, we cannot lose sight of the power of race to define. This means acknowledging "whiteness" as a means and an effect of racial transcendence that often enables its bearers to cross social and institutional lines.

I do not believe that these contradictions are easily resolvable; yet neither do I believe that they need to be disabling. Rather, we can use them to raise the important questions of affinity and solidarity, parasitism and gain, self-criticism and self-aggrandizement, that haunt our own theoretical praxis, particularly given the rise of the new "whiteness studies" as one of the "futures" of critical race theory. By the same token, though we should not be surprised that "racial passing" has come to visibility *now*—at the contradictory moment when race retains its power even as, in many quarters, the racial binary is increasingly subject to critique—neither should we forbear asking what the emergence of passing discourse brings to visibility, what it conceals. Of course, the project of "deconstructing" race is not a sure path to liberation from racial discourse. Yet neither is it clear that critiques of the black/white binary cannot contribute to the erosion of the authority of race, and hence to conditions that might allow us to live in a more just and equitable society.

ACKNOWLEDG-

MENTS

The number of people who have variously assisted, encouraged, influenced, reassured, scolded, or prodded me over the years (sometimes at the same time) is great, as is my debt of gratitude to and affection for them.

At Princeton University Andrew Ross and Cornel West oversaw the dissertation that served as the basis for this book, and I am grateful for their inspiration and example. Cornel agreed to advise me although I was in a different department, and I will remember our lively discussions as he negotiated innumerable phone calls, messages, and faxes. Andrew was instrumental in creating opportunities for me and for other graduate students in English to pursue work in cultural studies and popular culture; and while he offered ideas as well as friendship, he also encouraged me to see the value in finishing a dissertation.

At Princeton, too, I benefited from the examples and brilliance of my wonderful teachers, especially Kimberly Benston, Diana Fuss, and Wahneema Lubiano. Toni Morrison, who agreed to lend her time to a tutorial on "race" and American literature, read and commented on the seminar paper that eventually turned into a dissertation proposal. At the same time, much of the serious learning that I did in graduate school took place in the company of my peers. In particular, Gwen Bergner, Joanne Gottlieb, Janet Gray, Lisa Lynch, and Erin Mackie shared food and ideas in our feminist/Marxist reading group, and along with Judith Jackson-Fosset and Lee Talley shared their friendship outside of it. During and after those years in Princeton, Timothy Cottrell was unwaveringly supportive of all my efforts; and Sandra Yarock's encouragement was an anchor.

First at Trinity College and now at the George Washington University, I have benefited from the generosity, personal kindness, and intellectual camaraderie of my colleagues, especially of Maxine Clair, Miriam Dow, Jennifer Green-Lewis, Jeffrey Melnick, Jim Miller, Faye Moskowitz, Judith Plotz, Jon Quitslund, Ann Romines, Chris Sten, and Claudia Tate. As chairs of the English Department at GW, Chris and Faye have unfailingly supported my efforts as a scholar and teacher. Constance Kibler and Lucinda Kilby deserve my gratitude for their patience, assistance, and invaluable knowledge of the university. A GW Junior Scholar Incentive award provided funding that helped me through the summer of 1998 when I was working on revisions.

My greatest intellectual and personal debts are to Jennifer Brody, Patricia Chu, Andrea Levine, Melani McAlister, Daniel Moshenberg, You-me Park, Rajeswari Sunder Rajan, and Stacy Wolf. All of these friends and colleagues offered their support and encouragement, and Jennifer, Andrea, Dan, Raji, and You-me provided me with invaluable feedback on the drafts of various chapters. Cindy Fuchs and Josh Kun have been more than professional comrades; stealing time with them at conferences and talking music with them has helped to keep me sane. I have also learned—and continue to learn—a great deal from the wonderful graduate students at George Washington; I particularly wish to thank those in my fall 1998 Race Theory seminar. Thanks, too, to David Tritelli for his excellent research assistance.

Priscilla Wald and an anonymous reader at Duke University Press challenged me to live up to their high expectations, and I am grateful for their thoughtful and incisive comments along the way. Ken Wissoker has been a most patient and encouraging editor who early on evidenced a faith in my work that, in turn, spurred my confidence. For years my parents Max and Marlene Wald and sister Heidi patiently forbore asking me when "the book" was going to be done; I thank them for granting me that space, as well as for their pride in my efforts. These last several years I have been lucky, finally, to have enjoyed the love, wit, and friendship of Luyi Shao.

INTRODUCTION

Race, Passing,

and Cultural

Representation

Borders are set up to define the places that are safe and unsafe, to distinguish *us* and *them*. A border is a dividing line, a narrow strip along a steep edge.

—GLORIA ANZALDÚA, *Borderlands/La Frontera: The New Mestiza*[1]

We make our customs lightly; once made, like our sins, they grip us in bands of steel; we become the creatures of our creations.

—CHARLES W. CHESNUTT, *The House behind the Cedars*[2]

A benefit and a disadvantage of looking white is that most people treat you as though you were white. And so, because of how you've been treated, you come to expect this sort of treatment . . . falsely supposing that you're treated this way because people think you are a valuable person. So, for example, you come to expect a certain level of respect, a certain degree of attention to your voice and your opinions, certain liberties of action and self-expression to which you falsely supposed yourself to be entitled because your voice, your opinion, and your conduct are valuable in themselves.

—ADRIAN PIPER, "Passing for White, Passing for Black"[3]

In "White Like Me," one of his most popular skits from the television show *Saturday Night Live*, African American comedian Eddie Murphy conducts a mock-serious experiment in which he transforms himself into "Mr. White"—a brown-haired, Silly Putty–complexioned character who wears a conservative suit and carries a tan briefcase—and ventures out into New York City, endeavoring to "actually experience America as a white man." Beginning with sequences that depict Murphy being made over in a backstage dressing room and preparing for his role (primarily, it turns out, by watching the TV show *Dynasty* and reading "a whole bunch of Hallmark cards"), the skit follows him over the course of a single day, as he gradually uncovers evidence of a "secret world" of whiteness. First a white newsstand clerk insists on giving him a complimentary copy of the newspaper over his objections, and later, on a city bus, he finds himself amid a group of white passengers who celebrate the departure of the last black bus rider by partying to the song "Life Is a Cabaret," the music provided by an obliging white driver. In a final episode in which he applies for a loan at Equity National Bank, Murphy's character is rescued from rejection by a friendly white bank employee, who reverses the decision of an impartial black loan officer and immediately proffers Mr. White wads of free cash despite his lack of collateral, a current bank account, or even a valid ID.

Playing himself once again at the end of the skit, Murphy cites these results of his "experiment" as proof of the as-yet-unfinished promise of American democracy. Above all, he tells the audience, spending the day disguised as Mr. White has taught him that "we still have a very long way to go in this country before all men are truly equal." Then, without skipping a beat, Murphy follows up on this rather unremarkable observation with a more radical suggestion: racial passing as an answer to America's "race" problem. Reentering the dressing room where he was made over as Mr. White, Murphy reveals a row of black men and women undergoing similar "white" disguise. America may not be a land of equal opportunity, Murphy tells his audience, "[b]ut I've got a lot of friends, and we've got a lot of makeup." Then, with the familiar strains of "My Country 'Tis of Thee" welling up in the background, he delivers the skit's memorable punch line: "So the next time you're hugging up with some really super groovy white guy or even a really great super keen white chick, don't be too sure . . . they might be black."[4]

First aired in December 1984, at a time of waning public support for "race conscious" social policy such as affirmative action, "White Like Me" functions as a hilarious send-up of race in a putatively color blind America.[5] Updating and revising *Black Like Me* (white journalist John Howard Griffin's 1961 best-selling account of passing for black through the segregated South of the late 1950s), the skit gently spoofs African Americans' expectations of white entitlement and racial fraternizing by imagining such ridiculously improbable scenarios as the one in which a white loan officer eagerly dispenses cash to Mr. White. Yet as Murphy insinuates through his staging of these scenarios at politically reso-nant locations such as a bus and a bank—the former an icon of southern civil rights struggle, the latter a site of activism in the post–civil rights era—"White Like Me" also speaks to the realities that inform such ex-pectations. Ironically, the skit's conceit of "undercover" exposé calls to mind the actual strategies of investigation used by civil rights organiza-tions and public agencies to monitor industries (such as banking and real estate) that persistently have discriminated against racial and ethnic mi-norities. In pretending to catch white people engaged in various hyper-bolic displays of what George Lipsitz has called a "possessive investment in whiteness," Murphy's character thus calls attention to the pervasive-ness of both race and color consciousness.[6] He also humorously drama-tizes how in a society structured on racial hierarchy, a "valorization of whiteness," as Cheryl I. Harris terms it, may inform even the most rou-tine of social and economic exchanges.[7]

Yet "White Like Me" is not only a satire of racial hierarchy and hidden racial entitlement; it is also, especially in its narrative frame, a pointed inquiry into the visual protocols of racial classification. In the dressing room sequence that opens the skit, for example, Murphy moves beyond familiar racial burlesque to examine the assumptions about racial appearances written into the notion of color blindness itself. Drama-tizing the process by which he "becomes" Mr. White, he displays how whiteness is symbolized through an array of seemingly embodied signs, from "white" skin color to "white" ways of walking and talking. At the same time, by demonstrating the ease with which "whiteness" may be appropriated for his own interests, Murphy suggests that these signs of race may not be as secure or as reliable as they appear. Such critique of the fallibility of the racial sign becomes particularly pointed in the skit's closing scene, which conjures the fluidity of racial appearances as a threat to the stability of "white" racial authority itself. Here "White

Like Me" brilliantly evokes the radical possibilities of the body's failure to manifest, in its outward aspects, the "truths" that race would seem to represent. What if, as Murphy's parting shot and the very title "White Like Me" suggest, racially defined people were capable of appropriating "white" likenesses or appearances? How might "not being able to tell"—a prospect alluded to in the image of future Mr. and Ms. Whites—unsettle the social and representational authority of "race"?

The questions raised in a humorously contrived fashion by "White Like Me" resound in the "real life" performances of Adrian Piper, an African American artist and philosopher who has explored themes of racial passing in her creative and scholarly work on race. As a way of challenging the beliefs and prejudices of people who assume she is white, Piper had calling cards printed up, which she distributed to people who openly displayed racist attitudes they likely would have concealed from her had they drawn a different assumption about her racial identity. "I am black. I am sure that you did not realize this when you made/laughed at/agreed with that racist remark," Piper's card begins. "In the past, I have attempted to alert white people to my racial identity in advance. Unfortunately, this invariably causes them to react to me as pushy, manipulative, or socially inappropriate." Reversing the dynamics of racial passing, by which Piper has been made to pass involuntarily while her interlocutor has assumed his/her identity to be both stable and inviolable, the card concludes by establishing Piper's displeasure at having been witness to an "off-color" racial joke or comment: "I regret any discomfort my presence is causing you, just as I am sure you regret the discomfort your racism is causing me." [8]

Like "White Like Me," a prerecorded skit broadcast live before a national television audience, Piper's public and improvised performance impels us to scrutinize the work of racial boundaries in maintaining a certain racial "order." Capitalizing on her own experiences of being drawn into the circle of "whiteness" that Murphy's skit contrives to expose, Piper challenges the terms of racial representation, holding a mirror to others' assumptions about and *pre*sumptions of her and their "whiteness." Using her calling cards to call into question the stability of white identities, Piper furthers Murphy's critique by demonstrating how the racist joke/comment/remark functions as a means of white social bonding. By calling attention to the acts of or collaborations with racism that others allow to "pass," as it were, Piper's performance offers an interpretation of the dependence of "whiteness" on racist projections of the degraded "other." Finally, by underscoring the arbitrariness and frangibility of racial signs, Piper not only debunks the stability of race, but highlights her own ability to "disorder" the terms of white racial authority and privilege.

Contemplating Murphy's and Piper's performances, we are reminded simultaneously of race's power and of the possibility that subjects may undermine, question, or threaten this power through practices that mobilize race for various self-authorized ends. In both cases, race is represented in terms of its authority to define (that is, to ascribe identity, to assign the subject to a stable "place" in the racial order); and yet in both, too, the means of racial definition are shown to be susceptible to appropriation and rearticulation by those who are "normally" defined *by* race. Dramatizing their respective deployments of racial identity, Murphy and Piper portray race as both authoritative and unstable, dominant and yet usable. In short, each portrays a means of using race to challenge and complicate the social mechanism of racial definition.

Like "White Like Me" and Piper's calling card pieces, this study examines how subjects have sought to defy, rewrite, or reinterpret the scripting of racial identities according to the socially dominant narrative of the color line. As W. E. B. Du Bois famously prophesied, first in his address before the 1900 Pan-African Congress in London and later in his 1903 work *The Souls of Black Folk*, the fiction of this line has been of urgent concern to racially defined subjects throughout the twentieth century (and into the twenty-first), exploiting the notion of their visible, corporeal "difference" from a "white" norm to sustain and enforce social relations of white supremacy.[9] Arbitrarily ascribing race in accordance with the changing needs and interests of white supremacy, the color line has long served a variety of specific "territorializing" functions through its ability to impose and regulate social inequality.[10]

Yet as this study demonstrates, inasmuch as it depends on race to be stable, transparent, and visibly embodied, the very authority of the color line must also give rise to possibilities of racial transgression, or "crossing the line."[11] Such possibilities emerge, that is, to the degree that the dominant racial discourse insists on both the naturalness and the obviousness of what is essentially a social and cultural production. Exercising a "real" authority in the realm of social and material relations, the color line differs from a line drawn in the sand, a mark easily washed away by the changing tides. Yet its tenacity is not a sign of its absolute power. Indeed, the investment of the dominant racial discourse in the authority of a "line" that eludes stable or consistent representation is necessarily generative of contradictions that are also opportunities for challenging, appropriating, or unveiling its chimerical and arbitrary nature.

This book examines how such opportunities are both manifested and negotiated in racial passing, a practice that emerges from subjects' desires to control the terms of their racial definition, rather than be subject to the definitions of white supremacy. As implied in the African American colloquialism for passing that also lends this book its title, to pass is to transgress the social boundary of race, to "cross" or thwart the "line" of racial distinction that has been a basis of racial oppression and exploitation.[12] It is also, as this study argues, to capitalize on the binarism of the dominant racial discourse to negotiate the multifarious needs, fantasies, and aspirations that are mediated and expressed through the racial sign. Passing entails, then, not racial transcendence, but rather struggles for control over racial representation in a context of the radical unreliability of embodied appearances.[13]

As the foregoing definition of "crossing the line" implies, this study contributes to the emerging, multidisciplinary project of anti-essentialist racial critique through its focus on the *instability* and *fluidity* of racial representation.[14] I argue that racial passing can "work," in other words, only because race is more liquid and dynamic, more variable and random, than it is conventionally represented to be within hegemonic discourse. Even at close of the century that Du Bois predicted would be beset by the "problem of the color line," race is normatively thought to describe (rather than to construct) apparently observable (not actively "visiblized") markers of difference. As Robyn Wiegman explains, it is widely assumed that "even the inconsequential minutiae of the body speak the truth that race supposedly, inherently means."[15] The contradiction here is that race requires metaphor and thus is neither obvious nor unmistakable. Moreover, the social "effectuality" of race is largely determined by its ability to shape epistemologies of racial identity.[16] Or as Gayatri Spivak has argued in another context, racial "names"—names we are given and which we also put to our own uses—have histories that are not "anchored in identities but rather secure them."[17]

My project in the chapters that follow is to investigate how this instability and fluidity of race is negotiated in various exemplary cultural representations of racial passing. In particular, through readings of literary and cinematic texts that center acts of "crossing the line," I explore how the transgression of the black/white racial boundary is expressed in the form of cultural narrative. Such a focus on narratives of passing serves my contention, following the work of diverse literary and legal scholars such as Hortense J. Spillers, Dana Nelson, and Patricia Williams, that race itself must be continuously narrativized, or reproduced as a "true" fiction, in order for it to be made "real." [18] It also enables me to use methods of narrative analysis to illuminate the ruptures in racial discourse that are exploited, interrogated, and recuperated through racial passing. I am most particularly concerned with how passing narratives produce the sense of an ending or narrative resolution in the context of the contradictions that the subject-who-passes must inevitably confront in appropriating that stability on which the fluidity of "race" depends. In addition, in reading how these subjects negotiate the desire to pass, a desire that would seem to require their valorization of racial discourse (if not necessarily of "whiteness" or "blackness" itself), I endeavor to illuminate those "openings" which might also allow them to imagine new narratives of identity, agency, and subjectivity. In reading these narratives, I explore various imagined alternatives to the color line, even if these alternatives sometimes end up being no alternative at all.

In representing the enterprise of racial passing to be contradictory, self-defeating, or otherwise impracticable, the cultural narratives I examine actively grapple with the circumscribed efficacy of crossing the line as an "actual" mode of political or ideological critique. The instability of racial passing as a means of negotiating racial oppression and segregation is illustrated, for example, in two different works by Langston Hughes. In the first, a short story titled "Passing," Hughes critiques passing as an individualized practice that fails to address the collective nature of racial discourse, which derives authority from its ability to unite people of disparate origins and identities under a single "badge" of color.[19] Through the representation of the narrowly self-interested motivations and hurtful effects of one young man's decision to cut off ties to his mother and siblings in pursuit of a "white man's" success, Hughes satirizes passing as worship of whiteness as an emblem of social and class mobility. Even if the protagonist's decision to cross the line had been differently motivated, Hughes's story implies, the efficacy of passing as a mode of agency is undermined by constructions of color that render it beyond the purview of the "choice" of his family members. Whereas "Passing" represents race to be a fiction of identity,[20] it also suggests that the status of this fiction cannot be disengaged from a critical recognition of the impossibility of passing for the great majority of racially despised and degraded people. Because of this conditioning of the agency to pass on the "evidence," crossing the line of the visible body remains the private and individualized "dream" of the narrator.[21]

On the other hand, as Hughes observed in a 1958 *Chicago Defender* column, stories of passing might be sources of enjoyment and gratification to African American readers who could imaginatively revel in the prospect of "fooling our white folks." As Hughes makes explicit through his use of the possessive pronoun "our," the consumption of passing narratives—in the form of gossip and family lore, as well as in the more "official" forms of newspaper articles and fictional representations—also entailed the contemplation of owning that prerogative to name and possess usually assumed by whites. Moreover, insofar as racial passing was conditioned on white supremacy, it could be a resourceful—even morally justifiable—response to circumstances beyond one's individual choosing. As Hughes observed, "Most Negroes feel that bigoted whites deserve to be cheated and fooled since the way they behave toward us makes no sense at all."[22]

Notwithstanding the qualification of passing as a political project, following Hughes this study remains invested in the notion that cultural narratives of passing are productive sites for interrogating not only the dualism of the dominant discourse of race, but also the instrumentality of race to a wide range of projects, ambitions, and intentions. As I have begun to suggest, these representations do not simply reflect racial ideology, and yet they are intimately and inevitably bound up with it. Neither wholly subversive nor wholly complicit, they mediate desires that disrupt the crude opposition of racial power and racial resistance. In so doing, moreover, they encourage us to draw a line in our own critical and theoretical practice between the celebration of individualized acts of racial transgression and the discovery of a "way out" of white supremacy. Indeed, they illuminate the precise manner in which the color line operates as a collectivizing discourse that also encourages subjects' investment in national narratives of individual social and class mobility.

In contrast to recent arguments that conflate race and class—thereby problematically privatizing gender as a term of consideration in the analysis of U.S. social structures—my contention in this study is that racial, class, and gender discourses are mutually reinforcing and inextricably linked. Without white supremacy and racial patriarchy, I argue, racial passing would lack that particular "economic logic," as Harris puts it, with which it has been invested through "the historical and continuing pattern of white racial domination and economic exploitation" (277). For example, the raced and gendered class aspirations of Hughes's narrator in "Passing," or of the nameless protagonist in James Weldon Johnson's fictionalized *Autobiography of an Ex-Colored Man*, would be illegible outside of the social structures that authorize the economic authority of white men within the public sphere of socially legitimated work and commerce. Similarly, the desires of the female protagonist of the 1949 film *Pinky* are legible in the context of the history of the exploitation of the labor of African American women—a history primarily embodied in the visual frame of the film through the figure of Aunt Dicey, a washer woman who is also Pinky's grandmother. The argument I am proposing here presumes, moreover, the securing of U.S. class structures through what Spillers has ingeniously called the "American grammar" of race. As U.S. history readily demonstrates, the myth of a classless society, in which hard work and self-reliance may be depended on as the keys to individual success, is itself predicated on the racialization of African Americans as a "class" of non-citizens whose labor could therefore be exploited and appropriated.

The texts I have chosen to illustrate and explore these arguments date from the era of the New Negro to the early years of the civil rights movement, encompassing categories of high, low, and middlebrow culture. Mediated by the ignominious histories of racial segregation and racialized violence in the twentieth century, they force us to reckon with the ways that race historically has been used to manage and discipline *particular* (that is, gendered, classed, and raced) bodies. Equally important, they ask contemporary readers to consider their own political, theoretical, or ideological interests in race as a site of identification and political or cultural investment, its fictional qualities notwithstanding. I see this as a particularly urgent challenge today, in light of the emergence of arguments seeking to appropriate anti-essentialist racial critique to question the social relevance of race. In the academy, for example, literary critic and theorist Walter Benn Michaels has been among the most outspoken proponents of this view, arguing in a recent article, "Autobiography of an Ex-White Man: Why Race Is Not a Social Construction" (the title riffing on that of Johnson's *Autobiography*), that contemporary social constructionist critiques have perpetuated racial distinctions that might otherwise disappear were we to summon the collective will to renounce race as a philosophical basis of identity.[23] Asserting the logical impossibility of passing if we affirm that race has no biological basis, Michaels urges readers to "give up the idea of race altogether." "Either race is an essence," he declares, "or there is no such thing as race" (125).

Yet as this study endeavors to show, such arguments are only possible if we neglect the *dialectics* of identity, through which subjects appropriate "race"—a discourse they do not control—for their own needs, wishes, and interests. Furthermore, they are predicated on the notion that we may choose our forms of resistance to race, rather than face the necessity of constructing our choices and our agency out of the material of racial discourse itself.[24] Such investment in the "purity" of our resistance to race ironically contrasts the impurity of the racial binary, as well as, therefore, the practice of racial passing as a strategy of deploying this impurity to various "impure" ends. My point here is not merely to register the inevitable complicity of resistance, but to suggest that we focus on how this complicity is itself negotiated through social and cultural practices and texts. As I demonstrate in the following section, which explores the basis of passing in the "one-drop rule," the "problem" of the color line has always required that subjects produce resistance in the context of the narratives that define them.

ONE "DROP" OF BLOOD

As this study's opening epigraph from Charles Chesnutt suggests, race has the power to "grip us in bands of steel." Upon closer inspection, however, these "bands" are revealed to have been forged in history rather than nature, allowing them to change and adapt over time. Like the borders that both define and circumscribe the nation, the "boundary" of race is subject to ongoing contestation and mutation. Yet as both Chesnutt and Gloria Anzaldúa imply, these boundaries impose social distinctions whose power supersedes the fluidity and arbitrariness of racial representation. Indeed, it is precisely *because* it operates through representation that race acquires its authority to define.

It is with these insights in mind than we can begin to understand the significance of the "one-drop rule," the set of social and legislative practices that condition racial passing as both a social enterprise and a subject of cultural representation. Codified in the late nineteenth century, particularly in the years following Reconstruction, this rule designated as "black" any person seen as possessing even a single "drop" of "black blood," as determined by ancestry extending back (in theory, at least) an indeterminate number of generations.[25] According to the one-drop rule, for example, Chesnutt, a writer of diverse African and European ancestry (his paternal grandfather was a white slaveholder and his grandmother a free "person of color") and a man who was often taken for "white," was thus grouped together with people of dissimilar ancestry under the badge of "Negro" or "colored" identity. Although Chesnutt maintained that he belonged to a separate category of "mixed blood" citizens distinct from what he called "true Negroes,"[26] the binary logic of the one-drop rule mandated that if he were not "white," then he had to be "black." Such contradiction was of enduring creative as well as personal interest to Chesnutt, who never passed but whose work—including his novel *The House behind the Cedars*, from which the epigraph is taken—repeatedly centers the question of racial "customs" and their transgression.

In this novel the protagonist John Walden has a conversation with Judge Straight, a "white" slaveholder who traces his roots to some of North Carolina's first European settlers, on the subject of John's racial identity. The question under discussion is what constitutes "proof" of race: the visible "evidence" of John's complexion, which he displays by turning back his sleeve and extending his exposed arm to the judge, or the "customs" of North Carolina, according to which, as the judge paraphrases, "one drop of black blood makes the whole man black." By illustrating how Judge Straight's definition prevails in categorizing John, Chesnutt reveals how the will of the state (as embodied in the judge) ultimately trumps the "proof" of the visible body. Chesnutt's point is not exactly that John wishes not to be "black," but that he desires the opportunities denied him on account of the one-drop rule's fundamental asymmetry, by which a "drop" or even a preponderance of "white blood" doesn't render a person "white." Denied the sort of intermediate racial status that Chesnutt himself advocated (and which had flourished in certain parts of antebellum Louisiana, as well as in the slaveholding societies of the Caribbean and South America), John is thus defined according to a false standard of "white" racial purity, such standard casting his own identity as "impure."[27] Such definition turns out to be of urgent practical value for John, a shrewd and self-aggrandizing character whose chief desire—superseding bonds of personal loyalty to his mother or sister—is for wealth and social status.

As Chesnutt's novel demonstrates, the one-drop rule is a biologistic paradigm, enlisting the authority of scientific discourse to enforce the state's interests; yet formally as well as informally, it continues to structure racial discourse in the United States even as the dominant culture began to abandon "scientific" standards of racial definition beginning in the 1920s.[28] In the period under study here, the one-drop rule is crucially important to the enforcement of de jure racial segregation, which persisted until passage of national civil rights legislation in the mid-1960s. Indeed, the indispensability of the one-drop rule to Jim Crow practices was explicitly written into *Plessy v. Ferguson*, the case that became the national litmus test for the right of states to regulate the geographical, economic, and social mobility of those it deemed "black." In its 1896 *Plessy* decision, the U.S. Supreme Court not only found the defendant, Homer Plessy, guilty of having violated Louisiana's statute requiring the physical separation of white and "colored" "races" during rail travel (the statute in question being brazenly titled "An act to promote the comfort of passengers," which of course meant *white* passengers), but it also found Plessy—a man who in court had refused to identify himself as "colored," and who was described in court papers as having a "mixture" of "Caucasian" and "African" blood that was "not discernible in him"— to be legally declared colored under state law.[29] Hence the case that gave official license to the nefarious tactics of "separate but equal" also tacitly decided Plessy's identity, overriding his objections that employees of the Eastern Louisiana Railway were incapable of enforcing the Louisiana statute based on the simple visual inspection of passengers. ("We are not prepared to say," conceded Justice Henry Billings Brown for the majority, "that the conductor, in assigning passengers to the coaches according to their race, does not act at his peril.")[30] Demonstrating the power of official rhetoric to paper over contradictions in public policy and racial ideology, the Court would thus have to insist on the visibility and obviousness of the black/white distinction, even while publicly acknowledging the racial binary to be socially constructed.

The double entendre of the Court's affirmation of the railroad's power to identify where "the passenger belongs" is consistent with this book's understanding of racial ascription as a radically social practice (albeit one that cloaks itself in the mantle of "essence"). Moreover, it suggests that this practice is intimately bound up with questions of national identity, whether or not the agent of racial "naming" is the U.S. Supreme Court or merely a legal arbiter such as Judge Straight. National desire—that is to say, the desire to define as "citizens" only those whom the state exempts from racial definition—is thus written into the history and logic of Jim Crow, which by the mid-twentieth century would come to govern everything from railroad cars to restaurants, from jury boxes to Bibles "for colored witnesses to kiss."[31] Contradicting the constitutional ideal of a standard of "abstract," or depersonalized, citizenship, the imbrication of racial and national identity undermines the ability of racially defined subjects to imagine their "universality" through narratives of Americanness.[32] In *Souls* Du Bois famously coined the term "double consciousness" to describe an aspect of the psychology of racially subjugated people, who were forced to internalize this contradiction as a "splitting" of national and racial "longings": a division nowhere better illustrated than in the case of the writer Jean Toomer, who is well known to have insisted, following his literary success with *Cane* (1923), that he was not "Negro" but rather "just American." Whereas Toomer, who was legally "black" but able to pass by virtue of appearance, was merely claiming a right that "white" citizens took for granted, the context of "race," as defined by the one-drop rule, rendered his wish problematic. Unable to transcend the opposition of "Negro" and "American" identities because of the racial construction of national citizenship, Toomer felt himself forced to choose, such "choice" affecting his social and literary reputation, if not ultimately his place within African American letters.[33]

The one-drop rule is not the only standard of racial definition, yet it has disproportionately shaped the U.S. social and cultural imagination of race throughout the twentieth century and promises to affect racial discourse, I would argue, into the twenty-first. By representing "whiteness" as the absence of the racial sign, it has perpetuated the myth of white purity (a chimera that colors contemporary liberal language of the "mixed-race" offspring of "interracial" marriages).[34] In a complementary fashion it has rendered the political and cultural presence of Asian Americans, Latinos, and Native Americans invisible (or merely selectively and marginally visible), thereby enabling the hypervisibility of African Americans as that national "minority" group most often seen as "having" race.[35] Such emblematic "race-ing" of "black" people has produced various predictable "ethnic" antagonisms, as exemplified in the pitting of "unassimilable" and "unruly" African Americans against "assimilating" and "docile" Asian Americans; and yet it has also produced, in dialectical fashion, the political and ideological refashioning of the dominant racial discourse, with its pernicious narratives of the "tragic" determinism, congenital inferiority, and inherent undesirability of "black" identities. Such narratives are one reason why cultural representations of "black" racial passing have often been looked upon with anxious trepidation by racially defined readers. They additionally partially explain why such narratives themselves are so often concerned to represent passing as morally reprehensible, racially inauthentic, and destructive of bonds of family and community.

The unilateral nature of the one-drop rule ensures that in the United States "black" people disproportionately bear the burden of racial representation. Yet though it might follow from this that "white" people can have no pressing *social* interest in racial passing, as this study argues they have construed various cultural and political investments in "crossing the line."[36] A combination of complex cultural, economic, and political motivations, for example, inspired Janis Joplin, rock music's first female superstar, to model her stage persona after blues singer Bessie Smith. Giving the name "Pearl" to that identity she fashioned through the imitation of Smith's dress and voice, and through her identification with Smith's bisexuality, Joplin once told an interviewer that "being black for a while has made me a better white."[37] In this statement Joplin, who throughout her career struggled with and against the norms of bourgeois white southern femininity that had shaped her Texas girlhood, paradoxically references the stability of "white" identity as the product of an appropriation of qualities she romantically attributes to Smith. In claiming Smith's "blackness" as a conduit of her own "white" self-betterment, Joplin ascribes a moral efficacy to passing that centers the virtue and paradoxical selflessness of the "white" self. On the other hand, Joplin produces a critique of "white" purity in defining herself as a "white" woman who is also periodically "black." Assigning positive rather than negative value to "blackness," she violates the traditional moral symbolism of race, which opposes "white" purity and virtue to "black" impurity and vice. Whereas she still presumes race as volitional (a notion that belies her exemption from the very racializing imperatives that are constitutive of Smith's "black" identity), she also embraces a dynamic conception of race as an object of negotiation, not a static "essence."

Joplin's statement is shaped by the exigencies of her status as a white southern female blues/rock singer seeking to establish her voice in a burgeoning, male-dominated and male-defined rock industry. Yet it also exemplifies the moral, political, and theoretical dimensions of all passing narratives, not merely those that center "white" protagonists. Moreover, it establishes how these dimensions may fail to overlap, the cultural and political implications of her "becoming" black complicating the theoretical questions of racial fluidity and performativity that her statement brings to light. Critics of passing narratives have often chosen to ignore or simply downplay these discontinuities, producing a critical dualism of "subversive" or "complicit" passing that echoes the binary logic of race. As Joplin's statement illustrates, however, the desire to pass is rarely ever manifested as a monolithic expression of racial insurgency or self-interest; nor can the conditions or effects of passing be measured solely in "racial" terms. As this study suggests, Joplin's social location as a gendered subject is at least as important as her "whiteness" in shaping the terms of her cultural expression.

PASSING FOR WHITE, PASSING FOR BLACK

Just as Joplin's desire to pass is inseparable from the context that produces it, so in the following chapters my readings proceed from an assumption of passing as a historically and socially constructed practice shaped by the exigencies of Jim Crow and by the binary organization of racial discourse. Indeed, I find that the racial binarism, which distributes the burden of racial definition unequally, influences the very ways that passing has been imagined and interpreted within twentieth-century cultural representation. In particular, racial imperatives—or in the case of "white" identities, a relative *freedom* from such imperatives—

implicitly elevates "white" passing to the status of an educative and ennobling enterprise, while casting "black" passing as a form of racial disloyalty and ideological entrapment. This binary construction of passing explains why, politically speaking, passing narratives that center "white" subjects often depict passing as a progressive or at least a liberal undertaking, motivated by tacit esteem for "black" culture and identities, whereas those that center "black" subjects more often portray passing as narrowly self-interested and complicit with structures of racial oppression and domination. Whereas "white" passing narratives center the individual passer as social maverick, "black" passing narratives examine the status of individual acts of "crossing the line" in relation to the social and economic health of racially circumscribed communities. In contrast to "white" passing narratives, which embrace the efficacy of passing as a means of tearing down racial prejudice and establishing avenues of "cross-racial" understanding, "black" passing narratives cast doubt on passing as a form of racial "liberation," drawing on metaphors of concealment and disguise to highlight the compromised agency of the subject who "crosses over."

Implicit in this argument that the racial binary is itself narrativized in a dualism of compromised versus heroic representations of racial passing is a related claim that these different sets of representations are also profoundly and inevitably gendered. In particular, the following chapters demonstrate how the structurally disempowered position of the racially defined subject with respect to definitions of race is evidenced in the "feminization" of black passing narratives, while the social entitlement assumed by "raceless" white subjects over these same boundaries is reflected in the coding of "white" passing as a masculinized (and often masculinist) enterprise. I find such gendering of the narrative representation of passing most frequently expressed through tropes of domesticity and/or homecoming that take on shifting significance within heterogeneous social and historical contexts, but that generally cluster along lines of race. Hence whereas the closure of narratives of "passing for white" is typically predicated on the subject's self-recognition within binary narratives of race, a process of recognition that is conflated with a symbolic "homecoming" to black identity, white passing narratives —especially those of white middle-class male subjects—are contrastingly centered on the subject's ability to access passing as a means of leaving actual and metaphorical "homes" and symbolically disciplining the "other" as object of knowledge. In my reading of white jazz musician Mezz Mezzrow's *Really the Blues*, for example, I show how passing for black facilitates both Mezzrow's literal departure from the domestic sphere of his middle-class parents and his symbolic exodus from the Jewish identity that he associates with (feminized) expressive inauthenticity. In Griffin's *Black Like Me*, the subject of chapter 5, I explore how tropes of domesticity enable Griffin to maintain a stable distinction between "self" and "other" even as he occupies the symbolic space of "otherness" through his experiment in passing. Symbolically domesticating the "other" as such becomes a means by which Griffin crosses racial boundaries while constructing "blackness" as an object of auto-ethnography.

On the other hand, in *Pinky* and *Lost Boundaries*, the two cinematic representations I discuss, juridically black subjects are the objects of a redoubled trajectory of domestication, insofar as they must simultaneously embrace the logic of racial binarism (the title character of *Pinky* literally electing to stay at home in the process) even while they are constructed as objects of a gendered and racialized cinematic "gaze." The social imperatives that site the protagonists of these films within racial hierarchy also implicitly feminize them by centralizing the body as the ultimate location of their identity. The raced positionality of the passer as a subject to-be-looked-at (that is, to be scrutinized for invisible signs of "blackness") thus overlaps with the positionality of the gendered subject, whose identity is typically also imagined to be inscribed on (or in) the presumably sexed body.[38]

In arguing that narratives of passing are gendered, I am explicitly building on the work of scholars such as Phillip Brian Harper, who has argued that to the degree that the discourses of black racial authenticity are always gendered, then the subject who passes (that is, the racial subject who appropriates the discursive and ideological instability that dominant narratives must render invisible) is also fundamentally feminine.[39] Harper's persuasive claim for racial authenticity as a masculinized social construct sheds particular light on the high degree of self-consciousness about the presumed stability of gender and sexual identities, which is manifested in passing narratives that ostensibly centralize race and its relation to social or class mobility. Yet whereas Harper critiques cultural representations of racial passing for their "inevitable" recuperation of normative gender identities (for example, their insistence on the return to forms of conventional gendered domesticity for the "mulatta" and the foreclosure of potentially disruptive narratives of homosocial desire across the line of race), I read these narratives' construction of passing within the context of pressures placed on racialized subjects to establish gendered virtue in the face of stereotypes and myths of sexual deviance or promiscuity. Particularly in the context of representations of juridically black women faced with the (sexualized) "temptation" to pass, my claim is that racial passing also reveals the pressures to maintain and/or secure sexual and gender "respectability" as a means of *racial* self-assertion. To the degree that there is a correlation between the foreclosure of racial passing and the recuperation of socially normative codes of gender, I argue, such narratives also evidence the investments of white supremacy in the construction of the racialized subject through narratives of gendered and sexual deviance—especially through what Patricia Hill Collins names the "controlling image" of black women as Jezebels.[40]

In what follows I develop this and other arguments through readings of specific texts, situating the work of modernist literature with respect to that of various other kinds of cultural production. There is a sense in which modernist African American literary representations of passing have become overdetermined sites for contemporary scholarly debates about race, gender, class, and sexual identities; and though I welcome the broadening of interest in literary works that previously were either forgotten or marginalized, I am also interested in understanding how the social context and formal exigencies of literary production combine to determine the available cultural models for representing passing within African American literature. In contrast, the limitations of modernist literature with respect to the visual aspects of racial passing give way to the realization of different narrative possibilities for the representation of racial passing within cinematic texts, or in literary contexts that offer the possibility of illustration. I take up the question of passing and visual representation most pointedly in chapter 3, on the films *Pinky* and *Lost Boundaries*, and in chapter 4, on popular narratives of passing published in the black periodical press of the 1950s, and which occasionally appeared alongside photographs and quizzes testing the reader's acumen in discerning "white" people from those merely "passing for white." In particular, I suggest that the need of film to embody fictionalized characters who pass through the bodies of actual actors suggests that we may look to film for specific representations of the construction of race through visual representation. On the other hand, the status of film and magazines as objects of mass culture potentially imbues their depictions of passing with very different public cultural functions than those of more self-consciously literary works.

The centrality of traditional literary representations within previous analyses of passing has tacitly abetted the notion that the literature of passing is also culturally representative. My juxtaposition of literary, musical, cinematic, and journalistic representations renders visible the relation between cultural apparatuses and institutions and the racial passing narratives that are produced in and through them. Such a method also works to underscore the imbrication of racial discourse and modes of cultural representation, the latter of which are often treated as though they were racially transparent or neutral. Finally, my analysis of texts from different decades enables me to read passing narratives in relation to the developing, ever-changing discourse of race, which they mediate and represent.

Chapter 1, on modernist literary representations of racial passing by African American writers, confronts the gaps within literary scholarship that pits an ideological critique of the complicity of racial passing with white supremacy against the narrative analysis of what the theme of passing offers to African American writers producing literature within the context of white literary and patronage institutions. This polarity within the critical literature has, with few exceptions, disallowed for the possibility that narrative strategies are themselves ideological, or that literary narrative is itself conceived in and through the ideological constructs of race, gender, class, sexuality, and national identities. Taking as its starting point the notion of "home" both as a symbolic and an actual location that marks the limits of raced and gendered agency even while offering a site for such agency, this chapter shows how three modernist writers—James Weldon Johnson, Nella Larsen, and Jessie Redmon Fauset—represented racial passing in their fiction. I argue that the ideological instability of passing translated into an unexpected degree of narrative flexibility for these writers, who variously used the passing plot to construct tragic satires (Johnson), domestic parodies (Larsen), and, in the case of Fauset's short story "The Sleeper Wakes," narratives of burgeoning female political desire, negotiating in the process the notion that the rejection of passing signifies the foreclosure of agency. Such literary representations of racial passing elucidate how subjects negotiate agency, identity, and "freedom" within the terms of the dominant discourses that circumscribe their choices.

Chapter 2 uses the career of Milton "Mezz" Mezzrow, a jazz musician who got his start in Chicago in the 1920s, as the occasion for an extended critique of white Negro self-representation. The site of my analysis is Mezzrow's 1946 autobiography *Really the Blues*, ghostwritten by Bernard Wolfe, which memorializes his transformation from Milton Mesirow, the undistinguished, upwardly mobile son of Russian-Jewish immigrants to Chicago, to Mezz Mezzrow, a clarinetist and occasional tenor saxophonist who played with the likes of Louis Armstrong and Sidney Bechet. A narrative of Jewish assimilation gone awry, *Really the Blues* raises questions about the status of white participation in black culture, the voluntariness of white passing, the mediation of narratives of passing by masculinized discourses of white ethnic "difference," and the gendering of the white Negro enterprise itself. My chapter on Mezzrow engages these issues in the context of an analysis of the ways that the "voluntary Negro" (as Mezzrow called himself) must shroud the agency involved in his self-production, enacting a tension between individualist and collectivist discourses of race that the term "voluntary Negro" encapsulates. By tracing Mezzrow's narrative strategies in *Really the Blues*, I show how his text opens up a space for the historical analysis of the valorization of raced and classed "marginality" as a form of politico-cultural dissent. Distinguished by its extravagant display of mastery over imagined linguistic signifiers of "blackness," Mezzrow's text enacts, at the level of narrative, his own fraught exoticization of black identity and culture. Moreover, in a role reversal that ultimately erases the materiality of racial hierarchy, *Really the Blues* ascribes freedom to racially defined subjectivities, "discovering" in the romantic idealization of black male identities the agency, mobility, and musical virtuosity that Mezzrow believed eluded him.

Chapter 3 is concerned with cinematic representations that depict the social and economic mobility of racially defined subjects as a menace to the stability of the dominant social and racial orders. Focusing on two 1949 films, *Pinky* (Twentieth Century-Fox) and *Lost Boundaries* (Film Classics), this chapter interrogates the spectacularization and commodification of narratives of racial passing in the immediate postwar years, at a time when black subjects were rallying around the wartime con-

tributions of black male soldiers to mobilize opposition to racial segregation. Although both films capitalize on the spectacle of passing to
promote liberal narratives of political and social inclusivity that are consistent with a postwar Hollywood political agenda regarding questions
of racial integration, both also establish passing as the justification, in
retrospect, for further disciplining of the racially defined subject in the
name of national interests. Moreover, in both films, the embrace of inte-
grationist ideals is undermined by the use of white actors to play the
roles of the black characters who pass—a practice that, while conventional, also underscores the film industry's persistent reluctance to inte-
grate its own labor force.

Lost Boundaries, a documentary-style film based on the true story of
a New Hampshire family, centers its representation of passing within
a larger narrative of the patriotism of African American men, building
dramatic tension around the apparent conflict between their national
and racial identity. In contrast, *Pinky* represents passing within the
context of the young female protagonist's conflict between a desire for
marriage and domesticity, on the one hand, and loyalty to "race," here
conflated with labor and filial responsibility, on the other. Although not
explicitly concerned with war, *Pinky* nevertheless depicts passing as the
racially defined protagonist's interiorization of a larger, national narrative concerning the status of women's labor and their "proper place"
within a patriarchal society. Their differences notwithstanding, both
Lost Boundaries and *Pinky* envision a "solution" to the threat of "invisible
integration" as a redomestication of African American subjects—in the
former case, the domestication of the black family integrating an all-
white neighborhood, and in the latter case the literal domestication of
a black female subject whose ambitions threaten to exceed a patriarchal
script.

Chapter 4 provides a counterpart to this postwar cinematic representation of racial passing in examining literary representations that capitalize on the narrative of crossing the line to critique the racial exclusivity of the American Dream of upward social and class mobility. The
texts that I examine here raise the question of whether passing can ever
be recuperated as an aspect of a progressive cultural politics on the part
of minoritized subjects. In particular, this chapter studies the representation of passing in the incipient black magazine culture of the late 1940s
and 1950s, focusing special attention on middle-class black women's

confessional narratives. Whereas modernist literary representations and the Hollywood "problem" films equate passing with secrecy and internalized confusion about race, in this popular confessional literature, the "shame" of passing is recuperated as a means of constructing a newly politicized pride in black identity. As in the previous chapter on film, chapter 4 is concerned with visual representation, but in the context of mass cultural representations—from magazines such as *Ebony, Negro Digest,* and *Jet*—that explicitly position black middle-class consumers as their primary audience. A section of this chapter is therefore devoted to analyzing the cultural practices of these magazines, bearing in mind not only their desire to construct the "black consumer" as a new subject of capitalism, but their efforts to proliferate "positive" images of black achievement, affluence, and contentment in an era when African Americans were sharing many of the fruits of postwar economic abundance, including the loosening of segregationist laws and customs.

Chapter 5, which is explicitly concerned with passing in the context of the modern civil rights movement, considers white passing in light of the question of whether such an enterprise can be the source of white empathy for black experience. My exemplary text in this chapter is *Black Like Me,* written by white journalist and lay theologian John Howard Griffin, and a work that has been continuously in print in the United States since its publication in 1961. In Griffin's autoethnography of the weeks he spent in 1959 traveling as a black man through four southern states most infamous for their reactionary stances on integration, once again racial passing is represented as a heroic enterprise of white male self-discovery that is also predicated on the "domestication"—both literal and figurative—of black identity and knowledge. As an anthropological and literary performance of white racial benevolence, *Black Like Me* suggests the limits of passing as an epistemological strategy, as well as the limits of the discourse of cross-racial empathy as a liberal strategy of political alliance. At the same time, Griffin's own reevaluations of his "experiment" in passing (as he called it) raise the possibility that white attempts to speak for "minority" experience inevitably turn to strategies of silencing—both of "minority" subjects and of the very experience that such attempts purport to represent.

My analysis of *Black Like Me* is framed by the theoretical questions raised by the notion of "looking relations" structured in and through white supremacy. Griffin's passing entails a dual process of engaging the apparatus of vision: first, in his adoption of racial disguise (achieved through the use of medications, dye, and a sunlamp), and second, in his deployment of passing as a strategy of observing "others" as well as the self-as-other. The social construction of "looking" additionally informs the gendering of Griffin's experiment, which is explicitly concerned with the transcendence of both race and gender boundaries.

By the time that Griffin's book was published in 1961, passing was already beginning to "pass out" of style for African Americans, going the way of Jim Crow buses and segregated lunch counters, as one Doris Black argued in a 1972 article in *Sepia* magazine.[41] Black's prediction for the trajectory of racial passing in the post–civil rights era is that increasingly the only passing of note will be "passing for black." I interrogate this notion in an epilogue that considers current discourses of passing in an era of "multiculturalism" and the "blurring" of the racial boundary. In a brief discussion I explore the logic of "color blind" social policy and relate it to current discourses of affirmative action. In particular, I examine the claim that the legacy of racism is best transcended through strategies that reject identity politics in favor of the recognition and reward of "individuals," conceived outside of categories of race, gender, and the like. The questions I raise here concern the cultural imagination of social mobility in a context in which racial definition is no longer seen as an impediment to occupational or economic advancement. I additionally interrogate the assumptions that underlie the metaphor and the practice of color "*blindness*," arguing that neither adequately accounts for the exigencies of racial ideology. Finally, I examine a contemporary literary representation of passing—Danzy Senna's novel *Caucasia*—which critiques the concept of racial purity while acknowledging the dangers and difficulties of embracing volunteerist characterizations of the abstract, individual "self." Notwithstanding the complicated history of the color line, particularly in the contemporary era, Senna's novel speaks to the importance of ongoing and careful negotiation of concepts of race, racial identity, and racial definition.

With its exploration of the urgency that questions of racial identity continue to have in a racially stratified and color conscious society, Senna's novel sheds light on the danger of hastily embracing new millennialist prognostications of the approaching obsolescence of "race" in the twenty-first century.[42] As scholars of U.S. literature and culture, we need to be aware, in particular, of how notions of the social construction of race may be appropriated to discredit and trivialize our concerns as "identity politics," as if identities were not themselves the products of the histories they mediate.[43] At very least, that is, we need to practice a self-consciousness in the ways we use the concept of race and in the methods we develop to read race in cultural production, lest the practice of putting *race* in quotation marks as a sign of anti-essentialist critique become rhetorical. This study of racial passing narratives would not have been possible without this critique of racial essentialism, which has shaped U.S. literary and cultural studies of the last two decades. At the same time, in exploring the ongoing necessity of thinking through the value and costs of racial identity, it warns against the reification and appropriation of such critique.

Cultural representations of racial passing demonstrate that the stakes of struggles for the cultural ownership of identities are particularly high for those groups who historically have been least able to exploit the discourses of identity to express their own political will or social interest. For racially defined subjects, a strategic embrace of identities that are also sources of oppression may be a necessary precursor to the establishment of "lines" of safety and community.[44] For such subjects, "freedom" does not necessarily or in every instance lie beyond the veil of racial definition, in an ephemeral and problematically *disembodied* space that Du Bois describes, quite tellingly, as "a region of blue sky and wandering shadows."[45] At the same time, these representations confront us with the need to recognize how such interested mobilization of "identity" has invisibly and yet consistently served the interests of subjects who benefit from their exemption from the categorizing imperatives of race and gender. If we are interested in using the analysis of social mobility and agency as a potential tool of political mobilization, then we need to acknowledge that identities, though not etched in permanence or transcendence, nevertheless have multiple and competing histories, and that they likewise can be deployed to serve a variety of interests. In our analyses we cannot lose sight of the project of identity any more than we can fail to recognize identities as historically pliable and multiply articulated "fiction[s] of law and custom," as Mark Twain once put it.[46] Our analyses must indeed proceed—in the dual sense of "carry on" and "issue"—from such insights, situating critiques of identity within the context of a recognition of the work that identity historically has performed.

CHAPTER 1

> To Market, to Market
> To buy a Plum Bun
> Home again, Home again,
> Market is done.
> —Children's rhyme and epigraph to
> *Plum Bun: A Novel without a Moral,*
> JESSIE REDMON FAUSET

In 1926 Jessie Redmon Fauset decided to resign from her post at *The Crisis*, the influential NAACP house publication where she had served as literary editor since 1919. After seven years of energetically promoting the work of writers such as Langston Hughes, Countée Cullen, Jean Toomer, and Claude McKay, Fauset may have turned in her letter of resignation with the hope of securing more time to devote to her own fiction (her first novel, *There Is Confusion*, had been published in 1924). Yet if she harbored any such intentions, Fauset chose not to reveal them to Joel Spingarn, a friend and patron of the burgeoning New Negro Renaissance, whom Fauset solicited for help in finding new employment. In a letter to Spingarn, Fauset listed what she saw as her job prospects, in descending order of preference: to work as a publisher's reader, if the

pay were sufficient; to be a social secretary in a private family; to work
at one of the New York foundations; or to return to teaching French.
Knowing that her opportunities would be limited, she tactfully advised
Spingarn what to do if the "question of color" were to arise. "In the case
of the publisher's reader," she wrote, almost as an afterthought, "I could
of course work at home." [1]

Citing Fauset's letter to Spingarn in her introduction to the 1990 re-
issue of Fauset's novel *Plum Bun*, a work that centers an artistically ambitious female protagonist, Deborah McDowell writes that it "shows
Fauset combining an enterprising spirit with a sober, no-nonsense recognition of the realities of occupational segregation." [2] To this we might
add that the letter—and particularly Fauset's anticipatory offer to "work
at home" as a way of negotiating the protocols of a segregated public sphere—also resonates with multiple and subtle ironies. For one, it
anticipates the literary-critical legacy that has extolled Fauset for her
behind-the-scenes role as editor while casting a more equivocal eye over
her own literary production, which included four novels, children's
literature, and numerous short stories and essays. Echoing Langston
Hughes's famous description of Fauset (in his autobiography *The Big
Sea*) as one of the three people who "midwifed the so-called New Negro
literature into being," [3] scholars have typically assessed Fauset's "contri-
butions" to African American literary tradition in terms of her helpful encouragement of others. While protégés such as Hughes prospered,
Fauset would eventually be assigned to the ranks of African American
literature's "Rear Guard"—a term that paradoxically registers her importance in terms of her distance from the creative centers of modernist culture. [4] The self-seclusion suggested by Fauset's offer to "work
at home" thus resonates with her willingness to promote the work of
younger writers at the expense of her own literary reputation, which
suffered, by comparison, for being rooted in the genteel traditions of
nineteenth-century bourgeois domestic fiction, which it also critiqued.

We might also consider Fauset's proposition in terms of the capitalist scripting of "home" as that symbolic as well as literal location where
middle-class women are seen most to embody the private role that gender prescribes. Working "at home" as a publisher's reader is, of course,
not the equivalent of performing housework; nevertheless, the phrase
conjures the gendered construction of labor performed in the domestic sphere as nonproductive and therefore invisible. Her offer to work

at home thus links Fauset, a middle-class intellectual of old Philadelphia stock, with the majority of black women in the 1920s, who found their most ready source of employment in domestic labor, and whose "public sphere" of work was the private sphere of middle-class white women.[5] While it denotes the specific physical location where Fauset will do her editorial work, the word "home" is thus also suggestive of the place of black women within social hierarchies that delimit their agency within, and access to, the spheres in which socially visible and valued "work" is performed. Indeed, in Fauset's anticipation of staying at home as a condition of her work for a white publishing house, we can see these two spaces—home as a literal place and home as a symbolic social location— coincide and overlap.

Taking into account these convergences between the critical neglect of Fauset's published works, the construction of middle-class women's identities through domestic ideology, and the racialization of domestic labor through the restriction of African American women's opportunities for waged labor, we can begin to discern the multiple negotiations of power—the complex combination of resignation, self-discipline, and strategic resolve—involved in Fauset's offer to work at home. In particular, we can observe Fauset's resourceful response to her racial exclusion from the public sphere of literary production and "work" through the modes of gendered agency available to her via cultural ideals of middle-class domesticity.[6] As McDowell's use of the term "enterprising" suggests, she would indeed be reframing the privatization of her identity as a black woman in terms of professional and economic need and desire. In working at home, Fauset would be withdrawing from the racially segregated public sphere, even while deploying such withdrawal as a means of securing her role as a publisher's reader. Interpreted in this way, Fauset's offer to work at home is significant not merely as her pragmatic recognition of racism and gender discrimination, but as her resourceful appropriation of gendered norms and expectations of domestic virtue to assert herself as a black female intellectual, or "race woman." Relegated to a position of, alternatively, social invisibility or social marginality on account of both gender and race, Fauset contrives in her letter to fashion "home" as a space of intellectual productivity and cultural agency. Thus imagined, home, a space associated with the privacy and nonproductive labor of individual women, becomes a place where Fauset can continue to contribute to the collective project of "black" racial uplift, even while helping to secure the "room of her own" necessary to her own creativity.

The issues so powerfully evoked in Fauset's letter to Spingarn resound in the fictions of racial passing that she and her contemporaries James Weldon Johnson and Nella Larsen produced in the first decades of the twentieth century. In the three works I discuss in this chapter—James Weldon Johnson's novel *The Autobiography of an Ex-Colored Man* (1912), Fauset's short story "The Sleeper Wakes" (1920), and Nella Larsen's novel *Passing* (1929)—the issue of how racially defined subjects deploy race to their own ends and desires becomes a subject of narrative representation. In these texts the depiction of racial passing becomes a way of imagining the social and economic "wages" of whiteness (to use a phrase of Du Bois), and of envisioning, too, the rewards, stakes, and pleasures of a certain "chosen" identification with "blackness." In particular, all three texts offer readers sophisticated representations of the inevitable conditioning of such "choice" on factors outside of the subject's own, individualized choosing. In so doing, I argue, they also develop critiques of racial passing as a contradictory enterprise, one especially associated with the racially defined subject's cultural estrangement and forfeiture of opportunities associated with "home" communities and identities.

Although published over a period of almost twenty years, the texts that this chapter examines share a common concern with exploring racial passing as a source of political and ideological tension embodied in characters who quixotically seek "freedom" through the circumvention of racial definition. Each centers the development of an individual protagonist (or in the case of Larsen's novella, protagonists), juridically defined as black, as he or she confronts the implications—the rewards as well as the costs—of a strategic identification with whiteness. In all three texts, passing is shown to be a highly unstable means of transcendence, as each of the protagonists pursues a project of social and economic protection or "betterment," yet concedes an ability to mobilize this success as a "black" subject. Such contradiction, in turn, introduces a narrative instability that can seemingly be resolved only with the passer's rejection of passing. In Johnson's text this instability is allowed to prevail, as the male protagonist seeks an elusive solace in his success as a businessman and in the memory of his beloved wife, as she is figuratively reembodied in his two children. In Fauset's and Larsen's texts, on the other hand, the female protagonists are denied such "haven" in the fantasy of their economic and domestic success. Dissatisfied with the conditions of their domesticity despite the economic benefits of their marriages, both protagonists contrive to reestablish ties to the black communities from which they have, of necessity, distanced themselves. They do so in very different ways, however, and ultimately to quite different ends.

As this brief overview suggests, the interests and desires of the protagonists of these texts are quite complex. So, too, we might add, are the texts themselves. For one, they eschew idealizing representations of character, prompting readers to consider the limits and boundaries of their own identifications. Whereas each of their protagonists confronts exploitation and oppression (in the case of female protagonists, on account of race as well as gender), none is wholly a victim; indeed, all are the beneficiaries of a certain class privilege and power. Moreover, none of the narrative "resolutions" of these texts completely dissolves the instabilities, ambiguities, and tensions that the narratives raise. Even Fauset's story, ostensibly the tidiest in its conclusion, cannot neatly answer questions posed by the female protagonist's decision to sacrifice wealth and social status for a seemingly more humble dedication to her "people." Finally and most important, the figure of "passing" in these texts is produced and mediated not only through race, but through a variety of social discourses, especially class and sexuality. This is most explicit in Larsen's novel, the title of which is left radically ambiguous as a means of inviting multiple and even contradictory readings.

In highlighting the complicated set of factors that motivates each character to pursue and/or reject passing as an "alternative" to racial definition, I position my readings of these texts in relation to analyses that have argued for their overdetermination by racial ideology. As I show, however, although these texts are inscribed by race, inasmuch as it is the condition of their representations of passing, the narratives they construct are not therefore defined in the last instance by racial discourse. Written when conditions of racial segregation were encouraging many middle-class African Americans to embrace the political project of racial "uplift" as a means of encouraging collective prosperity and self-sufficiency, they represent the individual as well as collective value of the embrace of an imposed racial categorization. By centering the experiences of protagonists afforded a certain prerogative to choose what the one-drop rule has presumably already decided for them, they dramatize the process by which individual agency is negotiated in the context of prevailing social imperatives and restraints, including the ever-present threat of gendered racial violence (rape and lynching). In so doing, they also explore — through negative as well as positive example — the possibility that these imperatives might be reclaimed or refashioned as sources of collective mobility and "racial" affirmation.

LITERARY REPRESENTATION, RACIAL IDEOLOGY, AND THE "PASSING PLOT"

It is precisely because they grapple with such issues as the strategic embrace of subjects' gendered and classed racial identities that modernist passing narratives have acquired a certain significance within contemporary literary-critical debates about the power of racial ideology. In particular, feminist scholars of the last several decades have focused on such fictions of passing to critique racial essentialism, explore the representation of black female sexuality, and (especially in the cases of works by Larsen and Fauset) to reevaluate the previously overlooked or critically disparaged literary production of early-twentieth-century African American women. In this section, I identify and briefly examine two strands of such recent feminist scholarship, one of which has been concerned with African American women writers' strategic deployment of the "passing plot," the other of which explores the narrative limitations of this plot as, ultimately, a reflection of race and gender ideology. My concern here is to argue that so long as we valorize passing narratives according to their success in imagining the transcendence of social definition, we are bound to be disappointed by them. On the other hand, by approaching these narratives with the idea that they are concerned with questioning and redefining "transcendence" itself, then we begin to see how they elucidate the mobilization of social definition to articulate needs and interests that do not merely respond to or replicate the wishes of the dominant culture.

One of the first critical texts to explicitly broaden the terms by which scholars could understand the literary representation of racial passing was *Reconstructing Womanhood* (1987), Hazel Carby's pathbreaking study of African American women novelists in the nineteenth and early twentieth centuries. There Carby offers a compelling analysis of the preponderance of so-called mulatto protagonists in black women's turn-of-the-century literature in direct response to previous scholars' indictment of these characters/texts as "politically unacceptable."[7] Arguing that earlier criticism neglected the specific social and artistic restraints imposed on black women, Carby foregrounds the narrative function of such "mulatto" characters to the cultural and political work of black women's fictional texts. Reading the "mulatto" as "a narrative figure" who serves as both "a vehicle for an exploration of the relationship between the races and, at the same time, an expression of the relationship between the races," Carby argues that this figure "should be understood and analyzed as a narrative device of mediation" (89). Accordingly, she posits racial passing as a useful "narrative mechanism": a means of literary representation that enabled black women writers to transgress the boundaries that delimited the "proper sphere" of their storytelling (158). "The device that allowed a white character to darken his skin and move about the black community in popular fiction had no equivalent that would allow black characters equal access to white society, which could be accomplished only by the creation of a narrative of 'passing' " (147–48), she writes in a discussion of Pauline Hopkins's serialized novel *Hagar's Daughter* (1901–2). "Consideration of the formal aspects of 'whiteness' as disguise problematizes interpretations which consider the representation of white-looking black characters as an indication of acquiescence in dominant racist definitions of womanhood and beauty" (148).

Carby's arguments concerning the narrative deployment of racial passing echo the claims put forth by Deborah McDowell, in a widely influential 1986 essay on Larsen's *Passing* that spurred scholarly interest in Larsen's work.[8] Focusing on the explicitly eroticized relationship between Larsen's two female protagonists—as it is filtered through the narrative consciousness of one of these characters, Irene—McDowell similarly works to recuperate *Passing* from decades of critical neglect through an emphasis on the text's modernist articulations of ambiguity and irony. McDowell's argument is essentially that *Passing* passes, cloaking an artistically and politically risky exploration of black women's sexuality and sexual desire under the more conventional guise of the passing plot.[9] As McDowell explains it, Larsen "uses a technique found commonly in narratives by Afro-American and women novelists with a 'dangerous' story to tell: 'safe' themes, plots, and conventions are used as the protective cover underneath which lie more dangerous subplots. Larsen envelops the subplot of Irene's developing if unnamed and unacknowledged desire for Clare in the safe and familiar plot of racial passing. Put another way, the novel's clever strategy derives from its surface theme and central metaphor—passing."[10] McDowell raises a similar point in a subsequent analysis of Fauset's novel *Plum Bun*, claiming that it "displays a progressiveness and daring that few critics have noted." "As in so many novels written by women, blacks, and other members of 'literary subcultures,'" she writes, "indirect strategies and narrative disguise become necessary covers for rebellious and subversive concerns. Such writers often employ literary and social conventions that function as a mask behind which lie decidedly unconventional critiques."[11]

In distinguishing the narrative mechanism of racial passing from passing as a narrative subject, McDowell, like Carby, highlights the narrative agency of literary form and convention in mediating the cultural agency of black women writers.[12] Such distinction in turn enables both critics to make strong cases for revisionist readings of late-nineteenth- and early-twentieth-century passing narratives based on the argument that black women writers, facing considerable artistic and social restraint, appropriated literary forms and conventions as a means of cultural critique. And yet though it sets out to remedy the trivializing dismissal of black women's texts, such a formalist interpretation ultimately recuperates aspects of the earlier disapproval of the passing plot. For example, in her essay on *Plum Bun* McDowell echoes Robert Bone, a critic whose lack of admiration for Fauset helped to establish her as a "minor" figure, in asserting that "on its face *Plum Bun* . . . seems to be just another novel of racial passing"—a comment that insinuates a category of "minor" passing fiction. Later she repeats the point (again under the pretext of defending against the trivialization of Fauset's work), arguing that "[w]hile *Plum Bun* certainly displays the most salient features of the novel-of-passing, to read it simply as such is to miss its complex treatment of the intricacies of gender oppression, as well as the irony and subtlety of its artistic technique."[13] Ann duCille's *The Coupling Convention* (1993) takes this claim a step further in suggesting "that each of Fauset's novels transcends both its passing theme and its traditional form to become a novel of female and social development."[14]

My point here is not to dispute the rearticulation of dominant social standards and cultural forms as an important—perhaps even a preeminent—aspect of black women's literary production in the late nineteenth and early twentieth centuries. Given what we know about the cultural biases against black women artists, the racial politics of publishing, the pressures exerted by patriarchal expectations of women's writing, and a tradition of African American women's circumlocution and appropriation dating back at least to Harriet E. Wilson's *Our Nig* (1859) (indeed, to Phillis Wheatley), it would seem absurd to conclude otherwise. Yet in predicating the critical recuperation of black women's texts on the degree to which these writers "transcend" their own strategic depictions of racial passing, such revisionist scholarship assumes the "passing plot" as literary formula, downplaying identity as an object of critical interrogation. Moreover, and contrary to intention, insistence on the utility of passing to various "hidden" and/or subversive interrogations of gender, sexuality, and class obfuscates the mutual construction of such identity categories through racial discourse. Indeed, such framing of passing as a narrative contrivance belies anxieties about form and convention that previously were used to disparage black women's cultural production.

Whereas Carby and McDowell establish the "passing plot" as a formal instrument of black women novelists' critique of gender ideology, Valerie Smith and Phillip Brian Harper contrastingly assert the complicity of such "classic" passing texts with the normative scripts of both gender and race.[15] Smith makes this argument most directly, asserting that "[t]he narrative trajectories of classic passing texts are typically predetermined" by the master narrative of the one-drop rule, which dictates that the protagonists of these fictions must inevitably embrace a "black" identity as a condition of narrative closure. Insofar as these modern literary works fail to recognize "the intersectionality of race and gender," she argues, they "so fully naturalize certain givens that they mask a range of contradictions inherent within them."[16] Among these "givens" Smith points to the assumption of the "blackness" of the characters who pass, as well as to the frequent equation of "whiteness" with wealth. For Smith such representations ultimately reproduce "race" as a *social* (that is, not merely a narrative) imperative; they are "sites where antiracist and white supremacist ideologies converge, encouraging their black readers to 'stay in their places'" through the cultural opposition of passing with norms of racial authenticity and health.[17]

Situating the analysis of racial passing narratives within the context of a broad exploration of the gendered construction of "black" racial authenticity, Harper elaborates on this point, finding that such narratives "inevitably . . . support a conservative gender politics wherein black masculinity itself is conceived as fundamentally problematic."[18] Like Carby, Harper examines the cultural production and representation of the "tragic mulatta," arguing that passing narratives uphold the patriarchal construction of racial authenticity through their convention of racial "homecoming." For female protagonists, he claims, such narrative denouement typically reinscribes traditional notions of women's "place" within the home and their exclusion from the public sphere of commerce. The potentially radical interrogations of race and gender initiated by these narratives are thus ultimately foreclosed, according to Harper, in the texts' concession to patriarchal and heteronormative imperatives.

Whereas "revisionist" criticism overstates the mechanism of passing as a means of recuperating black women's texts, such ideological critique is perhaps more troubling in its claim—explicit and tacit—that passing narratives are racially determined. Smith's reading pits the "subversive" deployment of passing in contemporary cinematic narratives against its fundamentally conservative uses in modernist novels, which she claims downplay gender critique in order to recuperate a certain formulaic "public" narrative of race. Yet in arguing that the demand for politically stable "black" identities ultimately takes priority and even outweighs other interests, both Smith and Harper foreclose the possibility that passing narratives can amount to more than a cultural expression of race's power, including its power over gender. Both reject, in other words, a stronger reading of the varied (and often inconsistent) motivations that drive the protagonists of these texts. As a result, resistance to racial definition remains at best a remote possibility in these readings, which tacitly repeat the gesture of reducing passing to a formula. Once again, racial passing is construed as an obstacle to be transcended rather than as a site for the interrogation of racial transcendence as an important fantasy or desire.

As an alternative to readings that assert the "inevitability" of the complicity of passing narratives with racial ideology, I propose a method of interpretation that foregrounds the narrative representation of classed and gendered "racial" desire. Such an approach assumes neither the artistic limitation of the "passing plot" (a move that ironically subordinates race as a narrative concern), nor the ideological supremacy of the one-drop rule (a move that elevates race as a determining aspect of representation), but instead endeavors to understand how literary passing narratives thematize the fluidity and mutability of the "line" between capitulation and surrender, particularly for those gendered subjects who may be cast as outsiders to the sphere of overtly "political" resistance to racial definition.

To argue for the complexity and occasional irresolution of these texts is to reject the narrowly "racial" reading that both strands of feminist scholarship explicitly disavow, and instead to embrace the "intersectionality" that Smith proposes. This means, too, abandoning the notion that these texts are consistently or even necessarily critical of dominant discourses. Indeed, given the contradiction of the one-drop rule, which simultaneously constructs the possibility of "crossing the line" yet stabilizes the racial binary through the notion of "black" blood, we should expect that the complicity of identity with race will persist in some form in these narratives, whether or not their protagonists "choose" to pass. Indeed, in explicitly critiquing their protagonists' individualized choices, literary passing narratives build a critique of passing based on a theoretical and political cognizance of the collectivizing dimensions of racial discourse. In light of the fact that African Americans' choices were circumscribed by segregation (no matter their class, professional, or gender privilege), it is no wonder that racial passing was so prevalent a theme within the literary imagination of early-twentieth-century African American writers.

THE AUTOBIOGRAPHY OF AN EX-COLORED MAN AND
THE SATIRE OF "BLACK" MASCULINITY

I begin my discussion of specific texts by turning first to Johnson's *The Autobiography of an Ex-Colored Man*, a work that has the distinction of being not merely the first novel in the African American tradition to centralize the subjectivity of the protagonist who passes, but the first work by an African American writer to feature a sustained first-person narration.[19] Originally published anonymously in 1912 and then reprinted (with Johnson's authorship acknowledged) in 1926, at the height of the New Negro Renaissance, Johnson's text constructs a tragic satire of the collective fantasy of heroic black masculinity promulgated by such precursor texts as Frederick Douglass's 1845 *Narrative*, Booker T. Washington's *Up From Slavery* (1901), and W. E. B. Du Bois's *The Souls of Black Folk* (1903).[20] The *Autobiography* is frequently cited as a "prototypical" modernist passing novel—as the "classic" twentieth-century text against which all are judged—and yet as a work that centers on the failure of the nameless protagonist to live up to the standards of racial self-assertion associated with the heroic tradition, it also diverges from the narrative of racial "homecoming" that more typically signifies the successful resolution of the passing plot. Instead, Johnson's text renders the possibility of such homecoming outside the scope of its narration, which is told from the viewpoint of a protagonist (significantly, an *ex*-colored man) who has permanently "crossed the line."

As a result, the *Autobiography* both thematizes, and is actively structured by, a nostalgia for closure that lies forever beyond the unnamed narrator's reach. Try as he might, the "ex-colored" protagonist of Johnson's text is unable to assuage the "vague feeling of unsatisfaction, of regret, of almost remorse" (1–2) that haunts his narrative, depriving his voice of interiority and depth. Moreover, rather than fulfill the ex-colored man's desire for closure, the autobiographical enterprise, usually associated with the narrative production of a stable self, accentuates the instability of the ex-colored man's "I" through the circularity of his narration. Like the protagonist, who must merely reproduce his failure to secure a stable raced or gendered identity in the process of autobiographical narration, Johnson's text ends where it begins: in dissatisfaction and sorrow, as the ex-colored man contemplates his "yellowing manuscripts," "the only tangible remnants of a vanished dream, a dead ambition, a sacrificed talent" (154).

In its view of the protagonist as a failed "race man," the *Autobiography* explicitly engages the early-twentieth-century ideology of racial uplift. As Kevin Gaines has explained, racial uplift names that belief system that casts African American economic, educational, and professional elites as standard-bearers of the "race," and hence as prototypes for the social and economic rehabilitation of the "black masses," including the thousands of worker-migrants from the rural South.[21] In addition to imagining a solution to the collective experience of racial subordination and social exclusion in explicitly classed terms (bourgeois values and standards being those assigned political and ideological priority), racial uplift underwrote racializing national ideologies of progress and "civilization" that were implicated in the elevation of norms of gendered and classed domestic virtue as the political standards of "black womanhood." A response to de jure racial segregation, which imposed blanket restrictions on African Americans' citizenship rights, racial uplift ideology enforced self-imposed measures of racial authenticity and community, enshrining ideals of progress on the shifting and unstable grounds of "race." Yet racial uplift is more than a historical "backdrop" for Johnson's narrative; it is that specific class, national, and gender discourse of race that mediates his representation of the ex-colored man's "failure." By "mediates," I mean that it cuts both ways: Just as it is through the lens of racial uplift that the *Autobiography* interprets and critiques the ex-colored man's desire, so it is through the lens of this desire that the novel interrogates the project of "uplifting the race."

Throughout Johnson's text the central dilemma the narrator faces is how to reconcile legally and socially contradictory "birthrights," the first of which is associated with a musical tradition passed on to him by his mother, through her singing of spirituals and her encouragement of her son's musical talents; the second of which is associated with the economic and social entitlements of "white" patrilineal inheritance that are denied the ex-colored man although he is descended from "the best blood" of the South. This dilemma is seemingly resolved when, more than three-quarters of the way into his narration, the ex-colored man hears a German pianist improvise on a ragtime song in order to produce a "classical" piece. Inspired by the German's example, the narrator resolves to travel through the southern United States to conduct a study of black musical traditions, intending to put his talents to use as a "colored composer" of classical music based on "Negro" themes. Yet the prospect of narrative and personal closure that such a plan promises is abruptly interrupted when in the course of his travels the ex-colored man becomes the unwitting witness to the lynching of a black man:

> Before noon they brought him in. Two horsemen rode abreast; between them, half dragged, the poor wretch made his way through the dust. His hands were tied behind him, and ropes around his body were fastened to the saddle horns of his double guard. . . . Have you ever witnessed the transformation of human beings into savage beasts? Nothing can be more terrible. A railroad tie was sunk into the ground, the rope was removed, and a chain brought and securely coiled around the victim and the stake. There he stood, a man only in form and stature, every sign of degeneracy stamped upon his countenance. His eyes were dull and vacant, indicating not

a single ray of thought. Evidently the realization of his fearful fate had robbed him of whatever reasoning power he possessed. He was too stunned and stupefied even to tremble. (136)

The scene of the lynching, which Johnson based on his own experiences as a witness to lynchings as an NAACP representative, intrudes into the narrative in multiple ways. Not only does it literally interrupt the ex-colored man's travels, but it disrupts his fantasy of recuperating a stable "black" self through a self-conscious immersion in black musical traditions. More important, through the spectacle of the lynching the narrator himself is violently confronted with the contradiction of his own noncitizenship in a country that promises to be "the great example of democracy to the world" (137). In so doing, it therefore also unsettles the ex-colored man's fantasy that national identity affords him protection from racist violence, which is paradoxically committed in the name of national identity and authenticity. In spectacular fashion it demonstrates the predication of the national narrative on such secular rituals of racial "purification"—rituals that symbolically transform the African American male body (in this case) into a "beastly" presence that must be expelled.

The heroic tradition of black male autobiography—and, we might add, the ideology of racial uplift—require that the raced male subject resolve these contradictions around issues of citizenship at the level of *identity*. That is, they require the raced male subject to discover a solution to the problem of his noncitizenship (here rendered in particularly violent form) through the recuperation and/or rescripting of black masculinity. Within the tradition of black male autobiography, for example, Douglass uses the occasion of his violent physical confrontation with Mr. Covey, the notoriously sadistic "slave breaker," in order to reconstruct his social subjectivity within the space of his narration. "You have seen how a man was made a slave," he addresses the reader; now "you shall see how a slave was made a man."[22] More particularly, in drawing blood from Covey, Douglass effects the "glorious resurrection" not just of his spirit but of his masculinity, gaining retribution for the traumatic moment, early in his life, when he is forced to witness the brutal, sexualized whipping of his aunt Hester.

Whereas Douglass represents the fight with Covey in terms of the physical and moral triumph of black masculinity over white supremacy (as he reminds the reader, Covey never bothers him again), Walter White, the blond-haired, blue-eyed civil rights leader and longtime NAACP general secretary, depicts his own encounter with a white mob during the 1906 Atlanta riots as a benchmark of his identity-formation as a raced subject. In his 1948 autobiography *A Man Called White*, White recounts how he and his father readied themselves to confront the mob as its members stormed into their neighborhood threatening to burn down "the nigger mail carrier's" [White's father's] house.[23] White, who was then thirteen, portrays the scene in which he crouches in the darkened living room clutching a loaded gun not only as a crucial moment in his gendered coming-of-age (with his mother and sisters sent away for their protection, White and his father are "the only males in the house") but as a decisive turning point in his racial self-conception: "In that instant," he writes, "there opened up within me a great awareness; I knew then who I was. I was a Negro, a human being with an invisible pigmentation which marked me a person to be hunted, hanged, abused, discriminated against, kept in poverty and ignorance, in order that those whose skin was white would have readily at hand a proof of their own superiority" (11). Culminating in White's declaration of pride in "the knowledge of my identity," which is inseparable from his critical disidentification with "those whose story is the history of the world, a record of bloodshed, rapine, and pillage" (12), the scene of the riot thus establishes his text as the antithesis of the ex-colored man's autobiography. (Indeed, when later on in his life White does pass, it is in order to investigate lynchings for the NAACP.)

In the *Autobiography* Johnson refuses to satisfy the desire for such a stabilized black masculine subject who can embody the valorous tradition initiated by ex-slaves such as Douglass and carried on, into the twentieth century, by leaders such as White. Rather, by representing the lynching as the ex-colored man's incitement to pass permanently and purposefully, he allows the contradiction between the narrator's raced identity and his identity as a national subject to remain as such. Moreover, while the narrator's decision to abandon his musical ambitions to pursue "a white man's success" in the world of business (141) would seem to resolve the question of his masculinity (insofar as he is able to carve out a gendered refuge in the public sphere), nevertheless such success leaves him feeling further estranged from his "mother's people." Where the narrator might have been able to draw on his class privilege to fol-

low the example of his former schoolmate "Shiny," a man who embodies
gendered ideals of racial pride and confidence, his passing ultimately becomes the sign of a "wasted" (that is, effeminized) masculinity. Com-
pared to those exalted figures who "have the eternal principles of right
on their side," he writes, he feels "small and selfish" (154). In particular, he reserves his greatest praise for Washington, one of a "small but
gallant band of colored men who are publicly fighting the cause of their
race" (154).

Such allusions to the founder of Tuskeegee Institute and the era's
most influential proponent of racial self-help would seem to restabilize
the narrative of the *Autobiography*, if only by leaving readers with a sure
sense of the ex-colored man's tragic failure. In fact, however, it signifies
ambiguously. On the one hand, the figure of Washington makes more
poignant the narrator's fear, articulated in the last line of the text, that
he has "sold [his] birthright for a mess of pottage," choosing personal
wealth and safety over the collective security and prosperity of black
people. An important text within the heroic tradition, Washington's
own autobiography records his meticulous and irreproachable commitment to the very goals that the ex-colored man seemingly abandons in
his decision to cross the line.

Yet the *Autobiography*'s reference to Washington also potentially contains a fair bit of irony. The fact that the narrator, in his identity as a
"white" man, hears Washington speak at a Carnegie Hall benefit for
Hampton Institute (an industrial school for African Americans and Native Americans) alludes not only to the narrator's new social position as a
"white" patron of black (male) education, but to Washington's own successful fund-raising activities, which were notoriously dependent on his
tolerance of African Americans' social and political disenfranchisement.
Johnson himself criticized Washington's proclivity to grant concessions
to white benefactors in *Along This Way* (his own autobiography), where
he indicts Washington's infamous "Atlanta Compromise" speech of 1895
(made just months before the Supreme Court legitimation of racial segregation in *Plessy v. Ferguson*) for accommodating racial segregation in
the name of "mutual progress."[24]

In light of the ex-colored man's decision to seek his fortune as a white
entrepreneur, his admiration for Washington makes a certain sense,
however. Like Washington, the ex-colored man fashions his ambitions
according to what Du Bois (in his own scathing critique of Washington's

philosophy) called the "gospel of Work and Money" (*Souls*, 43), and like his idol, he predicates his survival within a racially divided society on his submission to the values of the marketplace. Yet whereas Washington's text ultimately legitimates his social and class aspirations in the name of racial uplift (that is, in the name of collective progress), Johnson's narrator is, finally, unable to subsume his personal ambitions under the stabilizing sign of race. Instead, the protagonist violates such gendered ideals of "race" pride and solidarity in the name of racial passing, trading in the possibility of "making history" with men like Washington (and Johnson) for the less glorious certainty of making money.

"THE SLEEPER WAKES": PASSING AND THE
INTERIORITY OF THE "BLACK" HEROINE

In my discussion of the *Autobiography* I have alluded to the assumptions of earlier, masculinist literary criticism, which tended to envision African American literary history in terms of Oedipalized struggles between black male literary forefathers (for example, Frederick Douglass, W. E. B. Du Bois, Booker T. Washington) and their modernist "sons" (for example, Langston Hughes and Countée Cullen). It is for this reason, among others, that Johnson's text has typically been elevated to the status of a progenitor of the modernist African American novel. Yet a crucial element of the critical attention historically paid to the *Autobiography* conceivably also derives from its explicit "masculinization" of the tradition of racial passing narratives associated with the literary production of late-nineteenth- and early-twentieth-century women writers. (Here we can see, too, how the Oedipal paradigm hinges on the symbolic "disappearance" of women's texts, which subsequently appear as background to the masculinized business of creating literary history.) In particular, Johnson centers the representation of the narrator's passing (that is, his decision to allow others to ascribe white identity to him) within the context of an interrogation of "public sphere" issues of race politics, the commodification of African American culture, and the proliferation of "capitalist" values.

In contrast, Fauset's "The Sleeper Wakes," a short story serialized in *The Crisis* from August through October of 1920,[25] explicitly explores racial passing as a figure that spans the gendered divide separating the "private" sphere of domesticity and the family, and the "public" sphere of work and politics. Like Johnson's novella, Fauset's short story centers on the development of a middle-class subject, and as in Johnson's text, in "The Sleeper Wakes" the turning point of the passing plot is structured around a scene (or in this case, scenes) of raced and gendered violence. Yet in Fauset's text such violence functions as an impediment rather than an incitement to passing for the young female protagonist, Amy Kildare. In fulfilling the conventions of the passing plot by staging Amy's return "home" (both literally—to the domestic sphere of the Boldins, the middle-class black family who adopted and raised her—and symbolically—to the "sphere" of a raced identity), Fauset's narrative seemingly returns her to her "proper place" within intersecting hierarchies of race and gender. Yet by mediating such homecoming through the protagonist's nascent critique of marriage and domesticity, "The Sleeper Wakes" also attempts to appropriate racial uplift ideology as a means of securing a political voice for its "black" female heroine. It does so out of a particular necessity, of course, since, unlike the ex-colored man, Fauset's protagonist cannot look to the public sphere of the marketplace as a gendered refuge from the contradictions of her raced citizenship. If within the heroic tradition of black male texts violence is a threshold to citizenship, in Fauset's text violence is "merely" a reminder to the heroine of her gendered powerlessness, and thus of her need to construct alternative modes of agency that circumvent both white supremacist and patriarchal scripts of her identity.

As does Fauset's *Plum Bun*, the novel for which it serves as a model, "The Sleeper Wakes" interweaves its narrative of racial passing with a conventional marriage plot, thus contracting the heroine's "crossing the line" with her first steps out of a patriarchal household and into a patriarchal marriage market. Within this context racial passing becomes a particularly gendered enterprise, associated with the heroine's passivity and with her mastery of "feminine" spectacle. It is precisely such pliability, in combination with the social value of her whiteness, that attracts the attention of Stuart James Wynne, the wealthy white scion of a southern aristocratic family, who offers Amy social status and material comfort in exchange for her willingness to grace his Virginia estate. Marriage thus not only establishes Amy's social legitimacy in highly gendered terms, but it ironically also enshrines her in the symbolic position of a white plantation mistress whose leisured domesticity is secured through the labor of her African American "servants." By passing, Amy does not elude her "destiny" as a gendered domestic woman (one of her original reasons for leaving home); rather, passing merely enables her to exchange one form of gendered domestic virtue for another.

Yet if Fauset might seem to be simply restabilizing the binary opposition of domesticity and mobility through the figure of racial passing, in fact the narrative of "The Sleeper Wakes" complicates this opposition through its representation of Amy's acquisition of agency as a raced and gendered subject. As she moves through a series of domestic enclosures—from Wynne's southern plantation estate to his New York town house to a modest room in a middle-class home in West Orange, New Jersey—Amy also sheds the emotional superficiality and materialism associated with her passing and is rewarded, in narrative terms, with the development of her interiority as a "heroine." In the particular scene in which she begins to win the reader's admiration, Amy allows the young black valet Stephen to flee from a certain lynching at Wynne's hands by telling Wynne that Stephen is her brother. Moments later, after Wynne has defensively boasted that "I know a white girl when I see one" (14), Amy rids him of this fantasy of his mastery over the signifiers of "race" by categorically asserting that she "*is* colored," even though (as she goes on to explain) she must infer her identity from the little she knows about the circumstances of her birth and adoption.

In post-Reconstruction sentimental novels structured around the discovery of serendipitous connections, Amy's claim might well have materialized in the revelation of previously unacknowledged kinship ties linking her to characters in spite of their different complexions and social stations.[26] The reuniting of estranged family members is both a theme and a formal device, for example, in Francis E. W. Harper's *Iola Leroy* as well as in Hopkins's *Hagar's Daughter.* Fauset's story actively reinterprets such conventions of black women's sentimental literature by grounding Amy's assertion not in biological certainties but in her nascent critique of patriarchal authority both within and outside of the "private" sphere. In effect, Fauset gains the reader's approval for her own narrative production of a stable "black" female subjectivity by conflating the moment in which Amy publicly asserts her "colored" identity with her first conscious act of disobedience to her husband—an act articulated through her willingness to cross lines of race, class, and gender to construct a space of solidarity with a male domestic worker.

Whereas Amy initially values her "blonde, golden beauty" as her "chiefest asset" within a competitive marriage economy, subsequent to her confrontation with Wynne, Fauset allows her protagonist increasing distance from such a racist, patriarchal narrative of her "value." Increasingly, that is, Amy comes to realize that her looks—along with her naïveté, her willingness to be objectified, and her indifference to politics and other "worldly" affairs—can only be sources of gendered agency and mobility so long as they are associated with her whiteness. Such "awakening" to the ways that whiteness secures female virtue, which entails a parallel realization of the patriarchal sexual economy of marriage, culminates in a scene in which Amy becomes the target of Wynne's sexualized violence. Realizing, for the first time, her "split" articulation as an object of *both* "hate and . . . desire" (22), Amy retrospectively equates Wynne's exploitation of her sexuality with the exploitation and oppression that characterize the Western colonial enterprise:

> Once she got hold of a big thought. Perhaps there *was* some root, some racial distinction woven in with the stuff of which she was formed which made her persistently kind and unexacting. And perhaps in the same way this difference, helplessly, inevitably operated in making Wynne and his kind, cruel or at best indifferent. Her reading for Wynne reacted to her thought—she remembered the grating insolence of white exploiters in foreign lands, the wrecking of African villages, the destruction of homes in Tasmania. She couldn't imagine where Tasmania was, but wherever it was, it had been the realest thing in the world to its crude inhabitants. (22)

As the tone of this passage suggests, Fauset is careful not to idealize Amy's "big thought," reminding readers through Amy's uncertain references to Tasmania that heretofore she has taken little interest in places or people that do not immediately serve her own ambitions. In addition, Amy's vision of a world simplistically divided between her "kind" and Wynne's reflects a defensive racial essentializing that primarily serves to naturalize her relation to an idealized version of the black "masses." On the other hand, the passage suggests Amy's ability to mobilize the knowledge she has acquired in the course of fulfilling her domestic duties to delineate connections among her own subordination within the domestic sphere, "domestic" (that is, nationalized) discourses of racial-ethnic difference, and the wrecking of African villages by "white exploiters." In particular, it illustrates Amy's growing wakefulness to notions of racial solidarity among such disparate subjects as herself and the "crude inhabitants" of a seemingly remote part of Australia. This shift in Amy's self-conception is outwardly symbolized by a corresponding shift in her habits of consumption (including her consumption of racialized labor), which are increasingly identified with the bourgeois values of thrift, industry, and moderation modeled in the story by her adoptive black middle-class family. Whereas Wynne is surprised to find Amy answering her own front door when he comes to visit her in New York, the reader is meant to understand that this simple gesture, in hearkening back to "the old days at Mrs. Boldin's," symbolizes Amy's rejection of the aristocratic entitlements that he takes for granted, and from which she herself once benefited. In fact, the allusion proves prophetic, since the end of the story finds a chastened Amy happily anticipating her move back to the Boldins' house after a nearly ten-year absence.

Given Amy's awakening to the possibility of refashioning a self outside the gendered imperatives of the bourgeois "coupling convention" and instead according to the tenets of racial uplift ideology, it might be tempting to conclude that, as with Harriet Jacobs, her story ends with freedom.[27] Moreover, unlike the awakening of Edna Pontelier, whose suicide marks the ironic closure of Kate Chopin's novella, Amy's awakening is not contingent on her self-extinction; neither, significantly, is it contingent on her racial homecoming, conceived in terms of crudely essentialist mandates. Amy's decision, at the end of the story, to dedicate her labor to the betterment of "colored people"—presumably that "class" of blacks whom she perceives as in need of uplifting—occurs in the absence of any such certainty about "race."

Yet Amy's dedication to the rehabilitation of "colored people" would seem a dubious solution to the "problem" of her racial passing, since in order to identify herself with the "folk" Amy must first naturalize "blackness" as an ideal. Fauset consistently foreshadows this dilemma through minor details such as Amy's preference for "colored" gems and her "natural" affection for "foreign"-looking children. But where this dilemma becomes most noticeable is in Amy's relation at the end of the story to the Boldins, the middle-class black subjects whom she previously left "without a word" (24). Within the context of Amy's symbolic domestication and objectification of the Boldins, the metaphor of her speechlessness can hardly seem incidental; indeed it could equally describe their relation to Fauset, who renders them, if not entirely silent, then problematically erased as speaking agents. The welcoming letter that appears from Cornelius Boldin in response to Amy's request to return "home" gives no indication of the dimensions of their response to Amy's absence, other than to provide assurances of their willingness to forgive any transgression, no matter how terrible. Meanwhile, even as Amy rejoices in having paid off her debts to Wynne, she never considers her indebtedness to the Boldins, or questions her entitlement to claim *their* home as her own.

The irony of "The Sleeper Wakes" is that in imagining an alternative to the narrative of gendered domestic virtue, Fauset's story also recuperates the terms of domesticity through its subtle domestication of "blackness." This is not to say that Amy's awakening to an ethos of service to the masses of black "folk" does not establish her as a newly politicized, newly purposeful "black" heroine in the tradition of such heroines as Iola Leroy, who ultimately dedicates herself to marriage (and tacitly to a degree of sexual agency) only insofar as it enables her work. Yet neither is it to say that her manner of acquiring interiority as a raced subject is without its costs. However sincere her plan to serve colored people, the paradigm of her intentions is still that of patronage and charity—ironically, a model that reproduces and even naturalizes the very hierarchical relations that racial uplift ideology means to dismantle.

PASSING AND DOMESTIC TRAGEDY

Of the three literary texts this chapter analyzes, Larsen's *Passing*, published in the waning years of the New Negro Renaissance, is arguably the most pessimistic about the possibilities for constructing "positive" middle-class black subjects within the terms of the passing narrative.[28] Their satire notwithstanding, Johnson's *Autobiography* and Fauset's "The Sleeper Wakes" are also marked in their optimism, both about the project of racial uplift and the appropriation of passing as a source of negative instruction to their protagonists (as well as, perhaps, to their readers). However ambiguously they may signify, both the ex-colored man's regretful references to Booker T. Washington and Amy Kildare's eager anticipation of beginning her work for the "race" allude positively to racial uplift values of racial solidarity, economic self-help, class assimilation, and service to the masses. Larsen's novella does not reject these values, but neither does it manage to portray the same confidence either in them or in its middle-class black protagonists as the arbiters of "race" progress. This shift in outlook is signposted through her text's very different representation of raced and gendered violence. By ending her book with Irene Redfield's likely murder of her "friend" Clare Kendry, Larsen primarily emphasizes the lack of solidarity between her two protagonists, only one of whom (Clare) is passing for white within her marriage. Insofar as we can assume that Irene pushes Clare out of an apartment window (such a move being foreshadowed in the meeting of the two protagonists on the roof of the Drayton Hotel), then it is possible to conclude that Irene quite literally extinguishes the agency of the passing plot in the narrative. Yet it is hardly clear that this act resolves any of the dilemmas (real or imagined) Irene faces, or for that matter any of the many questions—about the stability of race and gender identities, the construction of national citizenship, and the nature of "race" loyalty—that *Passing* raises.

In narrative terms, two elements distinguish Larsen's text from the earlier works of Johnson and Fauset (or even from Fauset's novel *Plum Bun*, also published in 1929). The first is *Passing*'s representation of Clare's desire for racial "homecoming"—rather than her desire to pass —as a primary source of narrative strife and dissonance. Unlike "The Sleeper Wakes," which ultimately demands Amy's homecoming as a means of bringing anticipated closure to the passing plot, *Passing* renders the status of such homecoming a primary site of interrogation. Accordingly, Larsen initiates the narrative proper with Irene's receipt of Clare's letter announcing Clare's desire to reinitiate contact with "Negro" society (a beginning that renders it necessary for the reader to go back in time through Irene's memory of their first reunion in Chicago). As a result, the focus of Larsen's text is not the development of an individual subjectivity through an act that ultimately must be repudiated, but the very status of racial "community."

The notion of community tacitly alludes to the other distinguishing characteristic of *Passing*: namely, its ingenious triangulation of the passing plot. Unlike both Johnson's and Fauset's texts, Larsen's novella explores the volatile relationship between two female protagonists, both of whom pass for white and both of whom see class privilege as a key to their survival as women within a patriarchal society. Primarily such a strategy of triangulation enables Larsen to filter her narrative through the watchful eyes of Irene, who is liable to wonder at the status of her friend's sudden yearning for "my own people" (182). In effect, therefore, *Passing* is able to translate the various anxieties associated with racial passing through the character of Irene, who voices them in the form of her own ambivalent censure of Clare's frank disclosure that she passes in order to acquire the wealth and social status that painfully eluded her in girlhood. Ambivalence, in fact, becomes a major theme of the novella, as Irene attempts (although with little success) to reconcile her fascination with and attraction to Clare with her discomfort at the various compromising positions that she feels compelled to assume in order to safeguard Clare's secret. Irene aptly sums up this ambivalent economy of aversion and desire—which could well describe the critical reception of modernist fictions of passing—in a discussion with her husband Brian: "It's funny about 'passing.' We disapprove of it and at the same time condone it. It excites our contempt and yet we rather admire it. We shy away from it with an odd kind of revulsion, but we protect it" (185–86).

As Irene's remark hints, the notion of "race" loyalty constitutes an important basis of Irene's critique of Clare's passing, and thus of her ability to establish herself as superior to her friend. A self-fashioned "race" woman, Irene distinguishes between her own occasional passing, which she justifies as a means of circumventing racial segregation, and Clare's seemingly more opportunistic and deceitful (because permanent) commitment to passing in her marriage. The difference between herself and Clare, as Irene imagines it, is that whereas Clare is primarily interested in crossing the line as a means of self-advancement, Irene's interests lie in working to secure the happiness of others, not merely her husband and her two young sons, but the "race" as a whole. Repeatedly the text contrasts Irene's perception of Clare's "having way" (a phrase that encompasses Clare's knack for acquiring things as well as the possibility that she is "having her way" with Irene's husband) with her own philanthropic work on behalf of the Negro Welfare League, a racial uplift organization modeled after the NAACP and the National Urban League. Additionally, the discourse of racial uplift provides Irene a ready vocabulary for establishing the authenticity of her "self" through a series of racialized oppositions to Clare. According to Irene, she and Clare are "strangers. Strangers in their desires and ambitions. Strangers even in their racial consciousness. Between them the barrier was just as high, just as broad, and just as firm as if in Clare did not run that strain of black blood" (192).

In order thus to see Clare as a stranger, however, Irene must also naturalize both her own passing and her status as a classed and gendered subject. Larsen hints at how Irene's censuring of Clare hinges on her ability to sustain a privileged relation to domesticity and to properly "domesticated" female sexuality. Notwithstanding her work for the Negro Welfare League, for example, Irene seems wholly unconcerned with the welfare of her black maid Zulena, and she exploits the fact of her marriage to Brian and the presence of their two young sons as a means of casting Clare's sexuality as "flaunting," "a shade too provocative," and "not safe." While she protests that Clare's passing irks her because it seems predicated on a blatant desire for gain, in fact Clare's rapid ascent up the class ladder violates Irene's middle-class belief in fair play and her tacit commitment to the American Dream of prosperity as a reward for sacrifice, self-discipline, and hard work. Like Amy in "The Sleeper Wakes" but unlike Brian, who harbors a "dislike and disgust for his profession and his country" (187), Irene is loath to give up her attachment to a national narrative.

Such trust in her own entitlement allows Irene to overlook the fact that for Clare, passing provides a relatively sure ticket away from the domestic sphere of her white aunts, who exploit her as a source of household labor, and into the ranks of the upper class. In Clare's narrative, however, it is precisely their disparate class locations as children, not any fundamental difference in their "race consciousness," that primarily distinguishes her passing from Irene's. "You can't know," she tells Irene, "how, when I used to go over to the south side, I used almost to hate all of you. You had all the things I wanted and never had had. It made me all the more determined to get them, and others" (159).

Through her depiction of Irene's growing animosity toward Clare, Larsen thematizes the clash between narratives of American individualism and racial uplift notions of collective duty and race progress. More particularly, she symbolizes the contradictions within racial uplift ideology itself: its attempt, on the one hand, to construct a class-based solution to the problem of African American citizenship, and its recognition, on the other hand, of segregation as a "leveling" narrative that ultimately triumphs over class distinction. Irene experiences this contradiction at the level of an interiorized struggle between the fulfillment of her own self-interests and the satisfaction of what she perceives to be the needs and interests of the "race." Much like the ex-colored man, in other words, she feels forced to choose between apparently irreconcilable options of self-preservation and self-sacrifice, the second of which is tied to loyalty to "race"; only unlike Johnson's protagonist, Irene has Clare to make her sacrificial victim.

In drawing the narrative to a precipitous close, Clare's "fall" from an open apartment window suggests that Larsen could imagine no resolution short of death to the "dangerous business" of her passing (195). Yet it remains significant that whereas this finale to the story would seem to guarantee Irene's safe return to the domestic sphere, Clare's death ultimately is not conducive to such a happy ending. Instead, by leaving the scene of Irene's own "homecoming" to the domestic sphere outside the narrative frame of the story, Larsen seems to be acknowledging the inadequacy of domesticity as a solution either to the specific "problem" of racial passing or to the more general problem of the agency of the raced and gendered subject. Indeed, the darkness and heaviness that descend on Irene in the last lines of the book suggest that through Clare's death, something of her own faith in the redeeming and protective power of gendered domestic virtue has taken a blow.

"HOME AGAIN"

"There is nothing more important to me than home." It is with these words that feminist theorist Barbara Smith initiates her introduction to the pathbreaking text *Home Girls* (1983), an anthology of black feminist writings that she also edited. Smith goes on to recall her childhood in a poor Cleveland neighborhood, where she shared a house with three generations of women, including her twin sister Beverly, her mother, her grandmother, and her great-aunt Phoebe, a cook who lived most of the time in the house of her white employers. Smith's representation of "home," filtered through the lenses of memory and desire, combines nostalgia with disenchantment and sorrow. On the one hand, home is associated with emotional nurture and political education: Thinking of home, Smith writes, conjures "this place that I miss and all the women there who raised me. It was undoubtedly at home that I learned the rudiments of Black feminism, although no such term even existed then."[29] On the other hand, Smith acknowledges the labor that supported and enabled her home — women who "cleaned, cooked, washed, ironed, sewed, made soap, canned, held jobs, took care of business downtown, sang, read and taught us to do the same" (xx)—as well as struggles that went on in the house, where she daily witnessed the spectacle of women "humiliated and crushed because they had made the 'mistake' of being born Black and female in a white man's country" (xxii).

Smith's introduction goes on to fashion an argument for the appropriation of "home" as a concept for theorizing solidarity and political community among black women. Having been accused of selling out her racial "home" on account of her feminism and her lesbianism, and having been excluded from mainstream liberal feminism on account of sexuality and race, Smith asserts that African American women—especially black lesbians—must strategically redefine home in terms of their own needs and desires, and in response to those who would bar them from (or conditionally accept them in) "homes" imagined according to rigid concepts of identity. The notion of home she envisions is fluid and conditional, and yet insofar as it is continuous with rather than separate from the "outside" world, it is a space that also encompasses conflict and contradiction. Although it emerges in response to essentialist indices of belonging, the home she postulates is not simplistically or romantically "inclusive" (a gesture that would only reinscribe essence through notions of "diversity"); rather, it is defined by the porous boundaries of "ourselves." As she concludes, "Home has always meant a lot to people who are ostracized as racial outsiders in the public sphere. It is above all a place to be ourselves . . . [to be] home girls" (li).[30]

Insofar as it is possible to generalize about racial passing narratives, the evidence of the three works I have discussed suggests that they, too, are concerned with elucidating concepts of "home" in relation to social categories of race, class, gender, sexuality, and nationality. In particular, they represent the struggles of subjects to imagine a "home" that would not demand their subjugation to, or confinement within, the various defining discourses alternatively imposed and wielded by the dominant culture. Such struggles are particularly—and perhaps not unexpectedly—complex for the female protagonists of these fictions, insofar as they must also negotiate domesticity; and yet they are no less important in the case of the ex-colored man, who attempts to realize a masculinist fantasy of "home" through an ambivalent embrace of national identity. Although it is sometimes postulated as being extraneous to the "core" concerns of these texts (that is, modernist alienation, middle-class propriety, eroticized jealousy and rivalry, respectively), racial passing is crucially related to their critiques of ideology. Indeed, it is through the representation of passing that they highlight the simultaneous instability and instrumentality of categories of identity, in the process exploring fantasies and desires (especially for "black" community and stable "black" identity) that are frequently shunned in contemporary theoretical discourse. Too often, that is, such fantasies and desires for "home" have been cast as hopelessly essentialist, rather than considered, as Barbara Smith's essay suggests, in terms of their political necessity in struggles against oppression.

Although the outcomes of these narratives differ, it is clear that their authors understood "crossing the line" not only or even primarily as a form of complicity with white supremacy, but as a legible, if contradictory, response to a social order that produces passing as a possibility. In light of this fundamental contradiction of the social order, passing elucidates the tension between subjects' capitulation to ideology and their constructive response to the exigencies of racism, segregation, economic exploitation or vulnerability, and patriarchal oppression. One conclusion we might draw from the foregoing discussion, then, is that we need to interpret the praxis of self-naming and strategic identification within the context of a recognition of the social and material relations that conditions subjects' agency and choice. More specifically, we need to consider how racial discourse conditions the opportunity, as well as the social, political, and ideological horizons, of passing. Or as Irene Redfield remarks to Hugh Wentworth, the white arts patron who also contributes to the Negro Welfare League: "It's easy for a Negro to 'pass' for white. But I don't think it would be so simple for a white person to 'pass' for coloured" (206). It is precisely this issue of "white" passing that I take up in the next chapter.

CHAPTER 2

Mezz Mezzrow

and the Voluntary

Negro Blues

They were my kind of people. And I was going to learn their music and play it for the rest of my days. I was going to be a musician, a Negro musician, hipping the world about the blues the way only Negroes can. I didn't know how the hell I was going to do it, but I was straight on what I had to do.

—MEZZ MEZZROW, *Really the Blues* [1]

As he attests in his 1946 autobiography *Really the Blues*, becoming a "Negro" musician and "hipping the world about the blues" were the related lifelong ambitions of "Mezz" Mezzrow (1899-1972)—the flamboyant clarinetist and sometime saxophonist, prolific weed pusher, self-professed opium eater, and prototypical "white Negro" hipster whose chosen name, also synonymous with the marijuana he sold, echoed the sound of the word "jazz." [2] Born to Russian-Jewish immigrants, who hoped that their son would one day take over the family drugstore business, Mezzrow (born Milton Mesirow) defied his family's expectations to pursue a career as a musician, immersing himself in the New Orleans–style jazz that he first heard as a teenager hanging out in the clubs and bars of Chicago's northwest side. For more than half a cen-

1. Milton "Mezz" Mezzrow, 1899–1972. Courtesy Rutgers University Institute of Jazz Studies.

tury Mezzrow "hipped the world about the blues" through his musical performance; his work as a composer, arranger, and impresario; and, not least, his memoirs, which double as an extended paean to his musical idols, Louis Armstrong and Sidney Bechet. Although by the late 1940s changing sensibilities and emergent styles such as bebop had rendered him obsolete as a performer, Mezzrow sustained an involvement with jazz culture well into his sixties, moving to Paris in 1951 and devoting his energies over the next two decades to promoting "all-star" blues reunion concerts throughout Europe, where the audience for music of the 1920s and 1930s remained strong.[3]

In *Really the Blues*, written in collaboration with Bernard Wolfe, a left cultural critic who originally met Mezzrow while seeking an interesting subject for a magazine article, Mezzrow tells the story of his career, from his discovery of blues in a Pontiac, Michigan, reform school at age sixteen, through his 1942 release from Riker's Island (where he had briefly done time on drug possession and trafficking charges).[4] Narrated in an engaging, if occasionally cloying, jazz jive that necessitates an appended glossary of terms for a presumably "unhep" audience, *Really the Blues* recounts Mezzrow's struggles for professional recognition, describes memorable performances (triumphs as well as disasters), and offers behind-the-scenes accounts of jam sessions involving famous performers. Positioning himself as a "keeper of the faith" (139), a purist devoted to the preservation of "real blues" in the wake of threats from both the commercial "mainstream" and the highbrow avant-garde, Mezzrow riffs extensively on his disdain for white popularizers of jazz ("out to make money, not music" [139]) and professes loyalty to the cult of self-taught, rather than conservatory-trained, musicians. Shamelessly self-aggrandizing, he boasts freely on subjects ranging from his musical and linguistic skills (at one point he even claims to have coined the phrase "jam session") to his friendship with legends like Armstrong to the quality of the "gage" he sold as a small-time Harlem drug dealer, even while admitting to insecurity, especially about the quality of his playing. Finally and most memorably, he recounts his self-styling as a "voluntary Negro," vying for the reader's acknowledgment of his "black" racial authenticity even while describing his attempts to secure the validation of African American colleagues.

In most respects Mezzrow's career was not significantly different from those of other young white jazz musicians coming of age in Chicago in the 1920s. Like Jimmy MacPartland, Bud Freeman, and Dave Tough, members of the Austin High Gang (named for the high school they attended), Mezzrow grew up emulating the music of such successful white bands as the New Orleans Rhythm Kings and Bix [Beiderbecke] and the Wolverines, and later (especially once he had moved to New York) such African American performers as Baby Dodds and Armstrong. Like many of these players, too, he found in African American music not merely an intellectually challenging and potentially lucrative set of expressive practices, but a set of "moral and cultural alternatives," in George Lipsitz's words, to the values of bourgeois individualism and upward class mobility promoted by the dominant culture and sustained through the discourses of white supremacy.[5] Equally important for Mezzrow, who was raised in a middle-class Jewish home, jazz culture nourished alternatives to paradigms of national identity-formation through ethnic assimilation, and offered models of raced masculinity through which to negotiate and deflect stereotypes of Jewish male effeminacy.[6]

Where Mezzrow was distinct, however, was in his belief that through his immersion in African American music culture and his participation in the life of the black community in Harlem, he had definitively "crossed the line" that divided white and black identities. According to Wolfe, Mezzrow went so far as to understand his racial passing in biological terms, finding in his identification with black music and people the source of an embodied "metamorphosis." Mezzrow, he writes, "was not unique in adopting the black man's music, slang, bearing, social and sexual modes—those cultural co-optations were to be observed in hundreds and hundreds of whites, sometimes in many millions. He was not alone in hanging around with blacks, moving physically into the closed black world, marrying a black girl and having a child with her. But search all the histories of personal 'negrification' as you will, you'll never turn up another case of a man who after extended immersion in the ghetto came to believe that he had actually, physically, turned black."[7]

"Case History of an Ex-White Man," a 1946 *Ebony* magazine feature article on Mezzrow based on Random House's promotional material for *Really the Blues*, takes a slightly different view. For one, through pages of carefully posed photographs of Mezzrow—including a series of idealized portraits of his domestic life with his wife Johnnie Mae Berg and their son Milton Jr.—the article emphasizes Mezzrow's intimacy with African Americans, contrasting Wolfe's claim of the insignificance of Mezzrow's personal relations. Furthermore, the article suggests that more important than Mezzrow's belief that "after his long years in and under Harlem" his "lips had developed fuller contours, his hair had thickened and burred, [and] his skin had darkened" (Wolfe, 390) is his interiorized and self-authorized transformation. "Physically speaking," the article observes, making explicit what the photographs tacitly illustrate, "Mezzrow couldn't pass for Negro by any stretch of the imagination; his skin is too white. His conversion to 'the race' has taken place largely within himself. In psychological makeup, he is completely a black man and proudly admits it."[8]

Taking its cue from *Ebony*'s characterization of *Really the Blues* as a "case history," this chapter inquires into Mezzrow's autobiographical representation of his "conversion to 'the race,'" paying attention to his text's valorization of "voluntary Negro" passing as a transgressive practice, although it is shaped by impulses and desires that reflect its contradictory investment in racial discourse. In particular, I trace Mezzrow's authorial agency in fashioning a romantic narrative of male self-discovery in and through a racial "other," examining his identification with "marginality" as, paradoxically, an attempt to elevate and distinguish himself.[9] As *Really the Blues* demonstrates, "voluntary Negro" passing is a theoretically and ideologically impure enterprise, in which notions of the permeability of the color line compete with the projection of inexorable and essential difference onto racially defined subjects, and in which masculine authority is maintained or even expanded through the eroticization of black men and masculinity.[10] Rather than merely condemn Mezzrow for his actively voiced desire to pass, this chapter inquires into his modes and strategies of self-representation, exploring his attribution of disruptive power to the cultural practices of racially oppressed and exploited people.

Whereas the previous chapter examined literary narratives that defined passing as an enterprise conditioned on secrecy and confidentiality, in this chapter I focus on a deliberately and self-consciously self-mythologizing text that defines passing as a fundamentally exhibitionistic enterprise. As the *Ebony* article observes, "There is nothing secretive about Mezzrow's passing. He has just written a remarkable book about it and some 25,000 copies are in book stalls across the nation" (11). Anticipating the attention that *Really the Blues* was likely to stir, the magazine predicted that Mezzrow's "amazing raw and racy saga [would] shock the book reading public [and] . . . send the book soaring into the best seller class." And in fact, *Ebony*'s premonition eventually panned out: in the first year of its publication, *Really the Blues* went through at least six hardbound reprintings before it was reissued in paperback. Rumor had it that Mezzrow had boasted (with no apparent evidence) that his book had been published in every language except Spanish; yet even if this clearly was not the case, there is evidence that Random House's promotion of *Really the Blues* as the "upside down success story" of a man who "crossed the color line, *backwards*" was itself a considerable success. In reviews the white press extolled Mezzrow's book for its authenticity, greeting *Really the Blues* as the "real" thing, the first jazz history by "an insider" (*Saturday Review*), and an "intense, sincere and honest book" that "makes all the novels with jazz backgrounds seem as phony as an Eddie Condon concert" (*The New Republic*).[11] *Newsweek* went so far as to venture to compare Mezzrow to Bessie Smith, asserting—without regard for Smith's own history—that whereas she "sang the blues," Mezzrow "lived them, brutally."[12]

In the context of this study's larger themes, what's particularly interesting about this aspect of the popular response to *Really the Blues* is not the elevation of Mezzrow's text per se, but rather the tacit divestment of "voluntary Negro" passing of the shamefulness, inauthenticity, or duplicity often associated with the passing of racially defined subjects. In part, of course, this is because Mezzrow's racial and class privilege facilitated the interpretation of his desire to "cross the line" as a courageous, sacrificial gesture (as opposed to one of self-aggrandizement, which it undoubtedly *also* was). Yet following the exhortation of Joan Scott, we might also take the emergence of such "white Negro" identities as Mezzrow exemplified as a historical event "in need of explanation."[13] What factors promoted such associations of "voluntary Negro" passing with moral heroism, and what role did such factors play in mediating dominant discourses of race?

James Weldon Johnson—author of *The Autobiography of an Ex-Colored Man* (from which the *Ebony* article derives its title), as well as a successful vaudeville composer and an astute analyst of African American musical traditions—once observed that white Americans had long been "doing their best to pass for colored," especially where music and dancing were concerned.[14] Yet it was not until the period when jazz first began to be incorporated into the cultural and commercial mainstream that black musical culture, valued or alternately disparaged for its appearance of being spontaneous, down to earth, and unaffected, would acquire a particular *symbolic* value as the site of individualized "white" self-discovery or self-mythologization. Whereas previously blackface minstrelsy had offered white performers and their working-class audiences a set of cultural practices through which to indulge, temporarily and conditionally, gendered and classed fantasies of "crossing the line," minstrel forms of passing were premised on the theatricalized lampooning of "black" identities and cultural practices, giving rise to a complex dynamic of attraction and aversion that Eric Lott has memorably called "love and theft."[15] By contrast, shifts in social and cultural relations made it conceivable that by the 1920s, when Mezzrow was first performing, not only would whites find jazz worthy of overt admiration and emulation, but "marginality" itself would become an object of "mainstream" cultural desire.[16] In effect, the nineteenth-century "love and theft" dynamic would be not only inverted and transposed but also internalized, such that performers such as Mezzrow could cast off the contrivances of blackface "disguise" and pursue fantasies of "being" black by means of what *Ebony* refers to as "psychological makeup."[17]

Within what Andrew Ross calls "the long transactional history of white responses to black culture, of black counter-responses, and of further countless and often traceless negotiatings, tradings, raids and compromises,"[18] Mezzrow's own performances of "blackness" were thus exemplary even as they were also audacious and extraordinary. Indeed, it was the thoroughness of Mezzrow's commitment to a hipster ethic he helped innovate that made him a readily available model for those postwar white male intellectuals whose romanticized appropriations of black culture were similarly instrumental to their development of a critique of the national social and cultural "mainstream." *Really the Blues* was read by such writers as Henry Miller, Jack Kerouac, and Allen Ginsberg, the latter of whom took in Mezzrow's autobiography at a counter at the Columbia University bookstore, finding in Mezzrow's experiences a precursor to his own downtown cohort's romance with "underground black, hip culture."[19] In Norman Mailer's 1957 "White Negro" essay, which *Really the Blues* helped to inspire, one can find reworkings of many of Mezzrow's conceits, including Mailer's justly infamous notion of jazz as "orgasm."[20] Wolfe himself went on to use Mezzrow's autobiography to elaborate a critique of what he calls "Negrophilia" and of black performers' negotiations of the "tryanny of expectancy," through which they were expected to "act black" for white audiences. Originally published in the French journal *Les Temps modernes,* Wolfe's essays caught the eye of a young Frantz Fanon, who went on to cite them extensively in *Black Skin, White Masks* (1952), especially in the chapter titled "The Negro and Psychopathology."[21]

This legacy of *Really the Blues* as a cultural icon for intellectuals and artists alike (Bob Wilber, a student of Bechet's, recalls that Mezzrow's book was considered a "bible" among aspiring white jazz musicians of the late 1940s)[22] serves as a reminder of the historical link between racial transgression and various projects of political and ideological critique, not least those that would challenge the elevation of individualism, upward mobility, and bourgeois domesticity as cultural ideals. "Crossing the line" has in this sense been constitutive of possibilities for rethinking alliances and identities in light of their contingency as social formations, not transcendent essences. Yet it would be reckless to attribute to Mezzrow's practice of "voluntary Negro" passing an inherently politically disruptive or subversive agency. Indeed, Johnson's remark, cited previously, regarding the normalcy of a certain "passing" among white Americans, points to a contradiction in the narrative of a hybrid American culture: namely, that even as African American cultural practices were being both commercialized and nationalized, in a process abetted by technological innovations such as phonographs and sound recordings, African Americans were also being excluded from national citizenship through racism and segregation and, indeed, were actively being stereotyped as having no particular "culture" at all. We cannot simply assume, that is to say, that the extolling of blues or jazz by those for whom, in Mezzrow's (and Johnson's ex-colored man's) words, it was not a "birthright" was itself necessarily linked to the reduction of the suffering of racially defined people, or indeed to any direct challenge to the structures of racial division and hierarchy.

This is not to impugn the sincerity or priority of Mezzrow's investment in the music—a quality that distinguishes him from writers on the left (such as Mailer) who primarily used blues as a metaphor, and that earned him the respect and admiration of African American musicians, including Bechet.[23] Although it could devolve into defensive posturing against the mainstream, Mezzrow's sensitivity to the commercial exploitation of blues and jazz was noteworthy in an era when most white Americans were content to crown Paul Whiteman, a popularizer of "European style" orchestral music, the "King of Jazz."[24] His fronting, in 1937, of the first racially integrated band (the short-lived Disciples of Swing) to play Manhattan's prestigious Savoy Ballroom was undoubtedly a culturally significant achievement. And he used his role as a promoter to disseminate his own abiding faith in jazz *consumption* as a conduit of social and political transformation. "I believe very strongly," he once told a British interviewer, that jazz "can do a lot to help crash the color barriers of bias and hatred"; it "can help evolve a new civilisation and culture . . . for to understand jazz you don't need to be technically minded, and it's evident wherever I've been that people from all walks of life and colours of skin enjoy jazz."[25]

Yet as I see it, such facts complicate—without resolving—the contradictions of Mezzrow's self-representation, whose condition of possibility (like that of all the passing narratives this study examines) is the very racial discourse that it also exposes as radically unstable. As I have begun to argue, although *Really the Blues* emphasizes the crossing of racial boundary as a mode of cultural critique, it also contradicts its own narrative of racially "transgressive" passing by demonstrating that defiance of social norms need not depend on any discernible disruption of classed and gendered racial narratives. Indeed, what is most remarkable about *Really the Blues* is its portrayal of the commensurability between certain modes and gestures of transgression and the preservation (or even expansion) of gender and race hierarchies. From the viewpoint of this study's concern with understanding the stakes and deployment of racial identity, then, the importance of *Really the Blues* lies not in its status as a superficially "transgressive" text, but in its complication of the paradigms through which we typically understand the transgression of, or resistance to, racial discourse.

A carefully composed photograph featured on the title page of the *Ebony* article dramatically illustrates aspects of this argument concerning the cultural, political, and ideological work of Mezzrow's autobiography. The photograph shows Mezzrow posing on a street corner with Milton Jr., alongside fellow musicians Sidney Bechet, Red Allen, and Baby Dodds.[26] In the men's relaxed postures and visible camaraderie, the photograph represents Mezzrow's ability to "blend in" with his African American companions. Clearly visible street signs above the men's heads

2. Mezz Mezzrow and Sidney Bechet. Courtesy Rutgers University Institute of Jazz Studies.

not only locate the photograph at a significant Harlem crossroads (West 132nd Street and Seventh Avenue), but reinforce Mezzrow's notions of jazz as a cultural "meeting-place," where "people from all walks of life and colours of skin" can converge. This convergence is additionally figuratively embodied by Milton Jr., who is positioned at the point where the men's gazes seem to intersect.[27] Not least, the intersection recalls the crossroads of blues legend: highly symbolic spaces associated with the blurring of boundaries between self and other, past and present, the spiritual and the material worlds.[28]

In the photograph these visual metaphors of confluence and intersection compete with the symbolism of a ONE-WAY sign positioned directly above Mezzrow's head. Pointing away from Mezzrow in the direction of Bechet, a man whom he admired second only to Armstrong, and with whom he collaborated on several recordings including his own signature "Really the Blues," the sign betokens the direction of Mezzrow's desire. On the other hand, the sign's lack of a clear end point alludes to the central problematic of his desire to pass, insofar as it was predicated on inherently unstable and endlessly deferred concepts of black (male) "realness" or authenticity. The sign thus alludes to the one-sidedness of Mezzrow's "voluntary Negro" enterprise, which operates through his unilateral appropriation of the very qualities that he himself ascribes to "blackness."

As the photograph suggests, Mezzrow's representation of essential "black" difference intersects with, undercuts, and shapes his depiction of the "flow" of identity across the color line. Insofar as Mezzrow's championing of "real" blues was inseparable from notions of cultural and racial purity, what *Really the Blues* leaves us to decipher is the impurity of Mezzrow's project and the desire that underwrites it. Such impurity is exemplified in the phrase "voluntary Negro," an expression that paradoxically conjoins notions of socially ascribed identity and conscious volition. It is manifested, too, in the tensions between nature and culture, identity and difference, and instinct and intention that structure Mezzrow's strategies of self-representation. In the following sections I explore these strategies in greater detail, focusing on themes of "realness," identity, and language. Having examined closely the instability of Mezzrow's discourse of passing, I then devote a concluding section to a discussion of the limitations and possibilities of such a "voluntary Negro" project as *Really the Blues* imagines for contemporary theoretical debates about identity and cultural politics, social marginality and power.

DISCOVERING BLUES

They taught me the blues in Pontiac — I mean the blues, blues that I felt from my head to my shoes, really the blues.

Like a blues lyric, *Really the Blues* can be interpreted as a set of narrative variations on a single, but never exhausted, theme: Mezzrow's lifelong pursuit of a standard of cultural or racial "realness," which, because it derives from his own idealized constructs of "black" authenticity, he can never really achieve. Yet it is precisely because "realness" can never be realized in Mezzrow's text that it can be posited as an important site of ideological production — a place to begin inquiring into the tensions that *Really the Blues* produces through the unresolvability and impurity of Mezzrow's pursuit of the "real." How, we might ask, does Mezzrow's text represent realness, and what shapes his perceptions of the "real"? What assumptions and desires authorize his representation? How are these desires themselves sites of conflict or instability?

The parameters of realness are established in the first chapter of *Really the Blues*, which narrates Mezzrow's discovery of blues music in the Pontiac [Michigan] Reformatory, where he was sent at age sixteen after being caught riding in a friend's stolen car. Although the reformatory is racially segregated by cell block, it sponsors a "mixed" band that Mezzrow is invited to join despite his lack of musical experience—only on the condition that he will learn to play the flute before moving on to the more popular alto saxophone. Flute or not, Mezzrow is soon consumed by the idea of making music, spending his days blowing "enough wind into those two instruments to fill the Graf Zepplin" (11). At night he stays awake studying the sounds of the blues as sung by the black boys in a neighboring cell block, the voices affecting him "like a millennium would hit a philosopher" (14). In prison, too, he hears his first jazz record: "Livery Stable Blues" by the Original Dixieland Jazz Band, a white group whose recordings predate the blues records of the 1920s.[29] By the time he is released from Pontiac after serving a year's sentence, Mezzrow has decided that his destiny consists in "sticking close to Negroes" and learning "their music" (14). Concluding the chapter with a flourish, he declares that although he entered reform school "green," he "came out chocolate brown" (18).

While Mezzrow's narrative of his experiences in Pontiac allows him to establish credibility as a jazz performer despite his middle-class background (Mezzrow being among the most economically privileged of the white "Chicagoans"), reform school also furnishes an alternative "public sphere" in which Mezzrow is encouraged to establish his first significant relationships with African Americans. The initial impression he conveys of Pontiac is that it fosters a camaraderie and intimacy among different identities that might not otherwise have flourished in the "outside" world. In particular Mezzrow fondly evokes the image of "Negroes and whites side by side busting their conks" (4) in the reform school band (anticipating his depiction, pages later, of the racially integrated Disciples of Swing), and conveys his initial experiences of blues through pastoral conceits that emphasize Pontiac's racial esprit de corps, even at moments that explicitly reference Jim Crow:

Night after night we'd lie on the corn-husk mattresses in our cells, listening to the blues drifting over from the Negro side of the block. I would be reading or just lying on my bunk, eyeballing the whitewashed ceiling, when somebody would start chanting a weary melody over and over until the whole block was drugg [depressed]. The blues would hit some colored boy and out of a clear sky he'd begin to sing them:

> Ooooohhhhh, ain't gonna do it no mo-o,
> Ooooohhhhh, ain't gonna do it no mo-o,
> If I hadn't drunk so much whisky
> Wouldn't be layin' here on this hard flo'.

. . . Many a time I was laid out there with the blues heavy on my chest, when somebody would begin to sing 'em and the weight would be lifted. (13–14)

What is most striking about such passages, and indeed about the opening chapter of *Really the Blues* as a whole, is the way that it grounds Mezzrow's desire to pass in both an attraction to African American forms of expressivity and a personal affinity with black people as a social group. Indeed, rather than establishing a single or unified narrative of "conversion," the chapter veers constantly between portraying Mezzrow's experience in Pontiac as his "discovery" of African American music, on the one hand, and his realization of something already latent within himself, on the other. The theme of latency is developed through anecdotes about the links between African Americans and Jews, which intercut the linear narrative of Mezzrow's musical initiation. Most important, Mezzrow recollects his friendship with Sullivan, a "colored boy" back in Chicago, who on one occasion accompanies the Mesirow family to synagogue, where he is told by the rabbi that Moses, King Solomon, and the Queen of Sheba were also "colored" (18). Mezzrow's sympathetic bonds to Sullivan are given a material basis at the end of the chapter, as Mezzrow relates an instance in which he and other Jewish boys, dirty from riding the rails, are called "niggers" and kicked out of a restaurant in Cape Girardeau, Missouri. Reinterpreting this experience in terms of his ambition to "become" a Negro musician, Mezzrow finds in it evidence of his own preordained kinship with African Americans: "[I]n Cape Girardeau they had told us we were Negroes," he writes.

"Now, all of a sudden, I realized that I agreed with them. That's what I learned in Pontiac. . . . I not only loved those colored boys, but I was one of them—I felt closer to them than I felt to the whites, and I even got the same treatment they got. . . . They were right for kicking me out of that beanery in Cape Girardeau. I belonged on the other side of the track" (18).

As this passage suggests, notwithstanding Mezzrow's use of personalistic idioms of "belonging" that speak primarily to his own needs and desires, his identification with the "colored boys" at Pontiac has explicit political as well as psychological dimensions. In particular, the passage represents blues and jazz as the *cultural* frameworks for Mezzrow's expression of political solidarity with black people based on shared experiences of racialization. This thesis of the cultural mediation of Mezzrow's political and personal desire to belong on the "other side of the track" is developed in a passage in which Mezzrow describes a race riot that breaks out at Pontiac after a group of southern white boys attack a black prisoner named Big Six for having a white "punk." Explicitly calling the reader's attention to the sexualized violence that links the attack and lynchings—although "I'm not going to apologize for Big Six," Mezzrow interjects rather defensively; "I'm just saying that the Southern boys had their punks, too, plenty of them, but they resented a Negro doing the same things they did with a white boy. It was the same evil that white Southerners have about a Negro man and a white woman" (15–16)— Mezzrow goes on to describe how the attack instills in him an indelible fear and hatred of the South, despite the fact that he himself is not a target of the violence. Hospitalized with dysentery after the riot, he speculates that his illness is exacerbated by a "nervous system" set awry by his witnessing of a "murdering hate" that continues to haunt him well after the violence has ceased: "All the time I was stretched out on the infirmary cot I kept looking at the blank walls and seeing the mean, murdering faces of those Southern peckerwoods. . . . It couldn't have been worse if they'd come after me" (16). The scene comes full circle when later, after he is released from the hospital, Mezzrow asks Yellow and King, the two black members of the Pontiac prison band, about their own experiences of racism and segregation.

Yet while Mezzrow's narration of the riot and its aftermath is noteworthy as an illustration of his development of empathy for black suffering (here, even in the context of homophobia), what is even more striking is the implication of his own highly romanticized narratives of such suffering in his culturally expressed resistance to white supremacy. For example, in a passage that immediately precedes his account of the riot, Mezzrow waxes philosophical about differences between "the white man" and the "Negro," establishing an ideal of "black" realness and authenticity that, though it mediates his identification with black culture, also depends on the inversion of racist stereotypes that cast African Americans as children:

> The white man is a spoiled child, and when he gets the blues he goes neurotic. But the Negro never had anything before and never expects anything after, so when the blues get him he comes out smiling and without any evil feeling. "Oh well," he says, "Lord, I'm satisfied. All I wants to do is to grow collard greens in my back yard and eat 'em." The white man can't feel that way, usually. . . . He's got the idea that because he feels bad somebody's done him wrong, and he means to take it out on somebody. The colored man, like as not can toss it off with a laugh and a mournful, but not too mournful, song about it. (14)

Laying the groundwork for his subsequent resistant reading of the riot as a disturbing spectacle of murderous and sexually vengeful "whiteness," this passage shows how Mezzrow's racial transgressions are shaped by his idealization of racial oppression as a source of "black" cultural authenticity. Contracting stereotypical imagery, aesthetic commentary, and a critique of the inauthenticity of "white" identities, the passage reveals how Mezzrow's own political disidentification from whiteness hinges on his mastery of cultural stereotypes that depict African American cultural practices as "natural" in order to render them sources of white liberation from the culturally stultifying effects of modernity and "civilization."[30] The point here is not merely that Mezzrow wishes to distance himself from the image of a neurotic white man, or even that he invests positive value in cultural stereotypes of the "happy-go-lucky" "Negro," but that he uses the *ideological opposition* of these two figures to underwrite the production of his own racially and politically transgressive identity. Ironically, by casting "black" subjects as outsiders to "culture,"[31] Mezzrow establishes the possibility of "choosing" blues as the cultural medium of both his own quest for authenticity and his expression of resistance to white supremacy.

In his book *Riding on a Blue Note: Jazz and American Pop*, cultural critic Gary Giddins observes that "the important thing about white jazzmen is not that they appropriated the black American's music—a narrow and paranoid sentiment that denies the individuality of all jazzmen, white and black—but that so many of them chose a black aesthetic as the best possible source for self-examination."[32] Yet this narrative of individualized "choosing," while investing a certain agency and authority in a "black" aesthetic, also runs the risk of aestheticizing the process by which Mezzrow mediates his own transgressive identifications through cultural stereotypes.[33] What Wolfe calls Mezzrow's "negrophilia" does not exist in a representational space separate from aesthetics, but is rather fully implicated in Mezzrow's production of a "transgressive" subjectivity through his attraction to African American musical culture as a source of individual self-discovery and self-expression.[34] As I show in the following section, such entanglements are made even more explicit in the second step of his "conversion": namely, his decision to become a professional musician.

TRADING PLACES

After serving a year's sentence in Pontiac, from which he is released on good behavior, Mezzrow returns home, working odd jobs and eventually gravitating to South Side clubs like the De Luxe and Royal Garden, then centers of Chicago's emerging jazz scene. There he mingles with some of the era's most important entertainers, including Bill Robinson, Al Jolson, Sophie Tucker, and the comedy team Williams and Walker, and gets his first taste of hearing Bechet play live, with the Original New Orleans Creole Jazz Band. Briefly imprisoned again in 1919—he's in the hospital faking appendicitis when the Chicago race riots break out that July—Mezzrow decides, upon his release, to pursue a career in music.

It is in a passage from this section of the narrative, one portraying Mezzrow's departure from the domestic sphere of his family, that *Really the Blues* further elaborates on the theme of his "conversion to the 'race'" in terms of a quest for "realness," defined in explicitly classed and gendered terms. The occasion for this next phase of Mezzrow's "voluntary Negro" enterprise is his attempt to transcribe the lyrics of several recordings by Bessie Smith to figure out the "great secret" of her singing. Initially Mezzrow works alone on this project, but his father later persuades him to ask his sister Helen for help, the rationale being that because she is a secretary, transcribing the lyrics in shorthand will be "a cinch" for her. Yet although Helen dutifully complies with his request, Mezzrow is infuriated at the results:

> If my sister had made a table-pad out of my best record or used my old horn for a garbage can she couldn't have made me hotter than she did that day. I've never been so steamed up, before or since. She was in a very proper and dicty mood, so she kept "correcting" Bessie's grammar, straightening out her words and putting them in "good" English until they sounded like some stuck-up jive from *McGuffy's Reader* instead of the real down-to-earth language of the blues. That girl was schooled so good, she wouldn't admit there was such a word as "ain't" in the English language, even if a hundred million Americans yelled it in her face every hour of the day. I've never felt friendly towards her to this day, on account of how she laid her fancy high-school airs on the immortal Bessie Smith. (54)

The passage is brought to closure with an act of revenge, as one afternoon, when he is attending a practice session with the recently formed New Orleans Rhythm Kings, it suddenly dawns on Mezzrow that he has "to cut loose in some way, to turn my back once and for all on that hincty, killjoy world of my sister's and move over to Bessie Smith's world body and soul" (54). In the middle of the rehearsal, Mezzrow goes home, steals Helen's Hudson-seal fur coat from a closet, and sells it to a madam for $150, using the money to purchase an alto saxophone (the first instrument he will own). When he returns, he breaks out the saxophone to play with the Rhythm Kings, imagining that every note is a "blast at my sister and her book-learning" (54). After rehearsal Mezzrow moves out of his parents' house for good, renting himself a room in a building across from a pool hall, where he briefly worked.[35]

Unlike the first chapter of *Really the Blues*, which highlights similar experiences of racial/ethnic definition among African Americans and Jews, this passage depicts Mezzrow's musical aspirations as inherently at odds with his social location within a middle-class Jewish household.[36] According to the logic of the passage, Mezzrow's departure from the domestic sphere, a space associated with the enforcement of bourgeois norms, is a necessary and important step in his artistic development.[37] In effect, becoming a jazz musician means adopting a certain oppositional stance with regard to those values (such as acquiring "good" English) associated with the class and social mobility of first-generation Jewish Americans of Eastern European ancestry. In the specific gendered terms of Mezzrow's representation, it means shifting his primary social and cultural identifications away from his sister, a speaker of "stuck-up jive from *McGuffy's Reader*," and instead associating himself with the figure of those "hundred million Americans" who would yell "ain't" in her face all day. In short, what constitutes a "step up" in professional terms also implies and mediates Mezzrow's willful "step down" the proverbial ladder of class and social prestige.

Here again, however, Mezzrow's formation of a socially and culturally "oppositional" identity ironically depends on his embrace of modernist culture's own racializing narratives of "black" sexuality as both "freer" and more instinctive (that is, more primitive) than "white" sexuality—and of black women, in particular, as sexually more "down to earth" than middle-class white women. This irony emerges most clearly in Mezzrow's structuring of the scene of his departure from the domestic sphere according to the formal conventions of the familiar "I've got a woman at home who treats me bad / I've got a woman in town who's good to me" blues lyric. Such narrative structuring pits Helen, as the embodiment of a sexually "uptight" bourgeois femininity, against Smith, the nondomestic woman who presumably knows how to please (and keep) her man. It also relies on an equation of middle-class Jewish womanhood with the creative (and sexual) emasculation of Jewish men, who are seen to find better outlets for the cultivation of normative masculinity in their partnerships (symbolic or actual) with black women. Through the opposition of these two figures, one a Jewish secretary, one an African American blues singer, Mezzrow thus constructs the raced and classed female "portals" through which he can establish his own powerful and transgressive masculinity, one associated with the gendered social spaces of the pool hall, the brothel, and the nightclub.

Even as the passage carefully deploys a series of interwoven binary oppositions deriving from this central opposition of Helen and Smith— that is, between spontaneity and affectation, autonomy and domestic "entrapment," creative freedom and artistic straitjacketing—so it also conceals Mezzrow's own agency by painting him as the victim of Helen's "betrayal" of Smith's lyrics. Contrasting his sister's stultifying conformity and philistinism with Smith's "native" genius, Mezzrow not only portrays himself as linguistically and culturally more compatible with Smith, he also positions himself as a protector against attempts to "whiten" her music. In differentiating himself from Helen, in other words, Mezzrow works to secure for himself a certain artistic legitimacy and license that he denies other "white" performers on the grounds that they are stealing from black performers. Meanwhile Mezzrow's theft of Helen's fur coat, an act that primarily serves his professional ambitions, is rationalized as a justifiable redistribution of wealth: what Mezzrow in another context refers to as stealing "good, like Robin Hood" (51). Mezzrow thus ensures his successful transition from amateur to "real" musician by staking his authenticity on his chivalrous defense of African American musical traditions as embodied in the sexualized figure of the "Empress of the Blues."

The scripting of this passage exemplifies how Mezzrow's self-fashioning entails a process of first securing the very boundaries he proposes to transgress. As *Really the Blues* portrays it, his "voluntary Negro" passing is thus not merely an expression of racial apostasy, but a means by which Mezzrow legitimates patriarchal desire through the manipulation of broader social and cultural narratives of "blackness." At the same time, the mediation of Mezzrow's desire through the image of Smith and through the visit to the madam frames his quest for "Negro" authenticity as heterosexualizing enterprise, although it is predicated on his emotional and bodily intimacy with black men. The terms of this representation of "interracial" male intimacy become clearer in the next section, in which I investigate moments of Mezzrow's "conversion" that emerge through his idealizing portrayal of "black" talk and musical collaboration.

"BLACK" TALK

I began this discussion of *Really the Blues* by proposing that it can be read as a passing narrative about the impossibility of passing. Scenes in Mezzrow's narrative script moments of "crossing over," yet because his passing is predicated on a wish to play jazz "the way only Negroes can," there is a constant tension in Mezzrow's text between performing and "being," a veering between merely imitating "otherness" and actually *becoming* "other." I have tried to show, too, how Mezzrow attempts to bridge this division between self and other through claims based in commonalities of knowledge or experience, arguing that these are invested in the very power relations that Mezzrow also wishes to transcend.

A final set of examples serves to demonstrate how Mezzrow confronts the difficulty of bringing to closure a narrative whose logical end point would seem to elude representation. How does Mezzrow manage the task of simultaneously speaking *for* and speaking *from* the place of the "other"? How does agency get figured and refigured in the process of negotiating between these two subject-positions? How is Mezzrow's passing finally made "real?"

Like all autobiography, *Really the Blues* is a deliberate and concerted fiction of the self. Yet what distinguishes *Really the Blues* from other autobiographical texts is the degree to which Mezzrow stakes the authenticity of his narrative on his ability to compel the reader's belief in the naturalness of his own performance. Passing is above all a social practice, predicated not merely on the "performance" of identity (that is, on the recognition of identities as socially produced), but on others' ability or willingness to affirm that this performance is also "real": that one "is," so to speak, the identity that one claims to be.

Mezzrow's autobiography involves the reader in this process of adjudicating identity by displaying his mastery of jazz jive. Not only is jive easily learned and imitated, but insofar as it is a hallmark of racial "difference" not ascribed to the body, Mezzrow can use jive to fashion a "black" self on paper.[38] Indeed, in that part of *Really the Blues* titled the "Jive Section," it is precisely the conceit of the indecipherability of black talk to white readers that Mezzrow invokes to establish the authenticity of his identity.[39] That the jive section serves such a strategic function is underscored by the fact that it serves no discernible narrative purpose aside from displaying Mezzrow's fluency. Occurring in the midst of a longer discussion of depression-era drug culture in Harlem, where Mezzrow had moved in 1928 (subsequent to developing his performing career in Chicago), it consists of several conversations that are later translated for the reader in an appendix whose title—"Translation of the Jive Section"—recalls Mezzrow's own fated attempts to transcribe Smith's lyrics. Ironically, however, where Mezzrow's translation of Sonny's voice might be seen to reproduce the "whitening" that so angers him when his sister transcribes Smith's lyrics, in the jive section Mezzrow's ability to shift in and out of the vernacular signifies the fluidity of his identity rather than his captivity to a bourgeois standard.

The jive section is a privileged passage in *Really the Blues* because it portrays an actual moment when Mezzrow "passes"—an impression highlighted by the shift to dramatic form, which conveys the sense that it is a transcript of actual conversations even while drawing attention to their staged, or performed, nature. In the following excerpt Mezzrow is at a Harlem street corner selling drugs when a regular (here called Fourth Cat) approaches him with a friend, Sonny, who is so impressed by Mezzrow's talk that he teases Mezzrow about having black "blood":

> FOURTH CAT (*Coming up with a stranger*): Mezz, this here is Sonny Thompson, he one of the regular cats on The Avenue and can lay some iron too. Sonny's hip from way back and solid can blow some gage, so lay an ace on us and let us get gay. He and Pops [Louis Armstrong] been knowin' each other for years.
>
> ME: Solid, man, any stud that's all right with Pops must really be in there. Here, pick up Sonny, the climb's on me.
>
> SONNY (*To his friend*): Man, you know one thing? This cat should of been born J.B., he collars all jive and comes on like a spaginzy. (*Turning to me.*) Boy, is you sure it ain't some of us in your family way down the line? Boy you're too much, stay with it, you got to git it.
>
> FIFTH CAT: Hey Poppa Mezz! Stickin'?
>
> ME: Like the chinaberry trees in Aunt Hagar's backyard. (217)

Here is Mezzrow's translation (from the appendix) of the voice of the character Sonny:

> SONNY (*To his friend*): Do you want to know something? This guy should have been born jet black, he understands all our subtleties and talks like a Negro. (*Turning to me.*) Boy, are you sure there isn't some colored blood in your family tree? Boy, you're too much to cope with, you keep plugging, you're bound to be successful in life. (355)

Much like the *Ebony* photograph that I described at the outset, the jive section of *Really the Blues* dramatizes Mezzrow's camaraderie with a group of African American men on a Harlem street corner. It conveys an impression of ease and familiarity, further establishing Mezzrow's belonging through the character Sonny, who mock-seriously asks Mezzrow whether there is "some of us in your family way down the line."

In another context such a question might be unwelcome, and yet here it contributes to the text's cultivation of a series of associative links between bodily proximity and racial "sameness" that operate within the implicitly homoerotic framework of Mezzrow's romanticization of African American male musicians as embodiments of creative (that is, sexual as well as artistic) power. The erotics of "interracial" male intimacy, made clearer through the text's exclusion of women *except* as conduits of male bonding and sociability (or as a means of establishing Mezzrow's heterosexuality), is at once a familiar conceit of male musical culture (in which the presence of women as sexual "distractions" is seen to inhibit or preclude the male creative process) and a crucial aspect of Mezzrow's "voluntary Negro" self-representation, which frequently depicts his homosocial interactions with black men as the sign of his own "realness." The character "Girl" (the girlfriend of a male customer) in the jive section draws the reader's attention to this erotics of interracial male intimacy when she teases Mezzrow about his relationship with Armstrong. "All the chicks is talkin' 'bout you and Pops," she says. "Sure it ain't somethin' freakish goin' down 'tween you two? You sure got the ups on us pigeons, we been on a frantic kick tryin' to divide who's who" (217). The "translation" only makes her insinuations that there is "somethin' freakish" about them more explicit: "All the girls are always talking about you and Louis. Are you sure there isn't something funny between you two? You sure got the upper hand on us young girls, we've been going crazy trying to decide which of you is the wife and which the husband" (355).

This passage (as well as several others that might be cited as supporting evidence) does not so much indicate Mezzrow's or Armstrong's homosexuality as it firmly establishes the homosocial plotting of Mezzrow's "voluntary Negro" self-representation, linking his "realness" as a jazz performer to both his nearness to "black" bodies and his deviance, via this proximity, from sexual norms prohibiting male homosexuality and governing the expression of "interracial" sexual desire. According to the logic of such homosocial plotting, moments when Mezzrow is physically closest to African American jazz musicians are also those when he comes nearest to realizing his fantasy of "crossing the line" (as Sonny's comment about "blood" alludes). Yet this ideal of interracial male intimacy as a conduit of "voluntary Negro" passing is consistently undermined in *Really the Blues* through the always threatened return of "difference." For example, although the jive section highlights Mezzrow's linguistic identity with Sonny, "Fourth Cat," and the other men gathered on the corner to buy his wares, its effect is ultimately double-edged: It affirms Mezzrow's insider status, but only at the risk of exposing his "black" identity to be obviously and self-consciously staged."[40] The purpose of the passage is to represent sameness, yet it can do so only in the most contrived and rehearsed terms, caricaturing "blackness" in a manner that recalls the ambivalent parodies of the minstrel stage. Designed to affirm Mezzrow's gendered and raced authenticity, it instead reveals his narrative to be structured around an anxiety of inauthenticity—a fear nourished by Mezzrow's implied cognizance of his inability fully to control the terms of his own racial performance.

It is during moments that portray homosocial proximity and intimacy, in other words, that *Really the Blues* reveals the *instability* of Mezzrow's embrace of deviance from bourgeois racial and sexual norms. At one point, contemplating his musical ability relative to Armstrong's— he "could make great music behind him with nothing but a washboard and a kazoo. I was no Louis"—Mezzrow admits to experiencing nagging anxiety about his masculinity and his artistic identity: "The race made me feel inferior, started me thinking that maybe I wasn't worth beans as a musician or any kind of artist, in spite of all my big ideas. The tremendous inventiveness, the spur-of-the-moment creativeness that I saw gushing out in all aspects of Harlem life, in the basketball games, the prize-fights, the cutting contests, the fast and furious games of rhyming and snagging on The Corner—it all dazzled me, made me doubt if I was even in the running with these boys" (239).

This anxiety comes to a head as *Really the Blues* is brought to closure through a series of events that complete the circle of the narrative, symbolically returning Mezzrow to the reformatory where he first discovered blues. Rapidly being outmoded by the development of bebop and facing obsolescence as a performer, Mezzrow once again returns to prison in 1940, this time to serve a three-year term on Riker's Island for drug possession (marijuana had recently been recriminalized). Initially assigned to the white side of the cell blocks (later he will tell the deputy that he is "colored" and have himself transferred to the Jim Crow block), Mezzrow reacts to the white inmates like Gulliver upon returning to England after his travels. Face-to-face with junkies, derelicts, and drunks—symbols of "the dying white-man's world" (304), he longingly recalls Harlem, "where the people [are] real and earthy" (306). "I could hardly listen to the talk of my cellmates," he writes, "their language and mannerisms and gestures were so coarse and brutal, they spoke with their lips all twisted up, in harsh accents that jarred on my nerves" (306). Yet whereas in Swift political satire opens up a space for critique, Mezzrow's investment in his own "realness" precludes self-ironizing gestures. In contrast to the jive section, where Mezzrow plays the dual role of interlocutor and translator, here such duality can only be construed as threatening to Mezzrow's critical disidentification from "whiteness."

Mezzrow's inability to indulge in self-parody on Riker's Island marks the imminent breakdown of his fantasy. Instead, however, of working to understand the politics of his "voluntary Negro" passing, Mezzrow resigns himself to the impossibility of ever crossing over through a scene of spiritual "possession" by the spirits of his jazz heroes. While playing with the prison's Ninth Division jazz band, he rises above not only musical memory and influence, but agency itself:

> And then, Jesus, I fell into a queer dreamy state, a kind of trance, where it seemed like I wasn't in control of myself any more, my body was running through its easy relaxed motions and my fingers were flying over the keys without any push or effort from me—somebody else had taken over and was directing all my moves, with me just drifting right along with it, feeling it was all fitting and good and proper. . . . And it was exactly, down to a T., the same serene exaltation I'd sensed in New Orleans music as a kid, and that had haunted me all my life, that I'd always wanted to recapture for myself and couldn't . . . and my clarinet and the trumpet melted together in one gigantic harmonic orgasm, and my fingers ran every whichaway. . . . And all of a sudden, you know who I was? I was Jimmy Noone and Johnny Dodds and Sidney Bechet . . . they were inside my skin, making my fingers work right so I could speak my piece. (321-24)

Mezzrow's narrative of falling into a "queer dreamy state" in which social distinctions between self and other fade in a single moment of openly homoerotic rapture extends his text's conceit of interracial male intimacy. Here it encompasses the blurring of both the physical boundaries that define the individual human body, marking it off from other bodies, and the boundaries that demarcate Mezzrow's own corporeality from the incorporeality of memory. Such rapture as Mezzrow experiences in this final "millennial" moment of his text also marks a homecoming, the completion of a circuit. Like the wandering Jew of the parable, Mezzrow writes, "I had been wandering for twenty years, looking for this fine fabled place, and suddenly I made it, I was home" (323). In contrast to the first millennium, in which Mezzrow comes out of reform school "chocolate brown," on Riker's Island he is restored to a previous greenness. "The rest of my life spread out in front of me smooth and serene," he writes, "because I not only knew what I had to do, I knew I could do it. . . . The millennium was on me—a small-size, strictly one-man millennium, but still a millennium" (324). Through the rehearsal of this final millennial moment, in other words, Mezzrow enables his narrative to arrive at a tentative ending, superimposing closure on a blues aesthetic marked by infinite variation on a single theme.

"VOLUNTARY NEGRO" PASSING AND THE POLITICS OF IDENTITY

Like a photographic negative, the white negro was an inverted image of otherness, in which attributes devalorized by the dominant culture were simply revalorized or hypervalorized as emblems of alienation and outsiderness, a kind of strategic self-othering in relation to dominant culture norms. . . . There is a whole modernist position of 'racial romanticism' that involves a fundamental ambivalence of identifications. At what point do such identifications result in an imitative masquerade of white ethnicity? At what point do they result in ethical and political alliances? How can we tell the difference?
—KOBENA MERCER, "Skin Head Sex Thing"[41]

The questions Kobena Mercer poses in the above passage—an extract from "Skin Head Sex Thing," an essay about photographer Robert Mapplethorpe's portraits of black male nudes—are also among those that *Really the Blues* impels us to ask. What are we to make of a narrative that is so deeply and obviously enacting what Mercer calls "racial romanticism" and yet at the same time positioning itself at the vanguard of a certain antiracist cultural politics? How do we determine whether Mezzrow's identifications are merely "an imitative masquerade of white ethnicity"? In terms of the goal of producing ethical and political alliances, what are the limitations and possibilities of Mezzrow's "voluntary Negro" enterprise?

As a way of beginning to answer such questions, we might look to James Baldwin's essay "The Black Boy Looks at the White Boy," written partly in response to Norman Mailer's 1957 "The White Negro" piece, in which Baldwin recalls a conversation he once had with an African American jazz musician. "Man," the musician tells him, referring to Mailer, "the only trouble with that cat is that he's white."[42] Baldwin parses this comment as a "shrewd observation" not simply about Mailer as an individual but about the social context that encourages white men "to believe the world is theirs" and that the world will "help them in the achievement of their identity" (183). Among the problems with such beliefs, Baldwin observes, is that the workings of power can only appear "helpful" and accommodating to those who are not under obligation to understand how power works *on* them. Symbolically returning the objectifying and eroticizing gaze of Mailer's essay, which celebrates "white Negro" identity as a transgressive alternative to postwar bourgeois culture, Baldwin thus suggests that the cultural elevation of "blackness" by those who are not thus racially defined may be an instrument and an effect of racial discourse, not only a means of imagining opposition to it.[43] Indeed, it may merely expand the possibilities for the dominant cultural expression of racial domination in the form of a professed admiration for "black" culture or style.

While also finding Mailer's essay "deeply reactionary," Mercer in "Skin Head Sex Thing" offers a means of interpreting the complicity of the "White Negro" as a historically and culturally specific expression of a larger dynamic he names "the ambivalent racial fetishization of difference." Clarifying his reading of the politics of Mailer's essay in response to a question, Mercer warns against the construction of a binary of complicity/resistance as a recapitulation of that oppositional logic that also structures racial ideology.[44] "One can't simply resolve the matter" of telling the difference between an exploitative appropriation of "otherness" and an enabling identification with it by insisting on a particular text's or author's goodness or badness, he argues, "because such binary thinking ends up with the static concept of identity rather than the more volatile concept of identification" (216). Condemning particular texts or authors, in other words, may leave us in the difficult position of also abjuring the very political possibilities associated with the transgression of race.

The urgency and difficulty of these issues are further compounded

in our own contemporary moment, when a certain narrative of social/
cultural "transgression" has become part of the logic of global capitalism in its pursuit of new consumers and markets. As cultural critic bell
hooks observes, in a context in which "race" and racialized identities
are "positively" objectified through the mediation of capital, identifying
with "difference" may in fact be a culturally normative means of expressing an alliance with power. As she writes, "To make one's self vulnerable
to the seduction of difference, to seek an encounter with the Other, does
not require that one relinquish forever one's mainstream positionality.
When race and ethnicity become commodified as resources for pleasure, the culture of specific groups, as well as the bodies of individuals,
can be seen as constituting an alternative playground where members
of dominating races, genders, sexual practices affirm their power-over
in intimate relations with the Other." [45] The idealization of otherness as
a strategy of global capital is, as hooks suggests, reason to be wary of
too easily attributing transgressive value to acts of "crossing the line"
that may not only be *merely* gestural, but fully supportive of a regime of
capital expansion that persists at the expense of subjects who are ruth-
lessly or even increasingly racialized within a supposedly boundaryless
global order. Moreover, to the degree that they, too, are mediated by
commodity culture, the spaces of "intimate" social relations cannot be
privileged as a space "outside" the dynamics of racial hierarchy.[46]

Yet the necessity of critiquing the consumption of racial "otherness"
as an imperative of global capital, even (or especially) as it infiltrates the
"private sphere" of personal intimacies, need not lead us to reject outright any articulation of racial transgression on the part of "white" subjects as merely another means of recuperating the stability of the color
line. To do so, as Mercer suggests, is to risk reinstating the racial binary
through critical gestures that disallow any possibility of acknowledging
the strategic "impurity" of resistance itself (insisting, in the meantime,
on the transcendence of the cultural critic).[47] Given that it is one of the
hallmark desires of "whiteness," it may be equally important, in other
words, to resist "purity" as a prerequisite of antiracist struggles.

My analysis of *Really the Blues* has revealed how Mezzrow mediated
his project of "voluntary Negro" identity through notions of blackness
that, despite being invested with "positive" value, were also entrenched
within racial discourse—indeed, the very discourse that enabled (and
even encouraged) Mezzrow to see in "Negro" identity a means of nego-

tiating masculinity and expressing defiance of bourgeois social norms.[48] At the same time, that "realness" that Mezzrow imagined to be embodied in African American jazz musicians, and which he pursued as an object of identificatory investment and pleasure, also offered him a rich symbolism for representing resistance to a dominant culture that held African Americans and African American culture to be inherently inferior.[49] Yet if we cannot resolve this contradiction of Mezzrow's project of "transgressing" race through a celebratory reading of his cultural politics (and even less so through a narrative of his "good intentions") neither must we ascribe to his passing a purely colonizing and exploitative desire. Rather, we might inquire into how the binary between resistance and power is itself mediated by racial discourse.

As the analysis of racial passing reveals, boundaries, as entities that must continually be produced, safeguarded, and maintained, are also active sites of negotiation, contestation, and struggle. "Telling the difference," as Mercer puts it, thus may not be a matter of recovering a stable or transcendent opposition between stability and fluidity, transgression and compliance, but of fielding heterogeneous and impure interests and desires, with the knowledge that these, too, are always provisional and always improvised. To rephrase Mercer's questions, What if Mezzrow was acting out classed and gendered fantasies of "blackness" and yet simultaneously constructing alliances? What if the sources of alliance that his text imaginatively projects are themselves inevitably impure?

The issue of impurity returns us, finally, to Mezzrow's depiction of his struggles to live up to his own impossible standard of "realness." A final irony of *Really the Blues* is that although it affects a tone of exuberant playfulness, ultimately it is weighted down by the impossibly high stakes by which Mezzrow defined the project of racial passing. As Bechet himself observed, Mezzrow took his wish to play blues "the way only Negroes can" so seriously that it got in the way of his playing. "Mezzrow, he'd had this rage of being King of Harlem for a while and that was wearing out some," Bechet writes in his autobiography *Treat It Gentle*. "When a man is trying so hard to be something he isn't, when he's trying to be some name he makes up for himself instead of just being what he is, some of that will show in his music, the idea of it will be wrong."[50]

Bechet's commentary on Mezzrow's obsession with "Negro" realness—an obsession, as Baldwin reminds us, that exacts an even greater toll on those expected to possess and perform it—underscores the ultimate pathos of Mezzrow's "voluntary Negro" enterprise. Reversing the "gaze," so to speak, Bechet relates Mezzrow's quest for authenticity to his struggles to give musical expression to contradictory and conflicting desires. Constantly professing to have "crossed the line" and yet never quite reaching the "millennium" he imagined, Mezzrow's life played itself out as a series of desperate and harried improvisations, his own Voluntary Negro Blues.

CHAPTER 3

Boundaries Lost

and Found:

Racial Passing

and Cinematic

Representation,

circa 1949

Don't hate me because I'm still tragic and beautiful (after all these years). Isn't it true I work best for you as a tragedy? You have your moment of showy guilt, then I'm out of your hair for another decade. You never have to face that this Frankenstein of yours is you also, is us, is America. But how could you? That renders you impure. So let it remain just me and my tragedy. The toxic mix of my blood.

—LISA JONES, "Tragedy Becomes Her"[1]

O f the many stories of racial passing reported in the black press throughout the 1930s and 1940s, that of Elsie Roxborough, born into Detroit's black upper class in 1914, was probably one of the best known, if not among the most sensational.[2] The daughter of Charles Anthony Roxborough, Michigan's first black state senator, and the niece of John Roxborough, who made his fortune as the originator of Detroit's numbers racket, Roxborough grew up surrounded by a kind of wealth that was rare, especially for African Americans, during the depression: a large house, live-in maids, summers at Idlewild (the black resort community in northern Michigan), and even her own Ford roadster, which she took with her when she enrolled at the University of Michigan in the fall of 1934. Talented, confident, and widely touted as beautiful, with a fair complexion and brown eyes, Roxborough grew up accustomed to the scrutiny of black society-page columnists, who followed her whereabouts and monitored her love life. When she was seventeen, rumor circulated of her engagement to rising boxing star Joe Louis, whose career her uncle John had sponsored; but as Roxborough told the *Chicago Defender*, she and Louis had no plans of matrimony and, in any case, she valued her "career as a writer" more than "the thought of marriage."

From the evidence of her early efforts, these career prospects looked promising. At college Roxborough studied playwriting alongside classmate and fellow campus newspaper reporter Arthur Miller, who beat her out of first prize in an April 1936 young dramatists contest in which she placed third. In the mid-1930s, when she was still in her twenties, Roxborough staged several plays (including *Flight*, her stage adaptation of Walter White's 1924 novel of the same name), formed the Roxane Players, her own black theater company, and developed a close friendship with Langston Hughes. The two fended off gossip of a romance, and although they eventually drifted apart, Hughes reportedly kept a photograph of Roxborough over his writing table until he died. Despite such auspicious beginnings, however, Roxborough's playwriting career never materialized. Critics panned her plays (one reviewer from the *Chicago Defender* complained that her work *Wanting*, in which the characters made plans to go on cycling trips in Italy and could afford yachts, sounded "ridiculous" in the mouths of "Race actors"), and Roxborough grew increasingly frustrated with the limited career opportunities available to black women who wanted to work—but not as performers—in the theater.

Some time in the fall of 1937, the year that Louis became the world heavyweight boxing champion and a household name, Roxborough dyed her hair auburn and "moved over to the other side" of the color line. On Christmas Day the *Baltimore Afro-American* reported that she had been "living in Gotham for the past few months as Nordic—much to her family's undisguised disgust."[3] Two years later she turned up as Pat Rico, a white model who lived in Greenwich Village; later she changed her name to Mona Manet, ran an East Fifty-second Street modeling studio, and occasionally contributed articles to various publications, including a short-lived style magazine called *Fascination*. When Mona Manet was discovered dead by a roommate in 1949, an uncle and aunt who could pass for white came to New York to claim her body, taking care not to reveal Roxborough's racial identity to her roommate. The *New York Times* carried no obituary for Manet, whose death certificate listed her as a "writer, white," but Detroit's black press displayed the story of Roxborough's untimely demise at age thirty-five prominently on its front page, attributing the cause of death to "nerves," in deference to her family and because Roxborough, in any case, had left no suicide note.[4]

The silences, elisions, and imposed invisibility that structure the "official" memory of Elsie Roxborough, whose story never crossed the color line, ironically contrasts with the public visibility and cultural agency of the two films, *Pinky* (Twentieth Century-Fox) and *Lost Boundaries* (Film Classics), that are the subject of this chapter. Released the same week that Mona Manet died, both center on the experience of racialized subjects who pass (or who are tempted to pass) for white, taking pains to deploy the passing narrative as a means of forwarding liberal parables about the ability of African Americans to establish themselves as justly "deserving" citizens within—and therefore despite—the construct of "race." In contrast to the sexualized "plot" of Roxborough's life, which suggests the intersecting roles of race and gender in circumscribing her choices despite her class privilege, in *Pinky* and *Lost Boundaries* the racialized protagonists assume bourgeois agency and (gendered) respectability, retaining many of the social and material "wages" associated with "white" identity even though they ultimately renounce crossing the line as a means of social and economic mobility.[5] In *Pinky* not only is the title character able to establish herself as an unmarried, middle-class female black subject in a southern context (that is, a context more typically associated with the sexual degradation and class oppression of black women),[6] but Pinky's fulfillment of her professional and class aspirations is predicated on her decision *not* to pass. Whereas Roxborough apparently passed at least in part as a way of dodging racism and sexism faced by black women working in theater, in *Lost Boundaries*, a film that centers on the frustrated career ambitions of an African American male physician, such impediments to black professional advancement are ultimately made to appear surmountable in light of a white community's goodwill toward its black neighbors. Indeed, although both *Pinky* and *Lost Boundaries* represent racial discrimination and exclusion as inducements to pass, the real heroes of the films are sympathetic whites and an American class structure that promises racially defined subjects the means of establishing themselves as successful citizens despite—and most disturbingly, perhaps, because of—their "difference" from the white majority.

In *Pinky*, directed by Elia Kazan, white actress Jeanne Crain, a performer best known to 1940s audiences as a "wholesome alternative" to Gene Tierney,[7] stars in the title role of a young black woman who returns to the South after passing for white while studying nursing in the North.[8] Although Pinky goes back to her childhood home intending only to say good-bye to her grandmother, Aunt Dicey (played by Ethel Waters), before she permanently crosses the line to marry her white lover, Tom Adams, she must confront her grandmother's deep disapproval of racial passing—"Pretending you is what you ain't," as Dicey puts it—and her insistence that Pinky owes a debt of service to her people (not to mention Dicey, who has helped to fund Pinky's education). Dicey makes no secret of the fact that she objects to Pinky's impending marriage and urges her granddaughter to break off her engagement; yet insofar as Dicey is never quite legitimized as either a political or maternal subject, her advice to Pinky is only ambiguously valorized. Rather, it is only through the agency of her growing friendship with Miss Em (played by Ethel Barrymore), an infirm white aristocrat, that Pinky begins to believe that passing represents a form of self-evasion. At her grandmother's request Pinky nurses Miss Em, and the two develop a surrogate mother-daughter bond. When Miss Em dies, she bequeaths the old plantation house to Pinky, provoking the latter's covetous relatives to bring a lawsuit against Pinky contending that she manipulated the dying woman for her own profit. In a penultimate courtroom scene, Pinky successfully defends her right to inherit Miss Em's property and then, swept up in a desire to live up to her patron's—not her grandmother's—expectations, concludes that her true vocation lies not in marriage and passing, but in converting the decrepit mansion into a hospital for black children.

Whereas *Pinky* maps the theme of passing onto the generic conventions of triangulated maternal melodrama (pitting an unlearned and poor black grandmother against an urbane and wealthy white mother-surrogate), *Lost Boundaries*, based loosely on the true story of a New England family, mediates its narrative of racial passing through the representation of a father-son dyad.[9] Directed by Alfred L. Werker and financed by Louis de Rochemont, best known for his documentary *March of Time* newsreels, *Lost Boundaries* stars Mel Ferrer as a black physician who, along with his wife, passes for white so that he can build a successful medical practice in a New Hampshire town. The plot of the film centers primarily on what happens when, decades later, the townspeople discover the family secret. Filmed in a documentary style, using a cast of mostly amateur actors from New Hampshire, *Lost Boundaries* also depicts the effects of the revelation of black heritage on the doctor's two children, who have grown up believing themselves to be white. The film focuses particular attention on their son Howard, who responds to his parents' disclosure by running away to Harlem to discover his "roots." From Harlem, represented as primitive, bleak, and degenerate, Howard eventually returns — via a kind black police officer — to New Hampshire, where he and the family are reunited and, ultimately, absolved for having committed a racial transgression.

As these brief synopses suggest, in both *Pinky* and *Lost Boundaries* the cinematic representation of racial passing is structured by the notion (ultimately related to national ideologies of the American Dream) that class and social mobility may be sources of racial transcendence for their juridically black protagonists. In these films, the first by white U.S. filmmakers to centralize the experiences of characters who pass for white, the narrative of racial passing, previously associated in Hollywood cinema with the sexualized threat of "invisible darkness" to "white" racial purity, is paradoxically retooled as a means of depicting the social and economic rewards of American citizenship for a national audience. I say paradoxically, because although *Pinky* and *Lost Boundaries* are eager to advance the notion of a United States in which industry and talent are the keys to middle-class success for all citizens, regardless of racial identity, they do so in a context that insists on the fundamental stability of the black/white binary. Both films construct narratives in which juridically black protagonists are disciplined for attempting to cross the line as a means of realizing social, economic, or professional ambitions — a narrative outcome that was, in any case, already predetermined by the infamous Hays and Breen offices, which threatened to censor any U.S. film that gave the appearance of tolerating so-called racial miscegenation.[10] At the same time, given their explicit commitment to popularizing a liberal postwar civil rights agenda whose goals included racial integration and the expansion of black citizenship rights, *Pinky* and *Lost Boundaries* are at pains to present their protagonists with alternative ways of entering (or remaining within) the ranks of the growing postwar middle class. In effect, the films enable their protagonists to realize their American "dreams" of professional success while also insisting that they remain in their "places," racially speaking.

The conclusions I draw from my analysis of *Pinky* and *Lost Boundaries* support this study's larger contention that the national narrative of class mobility as the opportunity of every deserving citizen is tied in complex ways to the stability of race as a means of collective social organization. According to this argument, the economic and professional successes of the protagonists in these films signal not so much their transcendence of racial discrimination and segregation (that is, the transcendence that is the promise of passing) as their incorporation into an occupational and reward hierarchy that can continue to use "race" as a means of social discipline and control. Indeed, in their respective narratives *Pinky* and *Lost Boundaries* suggest that even for protagonists who are phenotypically "white" (a fact hammered home through the use of white actors), this type of racial transcendence remains elusive. The only acceptable modes of "passing"—that is, those that are not seen as fundamentally opposed to the *national* interest—are those that remain firmly circumscribed by the "line" of the one-drop rule.

My analysis of how *Pinky* and *Lost Boundaries* both construct and resolve the narrative of racial passing is thus motivated by a desire to interrogate the racial narratives of liberalism itself, particularly that discourse of "Negro rights" that is both a product and a legacy of the postwar era. How, I ask, do *Pinky* and *Lost Boundaries* imagine the agency of title characters seemingly caught between competing demands of race "loyalty," familial responsibility, sexual desire (especially in the case of Pinky), and social, professional, and economic ambition? How do the films negotiate the representation of the protagonists' racial definition within the context of a liberal political narrative of race, one whose cogency depends on its ability to establish color blindness as a principle and prerequisite of American democracy? How does liberalism "see" race, and what are the stakes of its vision for our understanding of race's power?

SENDING A "MESSAGE"

From a contemporary viewpoint, it is tempting to categorize these 1949 passing movies as period pieces that have the look, as cultural critic Lisa Jones has suggested, of "fabulously tormented B-movies" without their camp sensibilities.[11] Yet to relegate *Pinky* and *Lost Boundaries* to the status of quaint Hollywood anachronisms would amount to dismissing them for precisely those qualities that made them progressive in their own time. More crucially, it would mean potentially missing the ways in which these films' respective representations of "crossing the line" express underlying contradictions within postwar liberal political discourses of the "Negro problem" as well as the ruptures within conventional cinematic practices of representing collective forms of social oppression through narratives that focus on the lives of exceptional individuals. Rather than read *Pinky* and *Lost Boundaries* exclusively through the lens of their filmmakers' "good intentions," therefore, we might instead interrogate how these intentions themselves shape the terms of their respective representations of racial passing. How did white U.S. filmmakers in the late 1940s come to conceive of racial passing as an appropriate narrative device for the representation of "minority" experience to "mainstream" audiences? How is their commitment to realism as a mode of cinematic storytelling implicated in the production of racial passing narratives that refuse to concede authority over racial naming to these same "minority" characters?

The answers to these questions lie in part in the changing assumptions of U.S. filmmakers with regard to their own cultural practices.[12] By 1949 the major studios had largely abandoned their discourse of film as "mere" entertainment and begun openly to advocate the role of the cinema as a powerful shaper of national identity, not only for the U.S. domestic audiences who were still the primary consumers of Hollywood products, but increasingly for foreign audiences around the globe.[13] If Samuel Goldwyn's infamous (albeit perhaps apocryphal) line "If you want to send a message, call Western Union" had previously characterized the studios' collective attitude toward films that were explicitly invested in social and political critique, then movies such as *Pinky* and *Lost Boundaries* signaled the industry's new espousal of what some called its "cultural responsibility"—a calling that was all the more readily embraced once it became clear that social criticism and commercial popularity could go hand in hand.[14] Two in a series of five "message movies" released between the fall and spring of 1949 (the others were Stanley Kramer's *Home of the Brave*, Clarence Brown's adaptation of Faulkner's novel *Intruder in the Dust*, and Joseph Mankiewicz's *No Way Out*, starring Sidney Poitier), *Pinky* and *Lost Boundaries* were thus the products not only of individual filmmakers who correctly sensed that changes in the postwar political economy placed the nation "on the verge of the most important peacetime era of race relations since Reconstruction," as Thomas Cripps has argued, but also of an emerging consensus about the potential efficacy of cinematic representation to shape public discourse about race and national identity.[15]

Darryl Zanuck, the influential vice president at Twentieth Century-Fox who had overseen the production of *The Grapes of Wrath* (1940), exemplified this new outlook in a 1943 address before Congress. Speaking of the role of Hollywood filmmakers, Zanuck reasoned, "We've got to move onto new ground, break new trails. In short, we must play our part in the solution of the problems that torture the world. We must begin to deal realistically in film with the causes of wars and panics, with social upheavals and the depression, with starvation and want and injustice and barbarism under whatever guise." [16] Philip Dunne, coauthor of the screenplay of *Pinky* along with Dudley Nichols and Jane White (daughter of NAACP executive secretary Walter White), echoed Zanuck's comments in a short piece titled "An Approach to Racism," which later came to double as promotional material for the film. "We have throughout [the making of *Pinky*] remained conscious of our obligation to society in projecting such a film," Dunne wrote. "The experience of the war has taught us that the motion picture is a powerful and persuasive vehicle of propaganda. What we say and do on the screen in productions of this sort can affect the happiness, the living conditions, even the physical safety of millions of our fellow-citizens." In fact, Dunne argued, given the success of the Hollywood studies in producing wartime propaganda, the embrace of social realism could be reinterpreted as a marketing strategy. "Neutrality," he went on to write, in language still heavily marked by wartime metaphors,[17] "is as sterile dramatically as it is politically. Liberal democracy stultifies itself when it rationalizes away all conflict and passion. . . . We are propagandists only in so far as we insist that every human being is entitled to personal freedom and dignity." [18]

Such an embrace of social realism had a variety of salutary effects, particularly where the cinematic representation of African Americans was concerned. Although neither *Pinky* nor *Lost Boundaries* explicitly critiqued racial segregation, their sympathetic portrayals of individual black characters were widely welcomed as alternatives to the more typical Hollywood fare of the mid-1940s, which included black-cast musicals (for example, *Cabin in the Sky*), dramas featuring minor black supporting roles (*Casablanca*), racist nostalgia (Disney's *Song of the South*), and wartime propaganda (1944's *The Negro Soldier*, a film that was used in military recruitment efforts). Whereas conniving or tragic "mulattoes" had been stock characters of U.S. film from D. W. Griffith's *Birth of a Nation* (revived in 1947 by the Dixie Film Exchange, despite protests in New York and Philadelphia)[19] to John Stahl's 1934 film version of Fannie Hurst's best-selling novel *Imitation of Life*, *Pinky* and *Lost Boundaries* took it upon themselves to individualize—and in that process of individuation, to humanize—their protagonists, encouraging their audiences to see "crossing the line" not as a mere flight from black identity (in such cases presumed to be a source of tragedy or pathos), but as a way of circumventing the limitations imposed upon African Americans' social, economic, and geographical mobility. Hence although they still portrayed racial passing as a form of racial self-denial, in contrast to these earlier films, *Pinky* and *Lost Boundaries* were able to furnish a social rationale for passing that transcended individual psychology, personal misfortune, or impersonal circumstance. In particular, the films' frank representations of occupational racial discrimination (in *Lost Boundaries*) and racialized sexual violence (in *Pinky*) won them cautious praise from leaders of the NAACP[20] and the general admiration of the nascent bourgeois black popular press, which also applauded their showcasing of such familiar black film stars as Ethel Waters (*Pinky*) and Canada Lee (*Lost Boundaries*).

In short, there could be little doubt that social realism lent itself more readily than melodrama or farce to the production of "positive" cinematic images of individual African Americans. On the other hand, Zanuck's and Dunne's conception of film as a cultural agency of both social protest and national unity also presented a number of rather glaring contradictions that were uneasily "resolved" in the figure of the "exceptional Negro," that character whose experience differentiates him or her from the masses of black people. Not only was racial passing itself an "exceptional" problem, as Ralph Ellison had suggested in an advisory letter to de Rochemont during the making of *Lost Boundaries*,[21] but the films' methods of avoiding the "crisis" of the breakdown of the black/white binary readily lent themselves to the discovery of unexpected and even "unrealistic" solutions to the problem of racism. For example, while Zanuck, Dunne, and others could boast that *Pinky*'s spotlighting of the story of "one particular Negro girl" was its greatest achievement,[22] the film's depiction of Pinky's victory (before an all-white judge and jury) in winning the legal rights to the property that Miss Em had willed her also obscured the fact that most southern blacks still had little hope of success in suing whites in civil litigation in southern courtrooms. Similarly, the integration of the Carter family into all-white Keenam, New Hampshire, where Dr. Carter would continue to serve as town doctor, papered over the fact that in 1949 black physicians were still not generally permitted to treat white patients or to join the American Medical Association.[23]

These problems of realism as a rhetorical mode of address were only compounded by the question of how "realistically" to cast the protagonists of the 1949 passing films. The selection of white actors to play black roles (including the roles of the tragic mulattoes) was a time-honored Hollywood tradition, one that endured for a number of reasons: the zealousness of film censors anxious to excise suggestions of "interracial" romance; the conviction of Hollywood liberals that white actors would have an easier time soliciting white audience compassion for black characters; and, not least, the greater ability of the studios to market and promote films featuring white stars. Yet given their commitment to social justice and to the "authentic" representation of racism from the viewpoint of those who are racialized, the continuation of these practices in the making of *Pinky* and *Lost Boundaries* was particularly egregious. Practically speaking, the selection of Crain, Ferrer, and others made it possible for the studios to advocate racial integration as a necessary step in the realization of the promise of American democracy without having to confront their own discriminatory hiring practices. As a result of the studios' refusal to use black actors in these roles, in other words, Hollywood made its first tentative forays into the "realistic" representation of racism without ever depicting "real" black people as the objects of racial violence or discrimination—or, for that matter, as visible political subjects who could advocate on behalf of "Negro rights." In response to dominant cinematic stereotypes of black indolence, black irresponsibility, and black lasciviousness (especially of the tragic mulattos), *Pinky* and *Lost Boundaries* thus fetishized "true" depictions of black experience at the expense of allowing blacks to inhabit this experience "realistically."

In fact, the apparent realism of the passing films served to obfuscate the critical absence of black people on screen, such that even among commentators on the left, the "authenticity" of the films' portrayal of social conditions would be touted as the measure of their political efficacy. For example, in a generally scathing attack on the "new stereotype" in Hollywood film, V. J. Jerome, a leader of the U.S. Communist Party, lauded the two movies' attention to the fact of racism as a defining aspect of black experience, but ironically failed to make much ado about the fact that in the films the victims of this racism are white actors. Hence the scene in *Pinky* in which Jeanne Crain is harassed by a white police officer (but only after he discovers that she is black) becomes for Jerome "a great overpowering moment of film realism," and the scene in which she is nearly raped by two white men "a rare flash of truth on the American screen."[24]

The lack of black dramatic leads in either of the films is particularly noteworthy in *Lost Boundaries,* in which the pretense of documentary (a pretense reinforced by de Rochemont's previous film work, director Alfred Werker's use of nonprofessional actors, and the fact that the movie was shot on location in New Hampshire and Maine) helped to construct an implied contract of realism with the white viewer. Thus it is especially ironic that the one scene in *Lost Boundaries* in which the film represents an actual act of discrimination involves intraracial conflict of a most unrealistic nature—that is, when a black physician at an all-black medical clinic in the South turns down Scott Carter's appointment to serve as an intern because he looks, sounds, and acts "too white."[25] ("I don't think you'll have any trouble getting into a northern hospital," the black doctor tells him. "You mean because I'm a northern Negro I can't get a job here?" Scott replies incredulously.) Ironically, this was precisely Ralph Ellison's complaint about Jeanne Crain in *Pinky.* "One thing is certain," he observed, drolly cutting to the heart of the matter, "no one is apt to mistake her for a Negro, not even a white one."[26]

According to most accounts, black actors were hardly even considered for the leading roles in either film.[27] Popular light-skinned black actresses with proven box-office appeal among both whites and blacks—

such as Lena Horne or Fredi Washington, known for having played the character of Peola in Stahl's *Imitation of Life*—were quite conspicuously overlooked for the part of Pinky, and apparently Werker, director of *Lost Boundaries*, wavered in his decision of whom to cast for Scott Carter until he found out that Ferrer was willing to play the part.[28] Ferrer, who professed in *Negro Digest* to having "about a 16th Negro blood in me, but it's not very noticeable," and who said that he took the part over the advice of his agents (who felt that *Lost Boundaries* was a B-budgeted movie with an incendiary theme), recalled that while he was pleased to get to work with de Rochemont, he harbored self-consciousness about the role and relied upon black actors to help him in "interpreting" it.[29] "A bigger thing for me," he told the magazine in 1951, "will be when Hollywood provides more opportunities for Negro actors, actresses, writers, etc. . . . And Negro actors must have featured roles, too—not the stereotypes now being perpetuated in an alarming degree."[30]

For contemporary viewers it may be particularly difficult to imagine Crain, a former Miss Long Beach and a cover girl of the *Ladies' Home Journal*, as an object of racial oppression. Yet virtually every positive review of the films praises the performers who played the roles of the "passing" characters; even Jerome, who is critical of the casting, writes that white actor Richard Hylton, as the Carters' son (the role of Albert Johnston Jr.), plays the part "poignantly."[31] Although Crain incurred professional risk in playing a "black" part on screen, her career was ultimately enhanced by *Pinky*, a film that enabled her to shake off her girl-next-door reputation as an actor. The *New York Herald Tribune* called Crain "a perfect choice" for Pinky, adding that she played the role with "restrained emphasis." "Jeanne Crain has risen to her Pinky role with no suggestion of her background as light comedy ingenue," wrote the reviewer for the *New York Telegram*. "She has suddenly matured into an intense, warm actress."[32]

RACIAL PASSING IN THE FIELD OF VISION

Thus far I have focused primarily on the practical contradictions that arise in the production of realist cinematic narratives of racial passing that use white actors to play the roles of the black characters who pass. Yet these contradictions are also played out at the level of consumption: specifically in the relation between the visual representation of racial passing and film audiences who "know" (and yet are asked to suspend their knowledge) that the actors playing these roles are "really" white people pretending to be black people pretending to be white.[33] These multiple layers of dramatic pretense in the cinematic representation of passing opens up complex questions about "race," knowledge, and the agency of vision that are not readily or easily resolved by contemporary theoretical notions of the performative nature of socially produced racial identities. This is not to dispute the notion that race is—and continually must be—performed in order for it to be made "real," but rather to underscore the degree of self-consciousness that exists in a context in which the "realism" of the cinematic spectacle threatens to disintegrate under the pressure of the audience's awareness of realism's own performativity.

At one level it could be argued that such self-consciousness about the constructed nature of both race and cinematic representation allows *Pinky* and *Lost Boundaries* to radically undermine the epistemological authority of the "white" gaze—a gaze which, as Fanon wrote, symbolically "fixes" the racialized subject as an object of fetishized interest and knowledge.[34] Vision is simultaneously the agency by means of which subjects come to "know" race (through visibilized and frequently biologized markers such as skin color, hair texture, and so on) and, as scholars more recently have argued, the way that "race" is normalized and naturalized, made to seem both obvious and socially meaningful—in a phrase, more than skin deep. Like "race" itself, this visual epistemology of race must constantly be amended and performed so that it can hold on to its status as truth. Hence longstanding provisions in U.S. racial discourse such as the one-drop rule, which produce the "evidence" of race beyond the most common visiblized signs, ascribing definitional sway over racial identity to invisible drops of blood.

Pinky and *Lost Boundaries* explicitly indulge this constructedness of the visual epistemology of race. Indeed, by flaunting the lack of an obvious, visiblized distinction between the characters who merely pass for white and those who "are" white according to the logic and demands of the plot, the 1949 passing films bring to critical visibility the agency of vision in the social production and reproduction of categories of racial identity. Moreover, by withholding the usual visual assurances provided by "black" skin, *Pinky* and *Lost Boundaries* invite viewers—here interpellated as privileged spectators of the "invisible" spectacle of racial passing—to realize their own reliance on vision as a means of drawing a stable line between self and other.

Yet whereas it is often assumed that such revelation of the visual apparatus of racial hierarchy might somehow dismantle or at least demystify the stability of "race," what is remarkable about *Pinky* and *Lost Boundaries* is the way that their self-conscious displays of the performed nature of race are finally irrelevant. We can infer this not just from contemporary reviews, which generally overlooked (or perhaps chose to ignore) the questions the films raised about the reliability of vision in the social ascription of racial identity, but also from their own ways of "resolving" the narrative tensions introduced by passing by reasserting the stability of race through other means. In other words, by making the "invisible blackness" of the passer a primary source of *narrative* instability,[35] *Pinky* and *Lost Boundaries* introduce questions of visibility and the visual economy of racial difference not primarily to destabilize the black/white opposition, but to restabilize this opposition by making its temporary unraveling into a narrative *predicament* that must be overcome in order for the films to achieve their "proper" closure. Brandishing the performativity of race, they do not provide the key to its undoing as a strategy of social power; rather, they dramatize the ability of racial discourse openly and self-consciously to display its performativity as merely one more demonstration of its power.

This ability of racial discourse to anticipate and accommodate challenges to its authority takes us back to the ambivalence of realist cinematic representation in critiques of racial discrimination and other kinds of racialized injustice. The staging of the performativity of race in *Pinky* and *Lost Boundaries* suggests that the films' "messages" may have been similarly staged, such that they realistically enact various modes of racial discrimination without actually deploring them and, at worst, actually reperforming them both through plot and through the spectacularization of passing itself. What I am suggesting here—that the performativity of realism as a mode of representation potentially undermines its claims to a certain moral or political authority—echoes the critique of a certain realist mode of fiction made by James Baldwin in his essay "Everybody's Protest Novel." There, in a discussion that centers on Richard Wright's *Native Son*, Baldwin decries the protest novel for reproducing, at the level of its own representation, the very discourses that it also seeks to critique. Such "consciousness-raising" art betrays its own purpose, Baldwin suggests, to the degree that it substitutes the "thrill of virtue" for "real" political engagement. Hence far from being disturbing, the protest novel "is an accepted and comforting aspect of the American scene."[36]

Baldwin's indictment of the social protest novel as a means of performatively iterating rather than disrupting stereotypes has bearing on our understanding of the 1949 message films, whose ethos of exceptionalism may actually serve to stabilize the very social hierarchies that the films' protagonists struggle to overcome. In both films, for example, the ability of the protagonists to transcend the social limitations imposed by racial hierarchy is vindicated by the presence of marginal black characters who figuratively embody the "blackness" that such hierarchy seeks to contain. In contrast to the passer, whose achievements are said to "transcend" race and thus earn him or her status as an "honorary" white person who may be integrated without difficulty into the "white" community, this character bears the burden of collective racial representation: he or she is the person who not only embodies racial difference, but gives the "race" a bad name. Hence even if social realism lent itself more readily than melodrama or farce to the production of "positive" cinematic images of individual African Americans, these images themselves contribute to the drawing of a "line" between characters who can demonstrate themselves to be deserving of equal treatment and those whose flagrant refusal to conform serves to retroactively justify their continued marginalization.

What distinguishes *Pinky* and *Lost Boundaries* from other realist "message" films is not the presence of such contradictions per se, but the fact that these contradictions are also allegorized at the level of visual representation. Thus while the "exceptional Negro" in each film is also that character who is able to pass, the person who gives the "race" a bad name and who is therefore portrayed as undeserving of the privileges of benevolent treatment is inevitably too dark-complexioned ever to be mistaken for white. In this manner—that is, through the visual trope of the character who looks white but who is "actually" and legally black— both films manage to bring forward their message of integration without necessarily unsettling the mechanisms of racialization (in particular, the one-drop rule) that also mark the black subject as *racially* unassimilable with the American nation, imagined as white.[37] Passing is allowed, we might say, but only to the degree that it does not assail the purity of the black/white binary, which is ultimately adjudicated through the rhetoric of blood as well as class.

Pinky and *Lost Boundaries* can arrive at this split resolution of the passing plot only by transposing onto the symbolic terrain of seemingly more mobile class and national identities the questions raised by the spectacle of a character who can transgress but not transcend the boundary of race. In both films the absence of an enforceable visual distinction between differently raced subjects necessitates the intervention of other means by which to return the passer to his or her "proper" place within racial hierarchy. In *Pinky*, the more explicit of the two films about the gendering of this process of the redomestication of race, the return of the female protagonist to a raced domestic sphere is explicitly and even crudely portrayed as the "logical" correlative of her class privilege. Whereas the impetus for Pinky's passing is her desire to leave the impoverished domestic sphere of her grandmother, which is also the place where her grandmother performs domestic chores for Miss Em, at the end of the film she is reinserted into a raced and gendered domestic economy—although this time the "home" to which she returns is Miss Em's reconverted mansion. Similarly, in *Lost Boundaries*, a film that centers on black male protagonists, the Carter family is permitted to remain part of the local community by virtue of Dr. Carter's class and professional status as the town's only doctor. Set against the events of World War II, *Lost Boundaries* additionally justifies this ethic of racial integration through the demonstrated loyalty of the Carter men to defending the nation's domestic interests in active military duty, even though they are excluded from service in the armed forces by virtue of race.

Part of my argument here is that the status of U.S. film as a purveyor of collective fantasies of individual social and economic mobility results in the production of passing narratives that differ in telling ways from their literary forebears. Whereas the protagonists of African American writers' literary representations of racial passing from earlier in the century were punished for having betrayed collective values of race progress as well as collective notions of racial identity, the protagonists of the 1949 passing films are rewarded to the degree that their renunciation of crossing the line can be made to complement notions of "individual" achievement and identity. Even in *Pinky*, which like the passing literature of the 1910s and 1920s affirms service to the "race" as the highest calling of the talented tenth, Pinky's founding of a hospital for black children is inseparable from her incorporation, by virtue of her inheritance, into an American class structure that continues to exploit black labor. At the end of the film we see Pinky's grandmother proudly outfitted in a new uniform—the symbol of her class and professional mobility —yet nothing has changed in terms of the film's conception of Dicey's role as a worker. The relations of raced and gendered labor to capital remain stable: Although she now works for Pinky, not Miss Em, Dicey continues to do the laundry.

PINKY, THE DOUBLE TAKE, AND THE DOMESTICATION OF PASSING

Pinky's opening images are of a white woman purposefully navigating the dusty, unpaved streets of a southern town, her high heels, suitcase, and perspiring brow (together with the sound of a train whistle overheard in the distance) initiating a series of narrative expectations and questions: Why has this woman come to this place? Is she a stranger, or has she once lived here? If the former, then why did she leave, and why is she now returning? Why does she appear distracted and worried, ill at ease with her surroundings? As the woman walks toward her destination, she pauses momentarily before the rusty front gate of a dilapidated mansion—once perhaps resplendent but now with an overgrown, untended lawn—before arriving at a small but tidy log cabin, from whose yard the mansion is still distantly in view. Approaching the cabin, she sees an older black woman (Ethel Waters), who is busy hanging laundry out to dry. At first the older woman greets her in a manner befitting a social encounter between two strangers, one young and white, the other old and black, in a southern setting, addressing her as "Ma'am" and commenting on the weather. A moment later, however, before the young woman has responded, the old woman looks up from her work and asks, "Pinky?" To which the young woman replies, "Yes, Grandmother, it's me."

With this opening reunion scene between Pinky, who has just returned from nursing school in the North, and her grandmother Dicey, viewers of *Pinky* are asked to revise their previous assumptions (supported by the dialogue and Dicey's own initial misrecognition) about the relation between the two characters on screen. In particular, once Dicey recognizes Pinky as her granddaughter, viewers are prompted to recognize that they have initially not inferred a relation of kinship between the two women based on the "evidence" of their skin (an infer-

3. Pinky (Jeanne Crain) and her grandmother Aunt Dicey (Ethel Waters) in *Pinky*, 1949. Courtesy the Museum of Modern Art.

ence supported, perhaps, by their additional knowledge of Crain's and Waters's racial identities as actors). In establishing consanguinity between the two characters, the scene thus radically undermines the epidermal "common sense" of race: the notion that skin is a reliable or stable source of knowledge, that color establishes the "truth" of racial identities or, in this case, the intimate relations among people who are presumed to belong to different races.

Significantly, this subversion of what Fanon calls the "racial epidermal schema" weighs more heavily on the viewer's ideas about Pinky than about Dicey.[38] Whereas Dicey's identity is and remains overdetermined by race, through the scene of recognition Pinky's "whiteness" is made the subject of a radical misrecognition and uncertainty. Consistent with the logic of the one-drop rule, which stabilizes the relation between "black" skin and "black" racial identity while rendering "white" skin an ambiguous and fluid signifier of race, Dicey remains fixed in her blackness while Pinky's identity is opened to speculation. From the spectator's perspective, this initial scene of recognition (quite literally, of re-knowing or reinterpretation) is thus also a scene of racial *(re)production*, but only where Pinky is concerned. More specifically, it marks the moment when the audience begins to "see" Pinky other-wise: not merely to make her physiognomy and her skin objects of scrutiny and knowledge, but actively and self-consciously to ascribe "race" to her.

In addition to revealing the scopic mechanism of racial ascription, this opening scene in the film is important because it establishes the double take as a narrative paradigm of the (mis)recognition of Pinky as a subject who passes. According to *Webster's New World Dictionary*, a double take is "a delayed, startled reaction to the unexpected, following initial unthinking acceptance"[39]—a definition that perfectly encapsulates the dynamic between the viewer's (and Dicey's) initial unselfconscious interpretation of Pinky's skin as the sign of her "whiteness" and her later revision of this assumption. In the specific context of Kazan's film, "double take" thus alludes to the process through which "race" must be repetitively assigned to Pinky, "blackness" continually reinscribed on her white skin. Because this skin is, in and of itself, unreliable as a signifier of her identity, Pinky must always be "seen" twice, this second sighting functioning as a moment in which she is re-sited within racial hierarchy.[40]

The double take serves a series of important narrative ends in *Pinky*. For one, it is the means by which the film distinguishes among the various "white" characters with whom Pinky comes into contact, establishing the trustworthiness of who can correctly read Pinky's identity (for example, Miss Em, played by Ethel Barrymore) from those less likeable characters who are apt to misread her embodiment and thus to project their own fears, desires, and anxieties onto her. In one telling scene, for example, Mrs. Wooley, a cousin of Miss Em's who wants to ensure that she will receive a chunk of the dying woman's inheritance, remarks of Pinky, "My goodness, she's whiter than I am. Gives me the creeps!"—a line calculated, among other things, to demonstrate that Mrs. Wooley is herself rather "creepy." The double take also becomes an effective narrative for advancing the film's political agenda of establishing links between black racial identity and second-class citizenship. Scenes in which Pinky is harassed by the police, treated in a patronizing manner by a white judge, or sexually assaulted (she narrowly avoids rape) when she is walking along a rural road at night are thus not only instructive in establishing Pinky's vulnerability as a gendered subject, but in teaching audiences to recognize the manner in which others' assumptions about her identity radically affect the ways that they treat her.

Most important for my reading, the double take becomes a narrative principle in *Pinky*, establishing a trajectory in which Pinky's "blackness" must inevitably be (re)secured in order for the film to achieve its "proper" narrative closure. Just as Dicey must inevitably recognize Pinky for who she "is," so the film itself must arrive at a similar recognition if Pinky is to be allowed to inherit the mansion that is dimly visible from Dicey's front yard. In other words, if the opening shots of *Pinky* are noteworthy for allowing Pinky to "pass," then the rest of the film is structured by a need to reestablish the stability of the racial binary in the absence of the most common visiblized signifiers of race. In short, this means that Pinky will be continually pressured to identify herself as a "black" woman.[41]

The project of assigning Pinky stable "black" identity is important to the development of audience compassion for her "tragic" plight, and sympathetic identification with her status as a cinematic heroine. To achieve these ends, *Pinky* explicitly capitalizes on the parallels between its own narrative of racial passing and the more conventional narrative of the "fallen woman"—that country girl who goes to the city, indulges in "shameful" sexual desires (in Pinky's case, an affair with a white man), and then makes an ignominious return to her birthplace, where she recuperates her reputation and makes amends for her sexual transgressions. Because in Pinky's case these transgressions are not primarily sexual but racial, the process of her moral and personal rehabilitation consists of both her recuperation of a previously threatened gendered domestic virtue and her renewal of a previously held commitment to be of service to her "race." As the film demonstrates at several points, moreover, these two goals are intimately and inextricably linked through the racialization of gender and the gendering of race. In deciding to cut off her engagement to Tom and devote herself to nursing Miss Em, for example, Pinky simultaneously cuts off the threat of marriage and/or sex across the color line and takes up a more conventionally raced and gendered position as servant to a wealthy white woman.[42] In becoming a more obedient black female subject, she goes from being defined primarily in terms of her sexualized racial transgressiveness to being defined in terms of her more "proper" role as gendered and racialized laborer.

From these descriptions it might seem as though the ideological work of the film with regard to the implied threats (sexualized and racialized) of racial passing were rather straightforward. Yet as the paradigm of the double take suggests, *Pinky* is quite self-conscious about this process of the racial and sexual inscription of its heroine. Visual metaphors recalling the roles of slaves in the "big houses" of southern plantations repeatedly spur both Pinky and the audience into an awareness of the ways that her geographical homecoming is also a symbolic return to, and repetition of, a previous servitude—an overlap that is only reinforced by the fact that Pinky is not being paid for her labor, but is volunteering to help Miss Em as a favor to her grandmother. Thus the problem the film must work out is not primarily how to get her to perform the roles that are expected of her, but how to recuperate these roles so that they are no longer circumscribed within an economy of expectation. At the same time, the film must work to ensure that the stabilization of Pinky's racial identity does not compromise her status as an object of audience identification. She must accede to the expectations of race and gender, but not so much that the audience will be unable to see her as a worthy film heroine.

The scene that is most effective with regard to both of these goals follows the paradigm of the double take, this time primarily organized along lines of class, not race. The scene is actually a test, in which Miss Em (who is in the process of taking stock of her wealth and writing her final will) shows Pinky an ornate brooch and asks her what she thinks of it. Obviously under constraint to tell Miss Em what she wants to hear, Pinky forces herself to say that she finds the piece very impressive. In turn Miss Em, who is able to detect that Pinky is lying, responds by revealing what she correctly suspects that Pinky already has deduced—that the brooch is not a family heirloom but a cheap imitation. Moments later she repeats the brooch test on Mrs. Wooley, whose false answer hints that Pinky is actually more "deserving" of becoming Miss Em's rightful heir. At this moment, Pinky and Miss Em share a surreptitious smile, united in their common ability to discern real objects of value from those that merely "pass" as such.

Pinky's recognition of the brooch paves the way for the film's "reso-

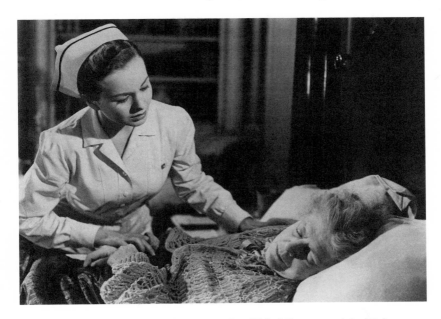

4. Pinky (Jeanne Crain) tends to Miss Em (Ethel Barrymore) in *Pinky*, 1949. Courtesy the Museum of Modern Art.

lution" of the passing plot through the narrative of class mobility. Not only does the scene portend her eventual inheritance of Miss Em's fortune (that is, the event that guarantees her passage into the middle class), but it fully justifies her ultimate status as a middle-class subject by demonstrating that at the level of taste and cultivation, at least, she is *already* middle class. This "innateness" of Pinky's class identity is lent further credence through the gradual diminishment of Dicey as a central, maternal figure, and her replacement by Miss Em, the symbol of a dying white aristocracy. Following the logic of the Victorian illegitimacy plot, in which the right of an orphaned child to his inheritance is secured through the revelation of a lost or previously unacknowledged parent, the film from this point forward substitutes Miss Em for Dicey, implying that through this surrogate maternal link and the wealth it affords, Pinky can be made out to be symbolically, if not actually, "white."[43]

Such a substitution is further consistent with the possibility of Pinky's actual status as Miss Em's rightful heir (that is, as her closest "blood" relation). The film strongly hints at this potential link between Miss Em and Pinky through its representation of Pinky's uncertain parentage; that is, we know only that Dicey is Pinky's grandmother. At the same time, however, the film actively works to repress this conclusion, which would disrupt its depiction of Pinky as a subject torn between irreconcilable options and desires. In other words, were the film to acknowledge the larger history that it can only allude to in its representation of the decaying plantation house—that is, the history of sexualized violence as well as sexual relations across the line of race—then not only would Pinky *not* confront the same dilemma of "choosing," but her right to the inheritance of the land and house would not be subject to the same "racial" interrogation. Indeed, it is precisely the figure of the "miscegenated" nuclear family that the film must banish from its field of visual representation, since this family would serve as a metaphorical reminder of the "mixed" national family to which Miss Em, not less than Pinky and Dicey, ineluctably belongs. In turn, the suppositions that guide the film's representation of the "ownership" of inherited wealth—and by analogy, the wealth of the South itself—would have to be reconsidered in light of the rights of ownership and property of African Americans (such as Dicey) who produced this wealth through their accumulated and collective labor.

Pinky's inheritance carries forward a set of conflicting and even contradictory messages. On the one hand, it insinuates that the kindness and generosity of white benefactors, not the determination and courage of black political subjects willing to confront white supremacy and a racialized class structure, are the most important keys to "black" racial progress. As the reviewer from the *Daily Worker* complained, *Pinky*'s imagined solution to black social misery is that it will come "from the white ruling class" and that black people "will be rewarded individually by the measure of simple goodness, not by organization or political struggle."[44] The fact that Pinky acquires the house through inheritance further obscures the question of the relation between class mobility and property ownership and raced and gendered labor. Despite the lengths to which it goes to emphasize that the southern aristocracy that Miss Em symbolizes is in financial as well as cultural decay—like her house, literally on its last legs—the theme of inheritance papers over the fact that her particular wealth and status were built and sustained by black labor, and that the preeminent figure of this labor in the film is not Pinky, but Dicey. *Pinky* gets metaphorical mileage from the idea of the descendant of slaves inheriting the Big House,[45] yet it would make more sense were the house to be inherited by Dicey, since Waters's character embodies the toil upon which the house, as well as Pinky's upwardly mobile aspirations, were built. Dicey's work in the film is, quite literally, never done, from the scene of her encounter with Pinky, where she is hanging Miss Em's laundry to dry, to the scene that shows the interior of the hospital, in which Dicey is bustling about in a new black-and-white maid's uniform. For Dicey the transfer of wealth from Miss Em to Pinky does not signify the end of the need to labor, but merely the end of the need to labor for Miss Em.[46]

Although the conclusion of *Pinky* seems superficially to resemble the ending of Harriet Jacobs's *Incidents in the Life of a Slave Girl*, since Pinky's story ends "not in marriage but in freedom," the "freedom" that Pinky wins through her inheritance of Miss Em's estate is, at best, double-edged. Though the estate liberates Pinky from patriarchal expectations of marriage—indeed, from the need for any husband, white or black, to ensure her economic stability—it also represents Pinky's captivity to ideals of black women's service. The final frame of the movie —filmed in bright sunlight, in marked contrast to the shadowy cinematography of much of the rest of the film—shows Pinky, her eyes glazed over with what is meant to be joy, gazing at a sign that reads "Miss Em's Clinic and Nursery School." The image suggests not only Pinky's triumphant sublimation of prohibited desires into the desire to serve others, but her spiritual "marriage" to her benefactress.

Pinky's previously transgressive body, troublesome because it would not mind its proper place, is by the end of the film quite literally redomesticated through the inheritance of the Big House. In this substitution of Pinky's desire to pass with the more conventional desire to stay home and tend children, the film intersects with another narrative—the postwar need to renaturalize the domestic sphere for middle-class women, who were called upon to cede economic independence and career autonomy when the men returned home. (I say "intersects" here because Pinky's "fate" also depends on her *rejection* of domestic fantasy [the planned marriage], even as the initial career choice she makes [nursing] is also gendered.) This complex narrative of (re)domestication, which revises for the twentieth century the nineteenth-century ideology of "true womanhood," is implicitly a white women's narrative, since no parallel set of options existed for most black women in the 1940s, who had long both maintained their own homes and worked inside those of whites. *Pinky* nevertheless draws upon this narrative of white middle-class women's return to the private, domestic sphere by constructing an analogous set of options for its heroine. If in the narrative of postwar female redomestication national progress depends upon women's retreat from the public sphere of work and politics, then in *Pinky* black progress relies upon the successful redomestication of black female sexual desire —a theme that would indeed extend into the very patriarchal logic of the civil rights and black power movements of the following decades.

LOST BOUNDARIES: PASSING AND INTEGRATION

One of the paradoxes of *Pinky* is that the audience never actually gets to see Jeanne Crain's character pass. As much as it defines the drama being enacted on the screen, "crossing the line" remains outside the visual frame of the narrative, just as the train that delivers Pinky to her native town at the opening of the film is never pictured, but merely suggested through the added sound effect of the train whistle. Yet if the North that the train whistle vaguely alludes to is the symbolic space of sexualized racial transgression in *Pinky*, then Miss Em's former plantation estate becomes the site for her racial and gender rehabilitation— the place where she learns to reorder her desires in conformity with the needs and interests of a "new" (albeit far from socially reformed) South.

Whereas Pinky's inheritance merely facilitates her incorporation into an existing racialized class structure, *Lost Boundaries*, set in a fictional New Hampshire town, uses the narrative of racial passing to offer an explicit critique of Jim Crow segregation, a system that by the late 1940s was increasingly recognized as a national—not merely a parochial or southern—problem. Consistent with this shift in outlook and locale, de Rochemont's quasi-documentary film focuses on the Carter family's passing, which although it is constantly in the process of being represented on screen nevertheless cannot actually be "seen." This visual strategy of displaying the spectacle of "black" racial passing as a non-spectacle, an ideological production devoid of visible epidermal reference, carries over into the film's liberal analysis of Jim Crow as the systematic withholding of citizenship rights from those who are (and in this case who look) "no different" from whites. Yet as we shall see, it also carries forth a series of more problematic proposals—not least, that

5. Promotional material for *Lost Boundaries*, 1949. The theme of "white" skin as an uncertain racial signifier is represented in the self-scrutinizing gesture of Howard Carter (Richard Hylton). Courtesy the Archive Center of the Historical Society of Cheshire County, New Hampshire.

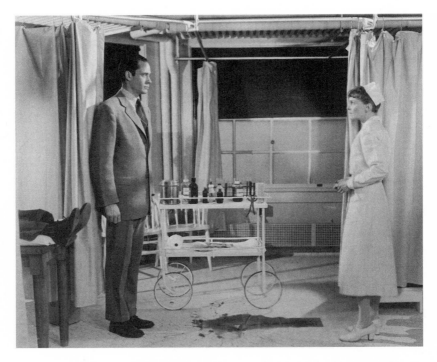

6. Dr. Scott Carter (Mel Ferrer) confronts a nurse who has intentionally dropped a container of blood from an African American donor in *Lost Boundaries*, 1949. Courtesy the Archive Center of the Historical Society of Cheshire County, New Hampshire.

black people will be worthy of inclusion into the symbolic "family" of the American nation so long as they agree to remain socially, culturally, and politically invisible.

This invisibility of black people as social or political agents carries over into the film's critique of racism and racial segregation, which is largely based on the notion that these run counter to the *national* interest, rather than to the specific interests of the nation's "minority" (non) citizens. This argument is made explicit in an early scene in which Scott Carter argues with a female nurse about whether the blood drawn from a black male chauffeur (class here emerging as an additional signifier of racial difference) may be donated to a local blood bank so that it may eventually help wounded soldiers. Although Scott insists that everybody's blood is the same, she trumps his argument by deliberately dropping the vial of blood on the floor, in effect rendering it "impure." Scott admonishes her by observing that "some fighting man may lose his life because of this"—a notion supported by a prominently displayed sign in the background, which reads, If You Can't Go to War, Let Your Blood Fight for You.

If this scene at the clinic establishes racism as un-American, then the film's turning point—in which Scott Carter, already proudly decked out in his navy uniform and ready to begin his tour of service, is peremptorily refused his officer's commission when it is discovered that he was in a black fraternity in college—develops the complementary notion that given the opportunity, blacks may develop into model citizens, "citizenship" here understood in conventionally gendered as well as tacitly racialized terms. Such privileging of male citizen-soldiers as exemplary national subjects is consistent with the film's abiding concern with the public, political sphere as the symbolic site of racial reform (a noteworthy departure from *Pinky*, which focused on the social reproduction

7. The Johnstons of Keene, New Hampshire—the prototype for the Carter family in *Lost Boundaries*. Photograph courtesy the Archive Center of the Historical Society of Cheshire County, New Hampshire.

of a black heroine's classed and gendered domestic virtue through her inheritance of a white woman's private sphere). It additionally links the film's rhetorical strategies to the strategies of contemporary civil rights leaders, who based many of their arguments against segregation on the demonstrated willingness of African American men to serve in the U.S. military—then still a Jim Crow institution—despite their national status as second-class citizens.

It is thus particularly jarring that although *Lost Boundaries* builds its case against segregation based on an emotional appeal to the patriotism of white viewers, invoking images of the masses of U.S. male soldiers fighting overseas to defend the national interest, the film contains no correspondingly sympathetic portrayal of the "masses" of black people. (The only scenes in which these "masses" are even symbolically present are those de Rochemont and Werker hastily patched together from newsreel footage of Harlem—the place Howard Carter runs away to to "find out what it's like to be a Negro"; and these associate "black" racial identity with criminality, poverty, and urban decay.) Such marginalization of black people from the visual frame of the narrative suggests that even as *Lost Boundaries* departs from previous representations of "crossing the line" to depict passing as a collective enterprise staged within the context of intergenerational familial relations, it ultimately reinscribes passing as a privatized (and thus symbolically feminized) endeavor. This notion of the privatization of passing is supported by the family subplot of *Lost Boundaries*, which is ostensibly intended to offer a "human" face to the drama that hinges on the revelation of the Carters' secret blackness. Yet what this subplot essentially offers, I would argue, is a convenient means by which the film itself may symbolically privatize precisely the sort of taboo sentiments (for example, of horror and revulsion at what Fanon calls "the fact of blackness") that threaten to undermine its liberal political narrative. In effect, by projecting these sentiments onto the Carter children—especially Howard, whose racial identity crisis also produces a crisis of masculinity—*Lost Boundaries* manages to contain them within the private sphere of the black family. The white public that ultimately will cast judgment on the Carters is thereby empowered, after an initial reckoning of its feelings of betrayal, to welcome the Carters into the wider community.

In addition to pathologizing the black "masses," the film's documentary-style Harlem interlude makes explicit the classed terms of its

8. The Carters confront their son, Howard, in *Lost Boundaries*, 1949. Ferrer's uniform underscores the film's rhetorical use of national symbolism to critique racial segregation. Courtesy the Museum of Modern Art.

representation of racial integration. For it is precisely these "masses" from whom the Carters must distance themselves—along both racial and class lines—if they are eventually to be recognized as legitimate citizens within the white public sphere. Consistent with this notion that class privilege offers a means of purchasing mobility across the "line" of race, the film offers Canada Lee, playing Howard Carter's preppy college buddy, as the only publicly black person who is ever allowed entrance into the Carter family home. Ultimately class privilege and racial transcendence are so inextricably intertwined in the film that it becomes something of a redundancy for the townsfolk to pardon the Carters for having passed for white. Indeed, the implication is that their racial transgressions can be forgiven precisely because the revelation of lost racial boundaries does nothing to compromise the authenticity or stability of the boundaries of class.

In light of the stated intentions of the "message" movies, it is perhaps appropriate that *Lost Boundaries* concludes with a sermon. Delivered by an actual clergyman and filmed on location (with regular churchgoers as extras) at St. John's Episcopal church in Portsmouth, New Hampshire,[47] the scene of the sermon is simultaneously the apotheosis of the film's "realism" and its most profoundly ideological moment, one that proposes Christian virtue, not social change, as a model for promoting racial equality. Or perhaps it would be more accurate to refer to the "simulacrum" of such equality, for in substituting the spiritual community of churchgoers for the imagined community of the nation, what the scene ultimately offers is less a prescription for how to interrogate the national "common sense" of race than a paradigm for the "conversion" of racialized citizens into a national imaginary that preserves the notion of "black" racial distinction. Although the Carters are shown taking their habitual places in the church's front pews, a sign that the revelation of their secret has not affected their standing in the town's social hierarchy, nevertheless such visual reassurance of their unchanged status is contradicted by the fact that they are now primarily welcomed into the church as objects of others' charity and benevolence. In this deeply "humanistic" moment of reconciliation, in other words, racial hierarchy is reinscribed through the positioning of the Carters as confessors and penitents. The black/white binary is thus restabilized through mode of address: implicitly, the sermon is not about whether they ought to forgive the community, but about whether they ought to be forgiven for their "sin" of racial trespass.

In establishing the white congregation as the privileged agents of Christian *caritas, Lost Boundaries* also recenters "white" subjects within the narrative frame, a move that subtly shifts the relation between spectators and cinematic spectacle. For the sermon is not merely a convenient means of bringing about narrative closure; it is also, as I have begun to suggest, an effective narrative device for reinstating hegemonic "looking relations" of race, in which whites are agents of the gaze and blacks its objects. By inviting the film's national audience to participate as witnesses to its representation of racial reconciliation, the sermon in *Lost Boundaries* thus also invites white viewers to become accomplices to a form of "looking" that insists upon black social invisibility. At the same time, the audience is transferentially absolved for having heeded the congregation's exoneration of the Carters. Assembled in the secular "church" of the darkened theater, the audience itself becomes the dispenser of racial goodwill.

PASSING AND THE PARADOXES OF LIBERALISM

Toward the end of his essay "Racism as Universalism," Etienne Balibar develops the idea of a "complementarity" between universalism and
racism: between the notion of the formal equality of all the citizens
of a nation, on the one hand, and a notion of racial "difference" that
is used to deprive subjects the rights to lay claim to this universality.
Within universalism, he argues, the project of fixing the boundaries of
the "citizen" (or the "human") cannot exist without the projection of a
latent hierarchy, hierarchy being a "structural constant" of all racisms,
whether genealogical, biological, cultural, or "differentialist."[48] Hence
whereas racism would seem to stand as a practical impediment and a
logical contradiction to universalism, it is also part of what constitutes
and enables universalist thought. It is more precisely what is *inside* universalism, securing universalism's own power and coherence.

In my own analysis of the 1949 passing films I have similarly sought
to demonstrate how liberal paradigms of universal citizenship can co-
exist with a racializing imperative that assures the ongoing "minoritiza-
tion," and therefore the hierarchical exclusion, of certain national subjects. This is not to say that the laws of racial ascription are consistent
or uniform, or that they need to be to assure the efficacy of racial hierarchy as a means of social organization; as the differential treatment
of darker-skinned and lighter-skinned black characters in both *Pinky*
and *Lost Boundaries* attests, some subjects may be more "racialized" than
others without significantly upsetting the racial binary. It is to argue,
rather, that some subjects are interpellated as "citizens" *through*, rather
than despite, their assigned racial particularity. Because of such complementarity between the universalism of national citizenship and the particularism of racial identity, Pinky and the Carter family must "choose"
a racialized subject-position as a condition of their symbolic inclusion
within the national "family" of citizens. Hence the difficulty, from a narrative point of view, of representing Pinky and the Carters in both their
sameness and their difference: as the bearers of conventional class and
gender identities, on the one hand, and racially marginal identities, on
the other.[49]

Where the idea of racial passing is concerned, the ultimate paradox
of both films is that the protagonists must be seen to acquiesce to racial
definition as a matter of personal volition, not state mandate. In order

for them to be represented as legitimate citizen-subjects, their embrace of "black" racial identity must appear to be wholly motivated by self-interest, not the interest of those who profit, racially speaking, from their racial marginalization. Not only would anything less leave the logic of racial ascription open to question, but more important, it would disrupt the films' respective representations of the nation/state as the benevolent proponent of the universality of black citizens (images that come through with particular clarity in the courtroom scene in *Pinky* and in the church scene in *Lost Boundaries*, which conflates nation and congregation). Balibar makes this point in more general terms, noting that as a condition of their social subjectification, "individuals have to 'choose'—by completely dedicating themselves to that task—something which is unavoidable, or compulsary." "This is the core of the problem of 'identity,' " he goes on to note, "which explains why it is always communicated with the sensation of 'destiny.' " [50] This notion of racial identity as destiny carries over into the films' portrayal of Pinky and the Carters (especially Dr. Carter and his wife) as their own worst enemies: Pinky because she would rather escape the gendered and classed racial oppression that has been the lot of her grandmother, the Carters because they have their sights set on a certain middle-class prosperity that eludes them as black subjects. Ironically, racial passing—that social practice that would seem to assure them of status as racially "universal" subjects—is depicted as the greatest impediment to their attainment of civic equality. Just as they are ultimately denied definitional authority over the *terms* of racial ascription, so both Pinky and the Carters cannot secure the terms of their entrance into national identity.

In this way the 1949 "problem pictures" illuminate problems within postwar liberal discourse, which, as I began to argue in the introduction, constantly veers between positions of affirming—or not—the "difference" that race makes in the lives of national subjects. Figuring race as the product of racialist ideologies, liberalism simultaneously acknowledges race to be an aspect of the social consciousness of racially defined subjects, and envisions such racial consciousness (along with racialist ideologies) as an impediment to the realization of the promise of American democratic ideals. By disseminating the image of the "exceptional Negro" as an argument for a limited and provisional racial equality, *Pinky* and *Lost Boundaries* embrace both sides of this paradox of liberal discourse, framing the representation of black citizenship within the context of a symbolic conversation between "white" benevolence and generosity and "black" self-discipline and gratitude.

As a result, neither film is capable of representing its black protagonists as capable of meaningful collective association with other black people. Yet although both films are reluctant to link black citizenship to the acquisition of collective social and political agency, in reality such links were being forged well before the films were released. Of particular relevance to *Lost Boundaries* was labor leader A. Philip Randolph's testimony before the Senate Armed Services Committee in March 1948. Speaking before the all-white body, Randolph, president of the Brotherhood of Sleeping Car Porters, threatened a massive civil disobedience campaign if Congress refused to recant its promise to pass a peacetime draft that preserved segregation in the armed forces. In closing he declared, "Let me say that Negroes are just sick and tired of being pushed around and we just don't propose to take it, and we do not care what happens."[51] According to contemporary accounts, white audiences who saw *Pinky* in segregated Atlanta movie houses cheered for her when she won the right to inherit the mansion from Miss Em.[52] Yet had *Pinky* or *Lost Boundaries* ventured to depict a man or a woman like Randolph, demanding jobs and inclusion in civic life and advocating physical resistance to white mobs, perhaps in the darkened movie theaters there would have been less cheering.

CHAPTER 4

"I'm Through

with Passing":

Postpassing

Narratives in

Black Popular

Literary Culture

[P]opular culture, commodified and stereotyped as it often is, is not at all, as we sometimes think of it, the arena where we find who
we really are, the truth of our experience. It is an
arena that is profoundly mythic. It is a theatre of
popular desires, a theatre of popular fantasies.
It is where we discover and play with the identifications of ourselves, where we are imagined,
where we are represented, not only to the audiences out there who do not get the message, but
to ourselves for the first time.

—STUART HALL, "What Is This 'Black' in Black
Popular Culture?"[1]

I could do anything I wanted, without question. No saleswoman would ever again refuse
to sell me a dress. No hotel clerk would refuse
me a room. No head waiter would deny me a
table. No man would ever look at me again the
way that producer had when I told him I was
a Negro. The sharp stabs which hurt so much
each time they happened would be ended forever. I would be free at last from the unremitting
hour to hour, day to day burden of prejudice.

—JANICE KINGSLOW, "I Refuse to Pass"[2]

In the preceding excerpt from "I Refuse to Pass," an article that appeared in the May 1950 issue of the magazine *Negro Digest*, the author, an ambitious young actress named Janice Kingslow, ponders the personal and professional advantages to be gained by crossing the color line. The impetus for Kingslow's contemplation of passing is an offer from a major Hollywood studio of a long-term film contract and star grooming — but only on the condition that she change her name and publicly adopt a white identity. Yet although she is frustrated with the obstacles she faces as a black woman trying to establish an acting career, and pressed for money to support her ailing mother, Kingslow questions the studio's stipulations. "What good was fame or money," she reasons, "if I lost myself? This wasn't just a question of choosing a pleasant-sounding false name to fit on a theatre marquee. This meant stripping my life clear of everything I was. Everything that had happened to me" (30).

Kingslow refuses to pass, telling the studio executive that she would like to work for him, but "openly, honestly and without deception" (31). In declining to "give in to easy temptation" (31), she chooses personal integrity over professional expediency, a felt sense of collective identity over individual self-interest, art over commerce. Shortly after she makes her decision, Kingslow's mother dies; yet her article ends on a note of optimism rather than grief or disappointment. Although she continues to struggle to find roles, she collaborates with other actors on a series of patriotically titled radio shows — *Destination Freedom, Here Comes Tomorrow*, and *Democracy, U.S.A.* — which win her awards and citations, including one from President Truman. More important, she claims to have found new strength in the affirmation of her pride in "heritage." "I would not deny my people," she concludes.

Unlike the representations of "crossing over" that previous chapters have considered, "I Refuse to Pass" is a story whose condition of narrative production is the author's disavowal of an opportunity to pass. Written after the style of popular confessional literature, the article restages the decision-making process that results in Kingslow's affirmation of "black" racial identity in the face of professional and financial pressures to conform to a hegemonic ideal of "whiteness." Refuting the notion that she would be better off passing, "I Refuse to Pass" interrogates dominant cultural assumptions regarding the inherent disadvantages of a "black" identity, instead depicting "blackness" as a source of positive identification. Bearing a resemblance to the stories of Pinky and Jessie

Redmon Fauset's female protagonist Amy Kildare in the story "The Sleeper Wakes," Kingslow's narrative of withstanding "easy temptation" serves to construct the refusal to pass as a sign of virtuous woman-hood. Moreover, in representing her success as a direct result of her grit and determination, Kingslow's narrative challenges cultural stereotypes of black women as lacking in industry, drive, or a commitment to the national work ethic. No "tragic mulatta" story, "I Refuse to Pass" instead depicts Kingslow triumphing over adversity, turning a potential source of conflict, bitterness, and sexualized shame into an occasion for the expression of patriotism and faith in the universal promise of the American Dream. Indeed, her narrative proffers a version of this "dream" in which the protagonist's steadfast "race pride" equips her to flourish within a patently racist society.

I begin with this brief interpretation of "I Refuse to Pass" because it points in the direction of a series of interrelated issues this chapter proposes to explore: about the representation of resistance to racial passing, the thematization of identity, community, and citizenship in representations that centralize the subject's refusal to "cross over," the cultural construction and marketing of gendered notions of racial pride, and the role of African American mass culture in mediating expressions of faith in national narratives of social mobility and civil equality. Like "I Refuse to Pass," my primary texts in this chapter are personal narratives published in the 1950s in popular black periodicals ranging from recognized sources such as *Ebony* and *Jet* to more obscure—and more often than not short-lived—titles such as *Color* and *Tan*, the latter a monthly specializing in the sort of "true confession" stories of which "I Refuse to Pass" is an example. My argument is that these articles, produced in an era of national economic prosperity and growing impatience with de jure segregation, deploy the trope of the *refusal* to pass (or to *be* passed, through the agency of others) as a means of giving voice to aspirations regarding African Americans' economic, political, and social well-being. On the one hand, such popular passing narratives mediated shifts in the U.S. postwar economy that betokened both the growth of the black middle class and, more generally, the expansion of African Americans' access to a class of consumer goods—including automobiles, refrigerators, washing machines, television sets, and suburban single-family houses—that symbolized middle-class status.[3] At the same time, and especially as the decade developed, these narratives expressed heightened optimism regarding the lifting of restraints on African American citizenship, projecting hopes that coincided with the goals of the burgeoning civil rights movement without explicitly referencing "politics" as such.

I refer to these articles as "postpassing" narratives, the prefix "post" referencing their collective interpretation of changes in the material and social well-being of black people as grounds for the obsolescence of racial passing as a social practice. In narrating personal stories of the refusal to pass, these postpassing articles address themselves to the concerns of racially defined readers, articulating collective values of pride in "Negro" identity and challenging the social and economic pressures that promote passing as an "alternative" to racial segregation. Whereas passing is conditioned on anonymity and privacy, such that one cannot publicly declare "I am passing for white" without thereby compromising the very enterprise that is named by such an utterance, postpassing narratives trouble the distinction between public and private identities, turning individualized self-disclosure into an occasion for collective representation. By invoking a "past" of passing, they name the economic and social circumstances that give rise to an interest in passing, establishing a relation between passing and white supremacy. Narrativizing the past, they also imaginatively project a future in which racially defined Americans will no longer have any impetus or need to pass.

This chapter uses postpassing narratives to gain an understanding of African Americans' cultural representation of "crossing the line" in an era in which passing was largely perceived to be "passing out," to quote a phrase from "Why 'Passing' Is Passing Out," a July 1952 article in *Jet* magazine. As the article observes, "Sixty percent of the Negro population of the U.S. is concentrated in urban centers, where agencies like the National Urban League, the NAACP, state employment offices and FEPC [Fair Employment Practices Committee], non-segregation clauses in Federal contracts, and private bodies have helped persuade and educate employers in eliminating the race factor in employment. As race barriers fall, the thousands of Negroes who 'passed' to find decent employment 'return' to their race."[4] Still others would peremptorily refuse to pass, the article continues, or pass only when socially or economically expedient, when buying homes or entering segregated educational institutions.

This chapter centralizes as its object of analysis the wishes and desires that are expressed in postpassing narratives' representations of individual negotiations of race and racial identity. As I have argued throughout this study, racially defined subjects historically have engaged in collective practices of rearticulating and reappropriating the racial signs circulated within a white supremacist culture in order to construct modes of political agency and establish sovereign definitions of racial identity. By necessity, practices of black self-naming have always been staged within the context of dominant definitions and ideologies, including and especially those that cast "black" identity (always differentially articulated through categories of gender, class, and the like) as a source of inferiority, shame, or degradation. Where racial designation is a means of social exclusion and oppression, racial self-definition becomes more than an abstract or superficial practice; rather, it acquires political significance as a public critique of racial ideology.

In postpassing narratives the refusal to pass designates racial definition itself as a site of such political and ideological struggle. The agency simultaneously manifested and established in the public circulation of such refusal rebukes the dominant culture in its belief that given the chance, racially defined subjects would choose to "be" white. In other words, such narratives construct what Stuart Hall calls a "different logic of difference,"[5] one that rearticulates the meaning of essentializing constructs that are also sources of oppression. They do so, moreover, even while actively participating in other modes of ideological production, especially those that underwrite national narratives of upward social mobility as a reward for industry and perseverence. The fact that the wishes and desires of these narratives were intimately bound up with hegemonic wishes and desires suggests that they pose questions about agency and resistance. Indeed, in centering "refusal," also sometimes expressed in terms of an exhaustion of the utility of passing, they raise the possibility of "resistance" that is expressed through the performance of an unwillingness or a "negative agency," even if this unwillingness is itself idealizing, ideological, and/or vulnerable to expropriation.[6]

This chapter's discussion of postpassing narratives foregrounds the modes and conditions of their production in black periodicals, a term that I use to refer to magazines that interpellated as their ideal readers audiences of middle-class and/or economically aspiring black consumers.[7] These magazines were not necessarily representative of the heterogeneous needs and interests of the audience they constructed. Nor did the diverse readership of these magazines consist of subjects defined as passive consumers of their images and narratives, which endlessly promoted the desirability and universal accessibility of a middle-class "lifestyle." Even as these magazines served to generate the "needs" of their readers, so I assume that readers themselves also interpreted their contents in ways that served their own negotiated interests, hopes, and desires.[8]

In other words, although postpassing narratives were vehicles of critique of the dominant racial ideology, they promoted the editorial stances of postwar magazines regarding the "proper" modes of raced, gendered, and classed citizenship, thereby advancing hegemonic narratives of nation, universal social mobility, and individual identity.[9] As I discuss at greater length elsewhere in this chapter, periodicals such as *Ebony*, the flagship journal of Johnson Publishing, were notable for being the first mass-market publications of their kind to treat black readers primarily as consumers. As John H. Johnson, the company's founder, was proud to point out, postwar black picture magazines acknowledged the presence of African Americans within capitalist society as recognized buyers of goods and services, not merely as sources of racialized labor, as blacks had been pictured virtually since the inception of magazine advertising.[10] In addition to circulating "affirmative" images of black Americans and fostering desire for various commodities, from automobiles to beauty products, the magazines in question thus also had a hand in mediating the creation of a new racialized national subject: the "Negro" consumer-citizen.[11] In the service of such a model, therefore, postwar black magazine culture recuperated notions of gendered domestic virtue and bourgeois individualism that were an aspect of the construction of postwar U.S. consumer society generally speaking.

These factors help to explain the critical omissions or silences within such postpassing narratives: in particular, their failure to represent class, their unwillingness to interrogate the specifically classed and gendered constructions of racial passing, and their reticence regarding the mutually securing relation between the racialization of "black" citizens and national myths of social mobility. Basing their optimism for the future on a vision of a color blind social marketplace in which individuals are rewarded for their determination, intelligence, and hard work, the articles often minimized the effects of racism and color hierarchy while downplaying class and gender divisions within apparently stable and homogeneous "black" communities. In so doing, they both mirrored and mediated the optimism of the age in which they were produced, expressing the wishes of a racially marginalized and exploited population to transcend the circumstances through which it had been relegated to second-class citizenship.

In short, these narratives mobilized fantasies of racial equality and racial justice in ways that supported dominant discourses while also offering readers a critical vocabulary with which to interrogate normative constructions of "race." As was the case with the fictional representations that I examined in chapter 1, they imagined "resolutions" to the problems that collectively confronted racially defined subjects in and through the stabilizing norm of the black/white binary. This is not to say that because these narratives were politically and ideologically "impure" they therefore were evacuated of meaning; rather, my argument is that the explicitly positive representations of black community, progress, and citizenship that such passing narratives offered were inextricably intertwined with the contradictions of the dominant social narratives with which they were also, and of necessity, in dialogue. Indeed, because the desires that such representations of passing embellished and displayed are themselves "impure"—in the sense that they, too, are mediated through ideology—we must expect that they will also be (in Hall's words from the epigraph that begins this chapter) "profoundly mythic" (474).

I raise this final preliminary point in light of the relative inattention that has been paid to modern commercial black periodicals in cultural studies analyses of mass-marketed magazines and their consumers. There undoubtedly are diverse reasons for this omission, ranging from the privileging of black cultural practices rooted in traditions of orality and kinesthetics (for example, music and dance) to the invisibility of forms of "minority" literary production that do not address or attract the attention of majority audiences. In light of what Fredric Jameson calls the "ideological vocation of mass culture," [12] however, it is apparent that these periodicals raise important questions about the possibilities as well as the hegemonic limits of popular representations of the expansion of dominant narratives of citizenship to include racially defined subjects. By raising questions about what it means to use the "end" of passing as an incitement to narrative production and about the use of the trope of the "passing" of passing as a moment in the development of a politically conscious "black" speaking or narrating self, I am therefore also interested in understanding the narrative conditions of the cultural construction of a collective "black" consciousness. Postwar periodical narratives of racial passing complicate these questions insofar as they circulated within magazines that generally eschewed explicit criticism of the dominant social order. It is to the conditions of the emergence of these magazines to which I first turn, then, before moving on to explore the dynamics of these representations of passing at greater length.

"THE HAPPIER SIDE OF NEGRO LIFE"

We wanted to emphasize the positive aspects of Black life. We wanted to highlight achievements and make Blacks proud of themselves. We wanted to create a windbreak that would let them get away from "the problem" for a few moments and say "Here are some Blacks who are making it. And if they can make it, I can make it, too."
—JOHN H. JOHNSON[13]

In order to understand the development of the postwar black periodical press, we must also grasp the material and political milieus that such mass circulation magazines inhabited, and that shaped, if not determined, their textual practices. As Thomas Holt has argued, black media outlets "have always existed in an uneasy and complex relation to the institutions of the white majority as well as to the ideology of democratic community, an ideology and value claimed by both whites and blacks but interpreted differently."[14] The practices of black popular literary culture emerge, as Holt suggests, within the context of struggles that ensue "over such competing meanings and values," struggles that give rise to the "separateness of black publicity" while also forging "intrinsic and inescapable links" that join the sphere(s) of "minority" cultural production with those of the dominant culture (327). It is only in the context of this dialectic between dominant and nondominant publics that we can begin to assess the cultural production of the postwar black periodical press. Likewise, only by interrogating the "conditions of possibility" of these magazines can we begin to understand how they negotiated notions of identity, citizenship, and freedom.

Holt's mapping of the black public sphere(s) as a space of productive negotiation with majority norms and conventions is particularly relevant to the study of commercial magazines, which have often been disparaged for their failure to construct a clear set of alternatives to the normative values of postindustrial U.S. society, with its rituals of advertising and celebrity worship, its idealization of marriage and patriarchal nuclear family life, and its fetishization of conspicuous consumption as an exercise of social agency. Such critiques are useful to the degree that they raise the issue of alternatives with particular urgency, pointing to ways in which dominant narratives (that is, of family, nation, progress, and the like) have often been predicated on the marginalization and even exploitation of racially defined subjects. One has only to look at the early twentieth-century culture of advertising, for example, to realize that the semiotic of bourgeois domestic consumption has long been dependent on the racialization of black Americans as a "servant" class who mediate the fantasies and desires that circulate around commodities.[15] Yet I also want to suggest that the terms of African American publicity, or blacks' entrance into the public sphere of cultural representation, must be analyzed within the context of their historical exclusion from this sphere as producers of their own images. The terms of such exclusion have dictated that when black subjects have become visible within dominant cultural representations, it is often as the symbolic embodiments of others' fantasies and desires. Within such a context, not only does the question of control over representation take on a certain heightened importance, but the subjective value of specific representations for consumers may shift or be amplified in response to their cognizance of the historical omissions, distortions, and impersonations of "blackness" and black identities within popular culture.

The question of alternatives is further complicated by the fact that black cultural productions are so often subjected to anxious speculation and policing surveillance within the realm of the public sphere. In part because of prejudicial beliefs about the naïveté of "minority" cultural beliefs and practices, such cultural productions are often interpreted — by dominant and nondominant publics alike — as mimetic representations of the subjectivities that they construct.[16] To the degree that realism is thus presumed to be the predominant mode of representation of black cultural production, such production often becomes the symbolic site for political debates whose stakes exceed the bounds of popular culture. Bearing the burden of "speaking for" as well as "speaking to," such cultural practices have therefore often been at the center of larger social and cultural struggles.

It is with such caveats in mind that we may consider the objections

of the black press's most well-known and vituperative critic, sociologist
and Howard University professor E. Franklin Frazier, whose scathing
appraisal of the content of *Ebony* and other postwar periodicals provided
cultural ammunition for his well-known 1957 study *Black Bourgeoisie*.[17]
Frazier's investment in these magazines is related to his book's attempt
to debunk the myths of "Negro business" and "Negro society" promulgated by middle-class African Americans, whose economic status, according to Frazier, belies "the essential fact that they still do not own
any of the real wealth of America" (11). Whereas the first part of his
book, "The World of Reality," documents the historical emergence of
class and economic distinctions among African Americans from slavery
through the modern period, in the second part, "The World of Make-
Believe," Frazier explores the cultural and social institutions, as well
as the psychological factors, that promote illusions of black economic
prosperity.

Frazier's specific argument about the postwar black periodical press,
to which he devotes considerable discussion in this second part, is that in
proffering images of middle-class black affluence, it serves the ideological function of obscuring the economic vulnerability and even powerlessness of black Americans, who do not own the "real wealth of America or play an important role in American business" (11). In addition,
Frazier impugns magazines such as *Ebony* for marginalizing the masses
of black people who do not have access to middle-class status (or who,
like Frazier, are critics of U.S. class structure), claiming that though
they pretend to speak to the interests of "the Negro group as a whole,"
they essentially give voice to "the interests and outlook" of a privileged
few, who in turn bask in the glow of their flattering representations
(146). Yet his most scathing contention concerns not the exclusivity of
these images, but their role in creating and perpetuating a false sense
of prosperity and comfort. The press's "exaggerations concerning the
economic well-being and cultural achievements of Negroes," he writes,
"its emphasis upon Negro 'society' all tend to create a world of make-
believe into which the black bourgeoisie can escape from its inferiority
and inconsequence in American society" (146). Arguing that they serve
a compensatory and even escapist function, Frazier thus implicates publications such as *Ebony* in the ongoing economic underdevelopment of
both the black middle class and of black Americans, more generally
speaking.

Frazier's ideological critique, which focuses on popular representations outside their conditions of production or consumption, is weakened by the fact that the escapism he so passionately derides was in fact openly and enthusiastically embraced as a marketing strategy by Johnson, whose company owned *Ebony*, the monthly *Negro Digest*, the pocket-sized weekly *Jet*, and the "women's service magazine" *Tan Confessions* (later renamed *Tan*). Indeed, the seductive power of Johnson's "escapist" formula was such that without compromising their popularity, the magazines could readily acknowledge the distance between the ordered and flourishing world they represented and the less reassuring economic and political realities that confronted readers. In his inaugural editorial in *Ebony*, for example, Johnson announced that the magazine would encourage reader optimism and eschew social critique, implying that the latter was the exclusive provenance of established national magazines such as *Crisis* and *Opportunity*, the respective house organs of the NAACP and the National Urban League. "Sure," the editorial reads, "you can get all hot and bothered about the race question (and don't think we don't), but not enough is said about all the swell things we Negroes can do and will accomplish. *Ebony* will try to mirror the happier side of Negro life—the positive everyday achievements from Harlem to Hollywood. But when we talk about race as the No. 1 problem of America, we'll talk turkey."[18] Whereas black journalistic outlets had historically served a "protest" function, articulating critiques of the dominant society through names such as *Defender* and *Whip*, Johnson's intention—as evidenced in the names he selected for his own magazines—was to eschew reporting on discrimination and segregation in favor of contents that emphasized racial self-affirmation: a strategy that, in effect, shifted the site and the construction of "politics" itself.[19]

Ebony's policy of running stories highlighting black "achievements," particularly in categories of "the first, the only, [and] the biggest" (for example, the first black entertainer to play in Miami Beach, the only black man in a small New York town, the biggest black landowner in the country)[20] was also a strategy of appeasing white corporate advertisers, on whose revenues *Ebony* and other popular black periodicals were increasingly dependent, particularly as circulation figures and printing costs rose. Already disinclined to do business with black-owned corporations, such advertisers were more reluctant still when they perceived these to be sowing seeds of popular discontent—a lesson hammered home to Johnson early on, when *Ebony* was rebuffed by advertisers for printing photographs of a 1946 Tennessee race riot that *Life* had obtained but had declined to publish. Hence even editorial decisions to avoid traditional polemic on the "race problem" were motivated by concerns about how best to balance editorial preferences against commercial exigencies.

To point out that *Ebony* was explicitly invested in representing the well-being and cultural achievements of blacks is not to argue that the images it proffered readers were therefore not also coercive, but rather to suggest that their ideological function is more complicated and potentially even more profound than Frazier's analysis allows. (It is also not to overlook the fact that though they emphasized stories and images of individual success, these magazines consistently referenced issues of racial segregation and discrimination as well as pertinent "current events.") Rather than scapegoat these magazines as agents of dominant ideology and purveyors of false consciousness, therefore, I want to suggest that their emergence dramatizes the particular tensions between structure and agency generated in the course of their representation of the middle-class "black consumer" as a newly visible citizen-subject within the capitalist public sphere. Such a notion was fraught with contradiction from the outset, of course, since even as black populations concentrated in northern urban centers were said to constitute new "markets" for capitalist expansion, segregation curtailed the access of urban residents to a range of goods and services. When he launched *Negro Digest* in 1942, Johnson recalls, African Americans "couldn't try on hats in department stores in Baltimore, [or] . . . shoes and dresses in Atlanta. . . . the only public place a Black could get a meal in the downtown section of the nation's capital was the railroad station" (Johnson, 118–19).[21] Johnson might have added that the corollary of such restrictions was the exclusion—or more precisely, the conditional visibility— of black subjects within popular magazines, which were predicated on the targeting of reader-markets. As Johnson saw it, the remedy was the creation of media outlets that would gratify the desires and needs of the very black consumer public which they would also help to create. Among these was a desire for representations of black participation and success within the political and corporate mainstream. In highlighting such achievements, the magazines thus would play to readers' economic and social aspirations while assuring them of their right to inhabit a world every bit as comfortable, welcoming, and convenient as that which was portrayed in their advertisements.

Black magazines such as *Ebony* emerged via a process of productive negotiation with dominant cultural practices, simultaneously responding to their elision of black subjects from their frames of representation while liberally—and in some instances literally—appropriating their forms. Conceived as "black" versions of the best selling "white" magazines among black consumers (*Negro Digest* was modeled on *Reader's Digest*, *Ebony* on *Life*, *Tan Confessions* on *True Confessions*, and *Jet* on *Quick*, a title it ultimately outlasted),[22] they embraced "mainstream" political and cultural values of the time—patriotism, anticommunism, faith in democratic institutions, the idealization of domestic motherhood, and trust in the free market as an agent of social equality—while alluding to structures of white supremacy that undermined the universality of these values. In so doing, however, they also tacitly called attention to the contradictory social construction of blacks as native noncitizens. As James Baldwin wrote in "The Harlem Ghetto," a 1948 essay, "It is the terrible dilemma of the Negro press that, having no other model, it models itself on the white press, attempting to emulate the same effortless sophisticated tone—a tone its subject matter renders utterly unconvincing."[23] Unlike Frazier, however, Baldwin contended that the black press brought to critical visibility problems that were latent within dominant representations. "[W]hatever contradictions, inanities, and political infantilism can be charged to [the black press] can be charged equally to the American press at large," he argued. "It is a black man's newspaper straining for recognition and a foothold in the white man's world. . . . Within the body of the Negro press all the wars and falsehoods, all the decay and dislocation and struggle of our society are seen in relief" (62–63).

In insisting that black periodicals be interpreted in the context of their affirmation as well as their interrogation of dominant norms and conventions, Baldwin's critique points to the necessary mediation of modes of black "publicity" in and through dominant cultural scripts. As I understand it, the issue here is not primarily that *Ebony* and other magazines validated these scripts, but that they did so as a means of constructing new scripts of black citizenship. Countering the dominant construction of "black" and "American" identities as incompatible, they produced new cultural narratives with multiple, uneven, and competing significations. On the one hand, their strategy of "benign passivity"[24] could lead them to embrace dominant narratives uncritically. On the other hand, and as Johnson and others tended to emphasize in defense of the magazine's contents, they were not merely publicizing a "world of make-believe," as Frazier asserts, but centering the prosperity of a growing minority to convey hope and optimism regarding the prosperity of the "race," more generally speaking. Johnson is particularly adamant about this point in discussions of the magazines' visual representations: "Black people wanted to see themselves in photographs. We were dressing up for society balls, and we wanted to see that. We were going places we had never been before and doing things we'd never done before, and we wanted to see that. We wanted to *see* Dr. Charles Drew and Ralph Bunche and Jackie Robinson and the other men and women who were building the campfires of tomorrow. We wanted to know where they lived, what their families looked like, and what they did when they weren't onstage" (Johnson, 156).

Contemporary poststructuralist discourses lead us to remark upon the essentializing premises behind notions of visible "racial" progress. Yet we can discover in such representations, in spite and even because of their endorsement of dominant norms and values, the expression of collective hopes for civil equality and economic parity shaped by the historical circumstances in which they were produced. This is particularly the case in Johnson's justification of *Ebony*'s editorial practices according to the ideal reader's zeal to "*see*" — through the medium of the mass-circulated photograph — African American social, cultural, and material prosperity. In a context in which such "positive" media images of black people were rare, the desire to publicize the image of "black" success therefore corresponded to a broader need to imaginatively construct and depict alternatives to the racial order. Interacting with the pleasures of both voyeurism and the surrogate consumption of commodities through the consumption of visual text, the practice of viewing photographs of "society" in *Ebony* thus became a means of envisioning the very rights of black people to share in privileges of wealth, social stature, and physical beauty.[25]

It would be understating the ideological operations of such periodicals to say that they did not attempt to wish away or "resolve" the contradictions of the American Dream by interpellating readers as the individual masters of their fates, capable of ascending the social ladder through hard work and determination; yet we might equally wish to acknowledge the value of their representations of equality and achievement as the basis for a broader struggle for social justice. These representations are "oppositional" not in the sense that they proposed explicit strategies of resistance, but in the fact that they circulated the sort of narratives and images of idealized bourgeois black citizenship that were often marginalized or invisible within dominant cultural representations. In so doing, they were simultaneously celebrating "black" success and responding to broader social and cultural imperatives that racialized minorities demonstrate their "worthiness" for citizenship by representing their compatibility with majority culture. As I attempt to show through the specific readings that follow, their social function was not necessarily to critique existing social structures, but rather to posit the right of "black" people, as racially self-determined subjects, to inhabit these structures—and in turn to potentially change the way these structures imagined race itself.

WHITE NO MORE: RACE, MOBILITY, AND THE "PASSING" OF PASSING

For 12 years I passed as a white girl. For 12 unhappy, frustrated years I dared to choose a double life, living in a way that could only bring me bitterness and complete vexation. Yet when I first stepped across the color line back in 1938 it never occurred to me that I was walking into a white world that I could never really become a part of—a white world that for me became a whole fabric of lies from that very first day when I walked into a downtown Chicago office building and took a job as a "white" secretary. —"I'm Through with Passing"[26]

Postpassing articles represented the aspirations of black subjects to be integrated into existing class, political, and social structures as first-class citizens. Politically and ideologically speaking, they expressed a liberal critique of African American oppression that was consistent with the liberal outlooks of the magazines in which they appeared. Calling into question the exclusion and/or selective inclusion of blacks from the public sphere, they manipulated the thematics of racial passing—especially of racial subterfuge, secrecy, and disguise—to imagine a world in which "white" skin would no longer be a prerequisite to equitable employment, fair housing opportunities, or personal freedom. They did so, moreover, in ways that emphasized possibilities for individual social mobility through, rather than in spite of, an embrace of "race" as a source of collective and personal identity. This simultaneous strategy of racial affirmation and optimism regarding opportunities for upward class mobility anticipates a world in which one need not transcend "race" in order to transcend racial oppression. Indeed, it suggests a precursor to contemporary liberal multiculturalist discourses, in which the recognition and appreciation of "difference" is seen as a complement, rather than an impediment, to social prosperity.

A good example of a narrative that entertains notions of class fluidity in the context of racial affirmation is offered by "I'm Through with Passing," a first-person testimonial piece that appeared without a byline in the March 1951 issue of *Ebony* under the long descriptive subtitle "Negro girl tells of her 12 years of bitterness and frustration while posing as white to get decent job, finally decides to drop mask and return to her people." [27] "I'm Through with Passing" frames its representation of racial passing in light of the narrator's economic hardship and her quest for employment as a gendered and raced subject. When she graduates from high school, the narrator immediately begins looking for work so that she can help her mother with expenses, yet she soon discovers that the jobs set aside for "colored girls only" are not only undesirable but economically exploitative. Later she finds substantially improved working conditions clerking at a South Side department store, but feels hurt and rejected when the other black women workers upbraid her for filling a "colored girl's" position when she could easily pass as white on "a good [that is, better paying] job" (23). Increasingly anxious at the growing burden of household expenses, the narrator eventually gets hired as a secretary for a downtown Chicago pension-plan firm by writing "American" on the application blank and merely letting her employer assume "white." She thereby embarks on a "double life," in which she is "white" by day, and "my real self again" at home at night (23).

The turning point in "I'm Through with Passing" comes more than a decade later, when the narrator is asked to type a business letter that ends with a statement of her boss's support for a colleague's Ku Klux Klan work (she tears up the letter and never sends it). Realizing that "there were not too many Negro businesses who could afford or were willing to pay the salary I had been accustomed to," the narrator nevertheless decides that she would rather be paid less than be obliged silently to tolerate the overt racism and deceit that she discovers "behind the closed doors of the white world." In the end she not only finds a job with a black-owned firm, but finds one "which offered even greater possibilities than I had hoped for" (27) (it seems possible that she is working for Johnson Publishing). Like "I Refuse to Pass" (the article I cite at the opening of this chapter), "I'm Through with Passing" concludes on this note of optimism, with the narrator assuring readers that "I've never regretted my decision [to leave the old job] and I can truthfully say that I'm happier now than I've ever been in my life, and grateful to my co-workers for accepting me just for what I am—a Negro" (27).

Fashioned as a self-help narrative in which the protagonist, confronted with a set of personal challenges, not only discovers a solution to her problems but is able to transcend the material circumstances in which these problems arose, "I'm Through with Passing" underwrites values of hard work, personal sacrifice, and race pride. Consistent with *Ebony*'s own bourgeois ethos, it associates success—defined in terms of the narrator's ability to earn a "white" woman's salary while affirming "black" female identity—with individual effort, perseverence, and economic ambition. Significantly, too, the narrator destigmatizes passing by framing it within the context of economic need, filial duty (through allusions to the economic hardship suffered by the narrator's mother), and intraracial social pressures, thereby avoiding the implication that she is merely interested in pursuing wealth and social status. The added detail of her substituting the sign of national identity for the sign of "race" on a job application also seems calculated to win over the reader's sympathy and trust (after all, she never tells a lie) while offering an eloquent yet succinct critique of the racialized construction of U.S. citizenship. These and other aspects of the article encourage readers to imaginatively identify with the narrator as simultaneously hemmed in by social circumstances and yet in control of her fate. Carefully weighing the representation of collective racial oppression against the portrayal of individual social agency, "I'm Through with Passing" thus manages to come across as a "realist" document that also promises a "real world" happy ending to the narrator's problems. Her discovery of an economically viable alternative to passing in 1950, twelve years after she first crossed the color line at work, further situates her repudiation of passing within the context of postwar economic expansion, suggesting that it is through the encouragement of black enterprise (later to be the title of another Johnson publication) that black workers will be able to discover opportunities that elude them in the "white" corporate marketplace.

At least two ironies belie the optimism of the article's ending, however. The first concerns the fact that even as the narrator declares that she is "through with passing," at the end of her article it is clear that her opportunities remain circumscribed by the material conditions of racism and racial segregation. Despite incremental changes betokening an atmosphere of diminished governmental tolerance for Jim Crow, the author of "I'm Through with Passing" ultimately expresses little faith either in official mechanisms for enforcing racial equality (at one point, for example, she cites her company's failure to follow the Fair Employment Practices Code [27]) or in the ability of her white employers or co-workers to transcend deeply ingrained beliefs in innate black inferiority.[28] "[B]ehind the closed doors of the white world" the narrator discovers "a brand of deceit" that not only renders her own passing "transgressions" venial by comparison, but that she interprets as a reason to mistrust even the most seemingly benign efforts of whites to welcome black co-workers into their midst. Significantly, her narrative's envisioned way "out" of racial passing lies not in the transformation of existing social structures, but in the emergence of independent "black" institutions that can nurture alternatives to these, if even on a somewhat diminished scale. In short, while her interest in passing arises from segregation and racial discrimination, she brings her story to closure by affirming traditional values of self-help and economic self-sufficiency rather than offering readers reassurances that black women will soon be welcome at "white" as well as "black" businesses.

A second set of ironies concerns the historical positioning of African American women within the U.S. labor market. Between 1940 and 1960 the status of black women workers, paralleling the status of all women workers, underwent a notable shift as domestic labor, previously a predominant source of employment for black women, steadily and significantly declined in importance. Frazier notes that whereas in the South black men and women were barred from holding service sector positions unless they were employed in black schools or businesses, in the North such jobs were generally more available; between 1940 and 1950 black women made the most visible gains, increasing from roughly one-twentieth to one-seventh of the clerical labor force relative to white women (46–48). Yet in the decades that followed, and as their presence as workers in private domestic households decreased, black women also experienced greater levels of gendered occupational segregation than did their white female counterparts, resulting in black women's dispro-portionate representation in "traditionally female" jobs.[29] The narrator of "I'm Through with Passing" alludes to these issues by observing a dis-parity in the incomes of black and white women secretaries, yet at the end of the article such concerns of gender and class are ultimately sub-ordinated to the interests of racial affirmation.

It is precisely the narrator's understanding of race as a basis of both self-definition and economic ambition, however, that renders her personal story compelling to readers. "I'm Through with Passing" not only sanctions readers' class aspirations, but it represents the narrator's ability to succeed and even thrive within a context in which she is being judged according to her merits, not her race. The narrator's allusion to her salary requirements near the end of the article complements this notion of the equality of her labor. The only time she is fired is when one of the companies she works for discovers where she lives. "It wasn't because of my work or because they suspected that I was colored," she writes, but merely because they discovered that "I lived in a Negro neighborhood" (26). On the other hand, she also demonstrates herself to be both more enlightened and morally superior to her white col-leagues by citing instances in which she must rebut their ignorant or intolerant remarks about black people. Finally, because the narrator's relation to "whiteness," even when she passes, is agonistic—that is, cir-cumscribed by her critical awareness that the treatment she receives is based on others' assumptions about her racial identity—she is able to represent her repudiation of passing as symbolic of shifts in the social and cultural construction of "black" identities more broadly speaking. By declaring herself through with passing, the narrator also implies that African Americans, as a racially defined group, need not accommodate themselves to the needs, interests, and social definitions of the white ma-jority, but may legitimately pursue their own interests and institutions.

The credibility of "I'm Through with Passing" as a true story is re-inforced by the presence of a photograph of the author among a group of seventeen professionally attired young women whose faces are indi-vidually numbered. The caption under the photograph challenges the

reader to discern "Which one of these girls is Negro?" promising to reveal the answer several pages later. (The author turns out to be "No. 9,"
positioned at the very center of the group and the only woman in the
photograph who is wearing glasses.) Complementing the written text,
the photograph doubles as a spectacular representation of the narrator's passing by portraying her "indistinguishability" from the (presumably white?) women among whose images her own upturned face is
framed. Yet even as the text offers assurances of the narrator's identity,
the photograph is also effective in undermining the reader/viewer's fantasy of being able to "tell"[30] by offering no additional information about
the other women in the photograph other than to note that they are
"girls at Chicago's Roosevelt College"—a private institution founded in
1945 with the mission of educating students regardless of class, race, or
ethnic origin. Alluding to the impossibility of the reader's "knowing"—
except according to the ambiguous authority of the printed word—that
the author of the article is No. 9, or that other women are not also passing, the photograph thus dramatizes the social construction of "race"
itself. At the same time, it intimates the instability of racial categories
by not providing the same "certainty" about the racial identities of the
other women.[31] Such illustration of the arbitrariness of dominant modes
of racial definition offered pleasure to readers collectively denied the social authority to mold these definitions according to their own interests and desires. Appropriating the conventions of race, photographic
"quizzes"—such as the one from an April 1952 issue of *Ebony* asking,
"Which is Negro? Which is White?"—thus supplied for their intended
audience a gratifying and amusing affirmation of the failure of these
conventions as well as a validation of alternative (even if no less unstable
or capricious) terms of definition and "knowing."

The visual ambiguities and equivocations of the photograph that illustrates "I'm Through with Passing" do not obviate the article's purpose of performatively ensuring the "truth" of the narrator's representation, however, but rather lend credibility to her observations that white
people she met while passing were easily fooled by their misreadings of
the visual "text" of her identity. In office discussions about the "race
problem," she reports, her colleagues "took it for granted that I was
not a Negro and never bothered to question whether I was or wasn't"
(23). Ambiguities in the photograph also indirectly support the claim

I'M THROUGH

Negro girl tells of her 12 years of bitterness and frustration while posing

FOR 12 years I passed as a white girl. For 12 unhappy, frustrated years I dared to choose a double life, living in a way that could only bring me bitterness and complete vexation. Yet when I first stepped across the color line back in 1938 it never occurred to me that I was walking into a white world that I could never really become a part of—a white world that for me became a whole fabric of lies from that very first day when I walked into a downtown Chicago office building and took a job as a "white" secretary.

My mother—for her job's sake—had always passed. A lot of my friends, too, had often said if they only had a chance to pass, they would do so without a moment's hesitation just to be free from color problems, poor-paying jobs and all the other vicious injustices that all too often go with being

a Negro. I, too, once thought that going over into the white world was a simple way out, an answer to my own personal problems. But after 12 years of having been "white" I can truthfully say that I'll never make that choice again. I'm through with passing—through with all the hiding, all the dodging, all the miserable lies that turned my life into a confused, frustrated existence.

Actually, it never occurred to me that I should pass, even though my mother had been doing it ever since she and my father separated and she had to go to work to take care of me and my sister. Of course, I had been mistaken for "white" many times because of my fair complexion, hazel eyes and unusually fine brown hair. But my family had always lived in predominantly Negro neighborhoods, and I never thought much

about trying to hide the fact that I w Negro. As far as I was concerned I been reared as a Negro, had attended cago's mixed schools as a Negro, and perfectly willing to go on being a N and probably would have had it not l for a series of incidents that changed pattern of my life.

As it happened I had to go to work high school to help out at home, so rally when I went job-hunting I looke places where other Negroes worked. A friend of mine who looks very much an Italian had recently been hired white firm which had advertised for ored girls only," so she suggested that apply for a job, but warned me that might be some reluctance toward hirin if they thought I was white.

She was right. When I went to h

Which one of these girls is Negro? The author of the article on this page is included in this group of girls at Chicago's Roosevelt College. Can you identify the

22

WITH PASSING

―iewed the personnel man took one look ―ne and began a sugar-coated apology ―ut wanting only colored girls. I insisted ―t I was colored and almost immediately ―attitude changed. Red-faced with em-―arrassment he threw an application at me, ―ing, "All right, all right, if you want to ―colored that's your own business!" I was ―ed, all right, but soon found out why the ―had insisted on Negro girls only. The ―k was unpleasant; the lighting was ―r; and the entire place—especially the ―shrooms—was the filthiest place I had ―e been in. I stayed exactly one day be-―e I decided to quit and my girl friend ―three days later.

―t wasn't long after that that I began to ―lize that where jobs were concerned I ―s a kind of racial misfit. And nothing ―ve this fact home to me more forcefully

―sing? The correct answer can be found on Page 27.

than a remark which was made soon after I had gotten my first steady job as a clerk in the South Center Department Store on Chicago's South Side. I had been working there only a few months when one of the girls said to me rather frankly: "I just can't understand why you would take a job here that a 'colored' girl could have when you could very easily go downtown and pass on a good job."

I knew that she was being sincere in what she said, but the words to me were hurting and unexpectedly cruel. All my life I had experienced inner conflicts as a result of people being so extremely color-conscious, and here was a co-worker whom I had thought of as a friend, suggesting that I quit the job I had tried so hard to get simply because she felt I was standing in the way of one more colored girl getting a decent job.

It seemed unkind to me at first, yet when I realized past incidents in my own child-hood I realized that there were differences like this and feelings against light-skinned Negroes that sometimes ran high among darker Negroes. I remembered how it had been with me in grade school, trying to be just another one of the kids in the neigh-borhood, yet being run home often by some of the less friendly kids who would taunt me with cries of "Think you're cute because you got light skin and good hair!" Nothing had disturbed me more than this feeling that I didn't belong, and it was an unpleas-ant, deep-felt emotion that followed me even until I was grown.

Yet, in spite of this, my decision to pass wasn't one that grew out of any racial in-cident or any other unpleasantness in my life. I simply did what some 50,000 other Negroes do yearly—pass for white in order to get a better-paying job.

In my own case it happened that a friend of my mother's knew about a secretarial job which was available with a pension plan organization in downtown Chicago. When my mother told me about it and I applied for it, I was hired as "white" simply by writ-ing in "American" on the application blank.

At the time it seemed that would be all there was to it. I could go on passing on my job during the day, and at night I could be my real self again at home with my mother, my sister, my Austrian grand-mother and my aunt who was somewhat darker than the rest of us. But that's the trouble with passing. It's never quite that simple. For once you begin to form ac-quaintances, there are times when you have to cleverly avoid socialization, and each lie you tell about your background, your fam-ily or some other vital statistic in your life

has to be followed with another lie and each has to be carefully remembered.

In the beginning I don't suppose I had any special feelings one way or another about working among whites, but it wasn't long before I began to openly resent the way they talked about Negroes with such utter contempt and complete lack of under-standing. Of course, no Negroes were hired there, so what was said was usually voiced in strong, uninhibited language. It so happened that this was at a time when Joe Louis was first coming into popularity, and actually their conversations concerning him and other Negroes became so bitter that I almost hated going to the office after one of his fights.

I remember once one girl who worked there had been out riding on the South Side and when she came back to the office the next day she reported casually that she had seen Joe Louis and that he was wearing a white suit. Someone asked her what he looked like in person, and her answer, in-tended to provoke a laugh, was: "Oh, I guess he looks about as good as a n——r can look in a white suit."

I was in a rage with anger and imme-diately got involved in a heated discussion about Negroes. Someone said that neither Joe or Marva were really Negroes and ar-gued that Joe was "too light" and Marva was "too attractive and too glamorous" to be colored. Another chimed in with "all n——rs are ugly," which prompted still an-other to add that "all n——rs are black and ugly." I was so beside myself that I could scarcely control my temper in telling them off.

Of course, from that day on, it seemed the office had suddenly become divided as far as I was concerned with those who liked me on the one hand, and those who didn't on the other. They took it for granted that I was not a Negro and never bothered to question whether I was or wasn't, but there was always the feeling that I was associat-ing with Negroes and was more concerned about them than they cared to be.

It was this resentment on my part, more than anything else, that made me decide that living among whites as "white" was more than I had bargained for. If I had followed the cardinal rule and kept quiet on racial discussions as most Negroes do who pass, I probably wouldn't have gotten so upset so often. But it was more than I could take to hear them speak so bitterly against Negroes without my saying any-thing in their defense. I just couldn't do it.

Like most people who pass for the sake of a job, I was always on my toes to avoid going to parties at any of my co-workers'

Continued on Next Page   23

9. "I'm Through with Passing," *Ebony*, March 1951. The caption asks, "Which one of these girls is Negro?" The correct answer (No. 9, the only figure wear-ing glasses) is the author. Reproduced from the Collections of the Library of Congress.

10. Photographic quiz, *Ebony*, April 1952. From the article "White by Day . . . Negro by Night," about "occupational" passing. The quiz is "a test of the reader's ability to identify a person's race purely by his physical appearance" (31). Reproduced from the Collections of the Library of Congress.

of her narrative that appearances simultaneously reveal and conceal interiorities. "[E]ven the most non-suspect white people can harbor deep-rooted hatred inside of them," she observes at one point, later adding the caveat that "[t]his hatred that at times seemed so intense was seldom revealed where Negroes could detect it" (26, 27). Interpreting the social text of "race," then, requires that one read appearances carefully, with the knowledge that they often conceal as much as they reveal. Moreover, identities are produced in and through the very contexts that also give them meaning and significance. These lessons of "I'm Through with Passing" carry over into the confessional story that is the subject of the next section.

FROM RACIAL PASSING TO DOMESTIC VIRTUE:
REVISING THE "TRAGIC MULATTA"

When love came to Betty, she was gripped by the chilling fear that she would have to reveal her racial identity and thereby spoil everything. But Steve, she found, had a secret, too.
—"I Passed for Love"

In its representation of female professional competency and ambition, its emphasis on racial segregation as an impetus to passing, and its construction of "black" identity as both a site of social agency and a source of personal and economic reward, "I'm Through with Passing" is a noteworthy departure from dominant cultural representations of the "tragic mulatta," that female subject who must typically "choose" between seemingly opposed options of the fulfillment of desire and the taking up of her "rightful" and expected place within racial hierarchy. In particular, "I'm Through with Passing" interrupts the conventions of such tragic mulatta representations by portraying racial passing as an expediency tied to the dominant occupational-reward hierarchy, not a predilection that results from an interiorized confusion about racial identity. Identity is never represented as a "problem" or a source of anxiety to the narrator; rather, the difficulties she confronts are external to her experiences of "self," arising from interlocking entrenched systems of racial privilege and racial exclusion that benefit those presumed to be white while operating to the disadvantage of "others." It is in this sense that we may read the final words of "I'm Through with Passing" not so much as a stabilization of the racial binary, but as a critical recoding of the symbolic value of "Negro" identity within the context of white supremacist myths of black inferiority, occupational incompetence, and desire to be white. Far from tragic in herself or tragically confused about race or place, the narrator of "I'm Through with Passing" instead is able to profit from others' assumptions about her appearance until that time when passing no longer seems necessary or advantageous. In other ways, too, her place within the article's imagined black community and her capacity for personal intimacy with black men and women are uncompromised by her decision to pass occupationally. Ironically, conditions of segregation are so rigid that she is not particularly fearful of "discovery" unless co-workers find out where she lives.

"I'm Through with Passing" is not alone among "postpassing" articles for revising the white supremacist and patriarchal narrative of the "tragic mulatta." Other postpassing articles in the black periodical press of the 1950s also engaged these conventions in a critical fashion, imagining their female protagonists' happiness, romantic fulfillment, and prosperity as alternatives to her prescripted, "tragic" fate. In so doing, such articles also challenged the longstanding cultural commonplace that a single, determining "drop" of "Negro blood" was an irreducible source of misery and heartache to its possessor, who presumably lived in a constant state of confusion about racial identity. Within these postpassing narratives the common thematic is not confusion, however, but a critical cognizance of the power of "white" skin in a racially bifurcated, segregated society. Because of this awareness of racial oppression, the protagonist's relationship to "whiteness" is defined not by envy or longing—the common tropes of desire in "tragic mulatta" fictions—but by knowledge that the advantages and freedoms she enjoys are based on others' hegemonic assumptions of her racial identity. Whereas dominant cultural representations understand the raced subject's inability, under the law of the one-drop rule, ever to "be" white as the root of her "tragic" circumstance (hence, the very term "mulatta," which Hortense Spillers calls a "neither/nor proposition"),[32] postpassing narratives revise this convention by representing the protagonist's ability to realize desire outside of the white supremacist script.

An example of such a postpassing narrative is "I Passed for Love," a melodramatic confessional piece that appeared in the March 1953 issue of *Tan* (previously *Tan Confessions*).[33] Similar to "I'm Through with Passing," "I Passed for Love" represents racial passing as a strategy of economic gain for the protagonist, a model named Betty who "crosses the line" occupationally so that she can save enough money to buy a house and pay for an operation for her ailing mother.[34] Later, when she is betrayed by a former acquaintance who reveals her identity to her employer, Betty moves from New York to Detroit, hoping that the anonymity of a new city will afford her a new opportunity to pass. Instead of putting money aside for her mother, however, Betty, forlorn and lonely, squanders what little money she has on dancing lessons for herself. To make matters worse, she quickly falls in love with Steve, a handsome dance instructor, from whom she conceals the "secret truth" of her racial identity. Their romance flourishes amid increasingly intimate dancing lessons and a trip over the Canadian border to visit the house that Steve is building on a small parcel of land—a cottage that resembles the one that Betty hopes to build for her mother. Resolving not to accept Steve's proposal of marriage, Betty meanwhile takes a modeling job that turns out to be a cover for a prostitution ring, later discovering that Steve has been falsely implicated—by the people who run the ring—in smuggling drugs across the U.S.-Canadian border. A series of further complications ensue, after which the narrative is brought to closure as Betty has the leaders of the ring arrested, then reveals her "secret" to Steve, who happily confides that he, too, had been passing for white.

"I Passed for Love" differs from conventional "tragic mulatta" stories in that it centralizes sexual desire, economic need, and filial responsibility as primary sources of conflict for its female protagonist. In particular, Betty perceives a contradiction between her sense of duty to her mother—a duty that would dictate, as she imagines it, that she "never marry any man—colored or white" (33)—and her own sexual needs, as embodied in Steve. Instead of being forced to choose between asexual self-sacrifice and sexual self-gratification, however, "I Passed for Love" ultimately represents these two trajectories of Betty's desire as complementary. Indeed, as in Jessie Fauset's 1929 novel *Plum Bun*, whose plot its own narrative loosely resembles, "I Passed for Love" ends happily, with Betty's various interests coinciding in the promise of her future marriage—the narrative here representing heterosexual union as a means of upward mobility, but not before assuring the reader that it is romantic love, rather than material interest, that compels Betty's desire. Meanwhile, Steve's revelation of his own "secret" not only ensures the legitimacy of their prospective union in racial terms, but it also assuages— at least in fantasy—the anxieties about money that were the source of Betty's desire to cross the color line. The past tense of the title of the article suggests that like the narrator of the *Ebony* story, Betty, too, is "through with passing," her previous need now remedied by her new-found prosperity.

Notwithstanding these ways in which it rewrites the narrative of the "tragic mulatta," "I Passed for Love" also recuperates elements of this narrative, particularly in its depiction of racial passing as a means of female sexual transgression. This is clearest in the article's association of Betty's—but not Steve's—passing with forms of transgressive (that is, nonreproductive or nondomestic) sexuality, such as modeling and prostitution. Implying that her ability to cross the "line" of race affords her complementary access to sexuality that lies outside the purview of patriarchal ownership or regulation, "I Passed for Love" suggests that Betty's passing is dangerous because it threatens to erode the stability of gender and sexuality as well as race. Although passing would seem primarily to be a trope of *racial* desire, in its different handling of the meaning of passing for Betty and Steve, "I Passed for Love" makes explicit the mediation of the discourse of "crossing the line" through discourses of gender and sexuality. For Betty the function of marriage is therefore twofold: not only does it enable her to forswear racial passing as an economic exigency, it also ensures the "successful" (re)domestication of transgressive sexual desire through her embrace of the more "properly" gendered roles of wife and caretaker.

Unlike "I'm Through with Passing," which foregrounds the female protagonist's negotiation of her identity as a worker, "I Passed for Love," as a confessional narrative grounded in the speaker's public disclosure of her private transgression, is more concerned with Betty's identity as a gendered sexual subject and with her successful negotiation of the identity of the "fallen" woman. As a result, although it does not explicitly engage changes in the postwar domestic economy as a factor in the "passing" of passing, "I Passed for Love" obliquely alludes to the status of black women's citizenship and their civil equality, through its represen-

tation of Betty's initiation into a 1950s era "feminine mystique" of gendered domesticity. By establishing the conditions that will allow Betty
to take up her "proper" place within the private sphere (a sphere where
she will presumably be protected from sexual exploitation), "I Passed for
Love" appropriates the raced script of postwar bourgeois femininity and
uses it simultaneously to stabilize Betty's racial identity and to solidify
her place, as a "black" woman, within the national cultural imaginary of
(white) bourgeois womanhood. Whereas the narrative denouement of
"I Passed for Love" conveys the promise of Betty's incorporation into
a national narrative that assigns women value according to their willingness and/or ability to embody such an ideal, its uncritical embrace of
marriage and domesticity as "solutions" to passing leaves open the issue
of whether these can really be "alternative" sources of economic agency
for Betty, especially within the context of white supremacy. In the interest of ensuring the inevitable conclusion of Betty's story of crossing the
color line, however, the formula of popular confession precluded the
asking of such potentially unsettling questions.

"I Passed for Love" renders the relation between "white" skin and the
narrator's social and economic security transparent, yet the demand for
a happy ending impedes its ability to be candid about the representation of passing as specifically classed enterprise. If we examine the narrative closely, we find, like "I'm Through with Passing," that it concerns
a subject whose class status is assured (or at least strongly implied) from
the outset. Indeed, one of the contradictions of "I Passed for Love" is
that although it associates racial passing with the attainment of a solidly
middle-class identity (Steve conveniently has a nest egg of savings stored
away to supplement his home and property), it also predicates the heroine's disavowal of passing on her prior embodiment of a bourgeois ideal.
Betty's taste and personal refinement contribute to the reader's sense of
her as a Cinderella figure whose prince will inevitably arrive to rescue
her from poverty and provide her with a private sphere of her own.

Like "I Refuse to Pass" and "I'm Through with Passing," "I Passed
for Love" appropriates the generic conventions of maternal melodrama,
appealing to readers' sympathies by framing its narrative from the viewpoint of a daughter seeking to protect and care for her mother, who has
in turn worked and sacrificed her own health to ensure her daughter opportunities. Yet ultimately the representation of Betty's repudiation of

passing in "I Passed for Love" is more conservative in its race and gender politics than either of the earlier narratives. We can attribute this conservatism in part to the narrative demands of popular confession, which emphasize the reconciliation of the individual with her community as a way of symbolizing the restoration of both narrative and social order. Nevertheless, although all three stories follow this narrative trajectory, "I Passed for Love" is distinct in imagining a privatized solution to the social drama of racial passing, Betty's retreat to the private sphere of marriage and domesticity contrasting the more "public" conclusions of the earlier narratives, which emphasize the individual protagonist's return to a (necessarily romanticized version of) racial "community." This contrast between the narratives suggests that whereas "I Passed for Love" is concerned with returning the narrator home in a literal sense, both "I Refuse to Pass" and "I'm Through with Passing" are interested in postulating "home" as a social space in which the characters no longer must negotiate rifts between public and private identities. Such themes of home and homecoming are further explored in the final narrative I wish to investigate, which takes the notions of "home," community, and identity as explicit objects of interrogation.

POSTPASSING NARRATIVES AND REPRESENTATIONS OF WHITENESS

I crossed the color line and lived as a white man in the worst part of the South — in Alabama, Louisiana and Mississippi. I passed for what some people may consider a strange reason: I hated white people, feared them and despised them. . . . Since so many people had suggested that I pass permanently, I took my life in my hands and went on a two-week journey into the world of my great-grandfathers, both of whom were white.

—"Why I Never Want to Pass: Southerner Conquers His Hate by Living as a White Man for Two Weeks"

In "Fooling Our White Folks," an article that appeared in the April 1950 *Negro Digest*, Langston Hughes defines racial passing as a practice of acquiring by guile what racially defined subjects rightfully deserve but are unjustly denied.[35] Recalling the story of a slave mistress who would not allow her house servants any biscuits, Hughes compares passing to the cook's practice of trimming off a narrow rim of every biscuit and distributing the resulting pan among her fellows slaves. According to Hughes, passing was a means of "trimming off the biscuits of race prejudice"—a method of redistributive justice that exploited white supremacy's own contradictions and vulnerabilities to construct alternatives to racial hierarchy. If whites were to continue to exclude, exploit, and marginalize black people, Hughes reasoned, then what was there to stop blacks, morally or practically speaking, from deliberately setting out to fool them?

The male narrator of "Why I Never Want to Pass," an article published anonymously in the June 1959 edition of *Ebony*, embarks upon passing in a comparable spirit of racial subterfuge.[36] His purpose, however, is not to appropriate the social and economic advantages that he associates with white identity, but to subject whiteness itself to critical interrogation. A southerner who grew up amid white racial hostility, the narrator previously had resisted his friends' occasional suggestions that he pass, protesting that he disliked whites and saw no benefit in attempting to "be" white. Yet it is precisely his own animosity that leads him to consider passing as a means of testing the "myth of white supremacy" (49)—a myth, he concedes, in which he nevertheless still half believes. Hoping to discover "if there was anything to being white," he therefore plans a controlled two-week experiment in passing during which he will travel from Washington, D.C., to New Orleans, anticipating by several months white southerner John Howard Griffin's more famous experiment of passing for black.

As the title of "Why I Never Want to Pass" alludes, the narrator's exercise in passing ultimately has a transformative effect. Not only does it leave him purged of debilitating racial hatred, but it more importantly extinguishes any potential desire the narrator may have harbored to cross the line permanently. As a primary reason for this turnabout in his outlook, the narrator cites his capacity, while passing, to gain the sort of insight into "whiteness" that later enables him to demystify it as an effect of "attitude" rather than aptitude. To underscore this point, "Why I Never Want to Pass" emphasizes the narrator's ease in mastering the forms of white masculinity despite initial fears of discovery, and in sustaining his masquerade in the presence of blacks as well as whites. After overcoming his reticence, he writes, he quickly "learned to talk to clerks and waitresses as though I was demanding service, was used to it and knew I would get it. I looked them in the eye and said in a firm, no-nonsense voice, 'I want this. I want that.' And I got it" (50).

Yet although he savors the experience of feeling "in a manner of speaking, raceless," ultimately the narrator easily decides that he never wants to pass. Having looked into "the heart of the white man" and discovered a heart very much like his own—full of hate "born out of a lack of knowledge" (54)—he instead comes away from his experiment committed to translating his private experience into political action. Assuring the reader that "race problems" have their origins in "man-made laws and man-made barriers that keep people from getting together and experiencing their common humanity," he confides his decision to "remain in the South and help fight for the day when peoples of all colors and persuasions can go anywhere they want to and talk to whom they want to" (54). No longer perceiving "whiteness" as a threatening or demonical presence[37] and energized by this political purpose, he therefore manages to bring his unconventional narrative to a conventional closure, by asserting that "for the first time in my life I am free inside and proud to be a Negro" (54).

"Why I Never Want to Pass" differs from the other postpassing narratives I have so far discussed insofar as it explicitly foregrounds the use of passing as a means of constructing an "affirmative" narrative of black identity. To this end the narrator establishes a series of symbolic connections between the critical analysis of "whiteness" and the cultivation of "black" racial pride. Deploying passing as a means of surreptitious observation, he not only infiltrates social spaces in which his presence otherwise would be unwelcome, but he subsequently draws on this privileged vantage point in order to represent the constructedness of "whiteness" to readers. In so doing, he disrupts the conventionally unilateral "looking relations" of white supremacy, according to which white people are designated as subjects of the gaze, black people as its simultaneously marked (and thus hypervisible) and invisiblized "others." In "Why I Never Want to Pass" the narrator contrastingly exploits the fluidity of racial categories to construct himself as a seeing and yet unseen presence: as someone capable, by virtue of his "invisible blackness," of rendering whiteness an object of critical interrogation. Such visual mastery as he wields over the "spectacle" of white supremacy in turn translates into the narrator's ability to claim a crucial epistemological authority over race itself. Confidently asserting that whites "cry about the same things as the Negro and the same things will make them laugh" (54), he establishes the authority of his own speaking voice through authoritative appeals to the universal subjectivity of all people and self-assured pronouncements about the nature of "white" identities.[38] Extending his narrative's metaphors of visibility as a source of power, the narrator reimagines black subjecthood in terms of his own capacity to "see through" myths of racial hierarchy.

In other respects—particularly the narrator's tacit appeals to masculine authority as a way of mediating the representation of passing—"Why I Never Want to Pass" is less critical of the power relations that shape the expression of racial hierarchy. Unlike the black women who were the subjects of the previous postpassing narratives, for example, the author of "Why I Never Want to Pass" is able to legitimate his passing as an exercise of politically motivated self-interest rather than as a means of fulfilling a perceived duty or loyalty to others. Together with his freedom to travel, the absence of such responsibility becomes a hallmark of the narrator's representation, enabling him to undertake passing as a form of quasi-ethnographic research. At times, moreover, his narrative conflates "white" racial authority with masculine entitlement, explicitly demonstrating the gendering of passing itself. For example, following his suggestion that "whiteness" entails the tacit expectation that others will heed one's desire, he at one point goes so far as to "test" the authenticity of his racial disguise by yelling at a "blonde" waitress despite the fact that she has done nothing to provoke him.

Ironically, it is precisely the narrator's masculine authority that enables him to represent overtly what the previous women's narratives can only allude to—that is, the translation of the subject's repudiation of racial passing into a sign of her political desire. Here the narrator's declaration of his resolve to fight for racial justice is particularly significant, insofar as it retroactively constructs the refusal to pass as a step in the broader narrative of the development of his political consciousness. Ending with an affirmation of racial pride, "Why I Never Want to Pass" represents the politicization of identity itself as the logical "end point" of passing. In this way, not only does it suggest the political outmodedness of passing (whatever its ongoing practical efficacy), but it hints at the possibility of a future in which "whiteness" will no longer function as the standard of subjectivity or citizenship.

"A DYING FAD": POSTPASSING NARRATIVES AND
THE PERFORMANCE OF AUTHENTICITY

Light-skinned Negroes often passed for white in job applications. Today, most agree that qualification is the pass-word.
—Photograph caption, "Have Negroes Stopped Passing?"

Proving to the world that individual talent, rather than the degree of white pigmentation, is generously rewarded with fame and fortune, American Negroes have practically dominated certain fields of endeavor.
—"Is Passing for White a Dying Fad?"

"Have Negroes Stopped Passing?" "Is Passing for White a Dying Fad?" Such are the questions posed by *Jet* (1956) and *Color* (1957) magazines in articles claiming that a "constant improvement of the Negro economic standard" has led to a noticeable decline in the rate of racial passing, especially among young people.[39] As examples of individuals who refuse to pass, *Jet* cites a twenty-two-year-old secretary named Audrey Saunders, a "fair Chicago beauty" who is also the magazine's cover model, and Basil Brown, a "$10,000-a-year lawyer" from Detroit, who confidently avers that in the four years since he graduated law school, he has "moved further than many of my white classmates will in forty." "There is no longer any need for a Negro to 'pass,'" according to Brown, "with the economic and employment barriers broken in most fields and fast breaking in others" (11). Likewise Saunders recounts how she once lost a job after holding it for only five minutes for pointedly asking her employer (who had tacitly assumed she was white), "Do you have any more Negro help?" but then reversed the misfortune within an hour by finding a new position that paid twice as much as the old job.[40]

The optimism of these articles is explicitly premised on a faith in postwar economic abundance—a faith not only in the mere fact of economic prosperity, but in the notion that such prosperity will have the power to promote racial justice. Such confidence is perhaps most explicitly expressed by one Marcus L. Wilcher, an Akron-based businessman who declares that black people "must realize that a lot of limitations are created in their own minds, and consequently they are defeated before they start. They must learn that we only have to offer as good a product on terms as good as the other fellow, and the customers will come

11. Cover of *Jet*, September 1956. The caption on the left assures readers that cover model Audrey Saunders has "no desire to pass." Reproduced from the collection of the Moorland-Spingarn Research Center, Howard University.

regardless of whether your skin is black or white" (*Color*, 49). With this statement Wilcher rewrites the script of blacks' exclusion from and circumscription within the public sphere, using metaphors of commerce to envision the equalization of social relations of race, in which the only salient social actors are buyers or sellers. The implication is that capitalist narratives will resolve the contradictions of embodied citizenship, thereby rendering the social practice of passing obsolete.

Throughout this chapter I have shown how postpassing narratives invest in the "American Dream" of democratic community as a means of representing the political and social aspirations of racially defined subjects. In portraying their protagonists' refusal to pass or to be passed, I have argued, such narratives not only question racial categories, but critique the hierarchies of social status and reward that "race" facilitates and mediates. Producing idealized counterrepresentations to deflect dominant stereotypes, they embrace "Negro" identity as a source of pride even as they imagine a society in which racial distinction will have been transcended. Centered on the narration of previous transgressions of the color line, they are also forward looking, foretelling future progress as well as present-day satisfaction. Although constructed as individual narratives of subjects who are exceptional by virtue of their talents, resources, and/or experience, they also manipulate the generic conventions of popular confession to articulate collective hopes and desires, an enterprise abetted by their publication in popular postwar magazines.

Each of the first-person narratives I have cited represents itself as a true story, yet it is clear that authenticity is also a rhetorical device of these representations, assuring readers of the credibility of their prognostications of a postpassing era of widespread prosperity and seemingly unlimited social opportunity. The confidence of these narratives was belied by the persistence of racism despite (indeed, perhaps because of) the economic gains of a small but burgeoning middle class: a fact nowhere better illustrated than in the case of William and Daisy Myers and their children, who were forced to leave their home in the original Levittown, in suburban Pennsylvania, weeks after they purchased it in 1957 because of the concerted hostility of their white neighbors. The access to affluence of a privileged minority of African Americans did not necessarily yield a hoped-for transformation in social structures or in social relations of race and gender.

Rather than be concerned with the verisimilitude of postpassing narratives therefore, I have instead inquired into their performativity: their mediation of collective fantasies and hopes regarding the inclusion of African Americans within national narratives of democratic community, meritocratic reward, and economic opportunity. Postwar black picture magazines proffered representations of racially defined subjects who had turned down opportunities to pass as a means of personifying such fantasies, using such individualized narratives to dramatize collective ambitions. That these ambitions were shaped by dominant values predicated on the marginalization and exploitation of racialized subjects, or that they were voiced through an often naturalizing rhetoric of racial "pride" and gendered domestic or sexual virtue, does not ultimately lessen their power as representations of future expectation and collective identification. In dramatizing how a certain refusal of racial passing could produce prosperity and happiness, postwar magazines also constructed a new cultural positionality for their readers, asserting their "rights" to profit from the narratives that had long excluded them.

CHAPTER 5

"A Most Disagreeable Mirror": Reflections on White Identity in Black Like Me

Between me and the other world there is ever an unasked question: unasked by some through feelings of delicacy; by others through the difficulty of rightly framing it. All, nevertheless, flutter round it. They approach me in a half-hesitant sort of way, eye me curiously or compassionately, and then, instead of saying directly, How does it feel to be a problem? they say, I know an excellent colored man in my town; or, I fought at Mechanicsville; or, Do not these Southern outrages make your blood boil?
—W. E. B. DU BOIS, *The Souls of Black Folk*

It is very likely that the Negroes of the United States have a fairly correct idea of what the white people of the country think of them, for that opinion has for a long time been and is still being constantly stated; but they are themselves more or less a sphinx to the whites.
—JAMES WELDON JOHNSON, *The Autobiography of an Ex-Colored Man*

have been arguing throughout this study that racial passing, as a social practice, is mediated by the "looking relations" of white supremacy.[1] In saying this, I have meant first to suggest that the specific conditions and modalities of racial passing are circumscribed by normative visual epistemologies of race, which assign meaning and value to visiblized traits of hair texture, skin color, and the like. Through my readings of various passing narratives, I have attempted to show how in the twentieth-century United States these visual epistemologies are also sites of ideological production and *re*production, such that one cannot pass (or, for that matter, "have" a racial identity) without also being implicated in processes of racial categorization and, inevitably, racial hierarchization. Yet at the same time, and more subtly, I have also wanted to emphasize the implication of passing in challenging and/or upholding racialized hierarchies of spectatorship. By this I mean the nexus of social relations that naturalize race and racial hierarchy in visual terms by investing subjects with—or in some cases divesting them of—critical agency with regard to "looking" itself. Here the racial binary is projected onto the field of vision in terms of a racialized dichotomy of (in Ralph Ellison's words) "seer" and "seen," complicating and overlapping with the ideological production of masculinity and femininity through the gendering of the "gaze."

Du Bois referenced this complementary axis of looking relations with the justly famous phrase "double-consciousness," a term that is often misunderstood as referring simply to the "double vision" of those who negotiate a "split" social inheritance, as both citizen and noncitizen, both "Negro" and American.[2] Yet as Du Bois explains in *The Souls of Black Folk*, double-consciousness also names the position of the subject who negotiates "his" identity in and through the social imperative of seeing himself through the eyes of the dominant culture. In the rigorously dialectical terms in which Du Bois conceives it, moreover, double-consciousness is both an encumbrance *and* a gift, imposing a burden of self-consciousness and at the same time enabling a perspicaciousness that confers if not necessarily social power, then a certain moral and even epistemological authority. In the preceding passage from *Souls*, for example, Du Bois implicitly conveys a sense of such authority to the reader in critically *representing* his invisibility to his white interlocutors, whose clumsy strategies of confronting his "difference" are altogether transparent to him. Likewise, in the quotation from the fabricated publisher's preface in *The Autobiography of an Ex-Colored Man* (which riffs liberally on Du Bois's prefatory "Forethought" from *Souls*), Johnson similarly alludes to the epistemological authority of "the Negroes of the United States," whose position of invisibility, though the sign of their exclusion and oppression, nevertheless renders them "sphinx"-like—beyond the bounds of everyday knowledge or understanding—in the eyes of "the white people of the country."

In this final chapter I focus on a passing narrative that deploys "crossing the line" as a mode of politically interested spectatorship of the "other" (and, ultimately, of the self-as-other). The text that I have in mind is *Black Like Me*, white journalist John Howard Griffin's autobiographical account of his ethnojournalistic experiment in passing for black. For a little over a month in late 1959—four years after Rosa Parks's refusal to cede her seat on a Montgomery bus, the year of Mack Parker's Mississippi lynching, and one year before the Greensboro lunch-counter sit-in—Griffin, a white male Texan and a devout Catholic, medically and cosmetically altered his skin color so that he could pass for black in some of the most segregated and impoverished regions of the Deep South. Comprising a series of entries from the journals he kept while traveling as a black man through Louisiana, Alabama, Mississippi, and Georgia, *Black Like Me* centers on Griffin's apprehension of "blackness"—his "own" as well as others'—as an object of intimate, clandestine knowledge.[3] By changing his appearance, and thus changing the ways that others perceived him, Griffin sought to understand what it was like to be an invisible man, to occupy a symbolic position of social invisibility. At the same time, he choreographed his experiment in passing such that he would also filter this experience through the lens of his "white" consciousness—that is, from the position of a privileged observer of racial "difference."

My reading of *Black Like Me* makes explicit an argument to which other chapters of this book have only alluded: that racial passing, in addition to signifying a manner of being seen according to the technologies of vision through which "race" is both constituted and experienced, is also and explicitly a *way of seeing*. In addition to depicting the failure of the agency of vision to represent race,[4] other narratives I have explored thus far have alluded to this aspect of passing; Larsen's *Passing* and Fauset's "The Sleeper Wakes" immediately come to mind, for example, as texts interested in representing not only how their respective female protagonists are viewed—or not—by others but how they in turn view the world. Yet it is in *Black Like Me* that the dialectic of seeing/being seen is made an explicit object of representation. We can attribute this centrality of looking relations in Griffin's text to his performance of racial passing as a mode of what might be called "critical voyeurism"— a way of looking at and analyzing the "other" without being observed in the process of observation. Of course, according to the Foucauldian argument about the productive qualities of spectatorship (especially of the panoptical gaze), such looking is also a means of constituting the "other" as such.[5] Indeed, as I argue, Griffin's enterprise of benevolent observation is disrupted by his text's investment in displacing the possibility of what bell hooks calls "black looks"—that is to say, of black people as agents and not merely objects of the (white) gaze. At the same time, by articulating "blackness" as a mirror of "white" identity, Griffin manages to turn the gaze on himself, albeit not necessarily in a way that interrogates the terms of whiteness as a "locus of panoptic power."[6]

In *Black Like Me*, "cross-racial" looking is invested with *political* importance as a privileged source of knowledge about racism and racial injustice.[7] The operative trope in Griffin's text is of "seeing [racism] with one's own eyes"—a way of magnifying and clarifying the expressions of racial hostility that are everywhere visible and yet treated as though they don't exist. Here *Black Like Me* is exemplary of texts of civil rights advocacy that take as an epistemological starting point the white subject's own self-conscious realization of racial difference. As Julie Ellison explains in a discussion of the public and private economies of "liberal guilt," narratives such as Griffin's rely "on visual practices of seeing pain and being seen to be afflicted by it" (that is, on the cultural display of sympathy)[8] as a means of unsettling social hierarchies of subject/object, seer/seen, which are mediated and enforced by social categories of race, gender, and class.

Yet as I argue in this chapter, *Black Like Me* also solidifies these hierarchies through its inscription of "blackness" as an object of surveillance, even though the motivation for this surveillance is its author's concern with documenting and critiquing social inequality. I read Griffin's journal entries as symptoms of the discursive productivity of the liberal (male) subject's sympathetic curiosity about the "other's" subjugation, an emotional investment that leads Griffin to the conviction that through passing he will be able to verify black experience (whether "black" experience is thus verifiable and why such verification might be necessary are subjects about which his journals have less to say). In addition to critically examining the terms of this desire, I am interested in interrogating Griffin's construction of passing as a means of performing his own political solidarity with an oppressed racial "minority." Given the rather ignominious traditions of cultural theft associated with white appropriations of "blackness," how does Griffin's text attempt to mobilize passing for antiracism, or for the production of antiracist sentiment in readers? To what degree does Griffin's experiment generate understanding of his complicity in racial hierarchy? The issues of "sentiment" implicit in these questions finally raise questions about Griffin's sentimentalizing representations of "blackness" and, not least, about the gendered construction of passing as a site for the public staging of "sympathetic [white] masculinity." [9]

This last point is particularly relevant given what I have been claiming is the gendering of white passing as an enterprise of "heroic" masculinity. Unlike Mezz Mezzrow, whose more ludic narrative of white Negro passing portrays the hipness of black male jazz musicians as a masculinizing alternative to white male (Jewish) squareness, Griffin's journals depict his experiment in passing in terms of a forfeiture of male authority and control. For Griffin, too, heterosexual masculinity and whiteness are so intextricably intertwined that he is led to interpret the "loss" of whiteness in terms of a fracturing of male identity and heterosexuality. There are at least two ironies to Black Like Me's representation of passing as a disruption of the stability of gender, however. The first is that Griffin should have experienced passing in emasculating terms despite the power that the role of invisible observer would seem to have conferred.[10] The second, more historical irony is that the phenomenal popularity of Griffin's book[11] would have the effect of elevating him to the position of a white spokesman for black experience. Here I am not discounting the interest of a narrative such as Soul Sister (1969), a direct spin-off of Black Like Me in which Grace Halsell, a white woman writer, recounts her experiences working as a secretary in Harlem and a domestic in Mississippi;[12] rather, I am attempting to underscore the gendering of the spokesman position as a public identity, as well as the gendering of the representation of "liberal guilt" in late-twentieth-century U.S. culture. Julie Ellison has argued that "liberal guilt" is masculinized insofar as it names a form of discomfort that takes on political significance only "when men suffer from it," yet I would like to go one step further, suggesting that Griffin's text dramatizes the gendering of that sensibility produced by the realization of the waning authority of the white male interpreter of black experience. As I show, Griffin's controlled "experiment" in racial passing preserves gender authority even as it experiments with a certain scripted relinquishing of "whiteness."

Widely hailed for his work in exposing the lie of harmonious "race relations" promulgated by southern conservatives in the 1950s,[13] Griffin, a religious man with a propensity toward monastic life, was propelled into the spotlight of 1960s civil rights activism. Riding on a wave of public approbation, he honed a public identity as an ambassador of interracial goodwill, making appearances on television talk shows, on college campuses, and in local community centers. Ultimately, however, Griffin would come to repudiate and even scorn his position as a white voice for the black voiceless. Such a change of heart was not merely the product of individual desire, but of historical changes that affected the tenor of civil rights activism and that led to the increasing marginalization of white liberals within local and national political campaigns. Griffin describes the process of disavowing this role in two 1973 *Sepia* articles, "What's Happened in America since *Black Like Me*" and "Why Black Separatism?" which were later combined and appended to the 1977 second edition of the book. The power of the spokesman role was such, however, that despite these late attempts to distance himself from *Black Like Me*, Griffin was ultimately unable to shake his reputation as the white man who had "turned" black. When he died in 1980 after a long and complicated illness, rumors circulated that the cause of death was skin cancer, fueling the popular image of Griffin as a paragon of sacrifice.[14]

Griffin attributed the commercial and critical success of *Black Like Me* to its strategy of undercover exposé, its unearthing of a secret face of white racism unknown, or so Griffin believed, to most white southerners. (This presumption of the innocence of whiteness would later seem remarkable to Griffin in light of his own changed perspective.) Convinced that Jim Crow had produced what he called an "area of unknowing" between whites and blacks, he believed that his project potentially mediated new avenues of communication and mutuality across the black/white color line. Notwithstanding the apparent benevolence of his intentions, however, Griffin's enterprise of passing invites critique

for the ways that it constructs blackness as a site of knowledge-production, a place where the "objectivity" of the (white) researcher encounters the nonthetic "experience" of the racially subjugated other, giving
rise to a symbolic exchange that ultimately contributes to the recentering of white male identities as the privileged interpreters of others'
truths. As Donna Haraway argues, though there may be "a premium on
establishing the capacity to see from the peripheries and the depths,"
there is "serious danger of romanticizing and/or appropriating the vision
of the less powerful while claiming to see from their positions." At the
same time, Haraway cautions, the very notion of "see[ing] from below"
inscribes a risk of essentializing the "being" of others—a "being" that
is itself never innocent or unmediated.[15] The following pages elaborate
these risks at greater length, paying attention to how Griffin's experiment precluded the fostering of opportunities in which black people
would elaborate their own narratives or even their own ontologies of
blackness, however necessarily partial or impure.

Yet though I am critical of Griffin's deployment of passing, I also map
those moments in Griffin's journals when he turns the "gaze" of passing back on himself. Such moments are important, I argue, to the degree
that they trouble the terms of Griffin's initial confident presumption
that by occupying the subjective space of participant-observer he can
control the distance between self and other, seer and seen. Indeed, the
unflattering self-image that Griffin takes away from this self-scrutiny
helps explain why he ultimately felt obliged to repudiate his position as
a spokesman for black experience.

GOING "NATIVE": *BLACK LIKE ME* AND THE FIELDWORK OF PASSING

*Liberals may pride themselves in their ability to tolerate others but it is only after
the other has been redescribed as oneself that the liberal is able to be "sensitive" to the
question of cruelty and humiliation. This act of redescription is still an attempt to appropriate others, only here it is made to sound as if it were a generous act. It is an
attempt to make an act of consumption appear to be an act of acknowledgment.*
—RON SCAAP, "Rorty, Voice, and the Politics of Empathy"[16]

Griffin arrived at a decision to pass for black while contemplating his
failure to initiate frank dialogue about race. On returning to Texas after
serving in the army during World War II, he was struck by the similarity

between white supremacy as practiced in the United States and Aryan supremacy as practiced to genocidal effect against Jews in Europe. The late 1950s found Griffin engaged in informal sociological research on what he termed the "suicide-tendency"—the apparent hopelessness—of young black men in the South, who faced dim employment prospects, the persistent threat of police harassment, and short life expectancy relative to their white peers. Though he had sent out a research questionnaire to prominent blacks and whites, Griffin was frustrated by the uneven and inconclusive results his survey yielded. In particular, he was perplexed by what he interpreted as the reticence of black respondents and the defensive posturing of whites. Convinced that no amount of dialogue could ever fully answer the question that W. E. B. Du Bois described as taboo but that is always tacit in conversation between whites and blacks—"How does it feel to be a problem?"—Griffin decided to attempt to find out through an experiment in passing. He justifies this turn away from sociology in the inaugural journal entry of *Black Like Me*, dated October 28, 1959:

> How else except by becoming a Negro could a white man hope to learn the truth? Though we lived side by side throughout the South, communication between the two races had simply ceased to exist. Neither really knew what went on with those of the other race. The Southern Negro will not tell the white man the truth. He long ago learned that if he speaks a truth unpleasing to the white, the white will make life miserable for him.
>
> The only way I could see to bridge the gap between us was to become a Negro. (2)

At various points in this discussion I return to the assumptions made manifest in this defense of racial passing as a methodology: primarily, Griffin's tacit faith in experience as a source of knowledge, but also his belief that racial passing affords the only means of authenticating racial oppression, his fixing of (male) "Negro" subjectivity as a passive object of knowledge, and his centering of the individual self-as-researcher as a bridge or conduit of social communication. It is particularly ironic that Griffin offers as an *impetus* for passing his realization of the persistence of white denial of the authenticity of black peoples' narratives of their experience, given that his own experiment ironically would lend support to such denial. What leaps off the page, too, is Griffin's implicit belief in his capacity for disinterested observation. For it is by surmising his own disembodied objectivity that Griffin unwittingly names "whiteness" as that identity that presumes its universality and neutrality relative to the embodied, particularist, and subjective identities of racialized others.

Griffin found support for his construction of passing as a mode of investigation in the conventions of modernist ethnography, whose method, according to Bronislaw Malinowski, consisted of "grasp[ing] the native's point of view, his relation to life . . . realis[ing] *his* vision of *his* world."[17] As modernist ethnography often engaged in an interrogation of domestic ideologies or institutions as it "unveiled" foreign cultures—in effect, troubling the very terms of the domestic/foreign binary—so Griffin discerned in racial passing a strategy of social criticism that would draw its authority from his experiences in the field, thereby disrupting the stability of the self/other distinction.[18] "It seemed to me," he wrote in retrospect, "that if one of us could take on the 'skin' of a black man, live whatever might happen and then share that experience with others, perhaps at the level of shared experience we might come to some understanding that was not possible at the level of pure reason."[19] Griffin's turn to participant-observation, a methodology similarly predicated on experience as a means of knowing, is anticipated in his semiautobiographical novel *Nuni* (1956), a book modeled after his experiences serving as an army liaison on a South Pacific island of the same name. For a year of his military service, Griffin lived on Nuni as the island's only white man and its only westerner; like John Harper, the stranded protagonist of the novel, he learned the local language, practiced local customs, ingratiated himself into the life of the people, and even married a Nuni woman, although Griffin's marriage was later annulled.[20] Griffin's inscription of his military experience in the character of John Harper, *Nuni*'s castaway-turned-casual-anthropologist, thus prepared him for his role as *Black Like Me*'s disguised-self-as-researcher engaged in more or less deliberate fieldwork.

Corresponding to this shift from an empirical mode of inquiry (the abandoned sociological study on the tendency toward suicide of black men) to a more personalized mode of inquiry based on his experience as a researcher, Griffin's appropriation of anthropological method in *Black Like Me* caused him to reenvision the relation between knowledge and the body. In the traveling "field" of the Deep South, Griffin's sweating, hungry, tired, and aching body—a body itself always in motion, never at rest—is represented not merely as an instrument of observation but as a source of evidence in and of itself. Having taken medicine (the drug oxsoralen, usually given to sufferers of vitiligo) to alter his pigmentation, exposed his flesh to ultraviolet rays, stained his skin with vegetable dye, shaved his head, and inserted himself into the field, Griffin transforms bodily sensations such as hunger, fatigue, and pleasure into symptoms or data. When he writes in his journal (as he often does) that his feet ache after walking two miles in search of a Jim Crow toilet, the reader is encouraged to understand that he is also writing, "This is what it feels like to *be* a black man whose feet ache from walking two miles in search of a toilet. This is how a black man's feet feel."

The conceptual centrality of bodily pain, discomfort, and fatigue in *Black Like Me* highlights Griffin's concern with representing race in terms of its literal embodiment.[21] In Griffin's narrative embodied pain is portrayed as a privileged mode of racial apprehension, one linked to the construction of circuits of shared knowledge that transcend the physical boundaries of individualized bodies. Embodied pain thus serves as a metaphor of the sympathetic bond that Griffin hopes to forge between himself and racialized "others." Through themes of pain, "feeling," both phenomenological and tactile, is inscribed on and in Griffin's body as it travels through social spaces in which his gendered "blackness" is scrutinized, objectified, exoticized, and feared. Contrary to what the notion of pain would seem to imply, therefore, the body in *Black Like Me* is not merely a site of primary or direct experience but a way of mediating experience itself.

At the same time, moments in the journals that draw attention to Griffin's body establish a series of unresolved tensions that result from Griffin's attempt to inhabit simultaneously the observing self's "scientific" position of speech and the experiencing self's subjective position of speech. Here Griffin's strategy of racial passing deviates from traditional anthropological inquiry, which seeks to maintain the authority of the observer over the subject of scrutiny, the segregation of participation and observation. Even among contemporary anthropologists, according to James Clifford, "the ethnographer's personal experiences, especially those of participation and empathy, are recognized as central to the research *process*, but are firmly restrained by the impersonal standards of observation and 'objective' distance."[22] By contrast, in the migratory field of his own research—variously composed of an Atlanta bus station toilet stall, a dilapidated hotel room in Hattiesburg, Mississippi, a shoeshine stand on a busy street in New Orleans, a rickety, two-room house in the swamp country between Mobile and Montgomery, and his own writing retreat in Mansfield—Griffin reproduces himself as both the subject and the object of his anthropological fieldwork. Through repeated experiences of internalized self-division—of contradictory and overlapping identifications as subject and object, participant and observer, black and white—Griffin recreates in himself what Du Bois at the turn of the century described as "the peculiar sensation" of "always looking at one's self through the eyes of others."[23] This "double-consciousness" born of Griffin's attempt to use self-erasure as a strategy of mastery in turn complicates his identity as a speaking and writing subject. As he traverses different temporal, spatial, and racial geographies, his journal begs the question of who occupies the shifting position of author-observer and what his position is with respect to his object of inquiry.

The vicissitudes of Griffin's identifications (as a white man passing for black? as a white man passing for white?) resound in his various and fluctuating narrative modes of address. A scene in which Griffin is pressured to relinquish his seat at the back of a segregated New Orleans bus to a white woman provides an example. At first Griffin "identifies" with the African American passengers, whose facial expressions urge him to refuse to give up his place. He writes: "If the whites would not sit with us, let them stand. When they became tired enough or uncomfortable enough, they would eventually take seats beside us and soon see that it was not so poisonous after all" (21–22). Through pronouns ("we" and "them") that effect a rhetorical distance from white identity, Griffin signals his collaboration with black people. Yet despite this participation in and identification with the black passengers' collective outrage, Griffin remains internally divided. Because the act of giving up a seat to a white woman functions as a crucial affirmation of masculine identity for the white Griffin, he also feels "tormented" by his "lack of gallantry" (21), unable to reconcile the exigencies of conventional white masculinity with the demands of racial solidarity. The scene on the bus ends with Griffin's outrage when the other white passengers confront him with a "silent onrush of hostility." Out of this experience, "I learned a strange thing," Griffin writes, shifting pronouns once again, now in a personalized and familiar appeal to readerly sympathies, "that in a jumble of unintelligible talk, the word 'nigger' leaps out with electric clarity. You always hear it and always it stings" (22).

Slave autobiographies such as Frederick Douglass's widely known 1845 *Narrative* are instructive here, because they demonstrate the variability of—and even the conflicts residing in—racial and gender identifications, as well as the dilemmas associated with the representation of psychical and physical violence. One scene in the *Narrative*, in which Douglass recalls observing the sadistic whipping of his aunt Hester by an overseer, Captain Anthony, provides insight into Griffin's particular ethnographic predicament: "I remember the first time I ever witnessed this horrible exhibition. I was quite a child, but I remember it well. I never shall forget it whilst I remember any thing. It was the first time of a long series of such outrages, of which I was doomed to be a witness and a participant. It struck me with awful force. It was the blood-stained gate, the entrance to the hell of slavery, through which I was about to pass. It was a most terrible spectacle. I wish I could commit to paper the feelings with which I beheld it."[24]

Though he endures the "horrible exhibition" of the whip, not its lashes, Douglass's spectatorship of Captain Anthony's sadism and his aunt's pain carries the weight of a physical violation, striking the narrator "with awful force." Such an account testifies to the young Douglass's empathetic identification with his aunt according to race, not gender. His description also articulates the inevitability of his voyeuristic participation in the scene of torture and thus his inability to master the scene through the activity of writing, to consummate his authority over it by assuming the identity of a disinterested or transcendent observer. In contrast to Griffin, who attributes to the white subject the privileged capacity to function simultaneously as participant and observer, Douglass's description demonstrates the imperative, for the black subject, of negotiating the same "split" subjectivity. In wishing that he could "commit" the scene "to paper" and thereby signify his authority over it (rather than its mastery over him), Douglass reveals the difficulty of ever being merely observer and not participant, participant and not observer.

As does Griffin, Douglass uses the trope of "bearing witness" to link the experiences of participant-observation to progressive social causes. Yet Griffin's journals also inscribe the difficulty he has in ever fully relinquishing the role of "white" observer. Despite his desire to use passing as a way of mobilizing and politicizing empathy, of linking individual sympathy for another's experiences with an ideological commitment to broad social change, he cannot ever resolve the two "unreconciled strivings" of his fieldwork: the desire to record his observations (to remain in a position of white mastery), and the desire to become a full participant by ditching his notebooks (to relinquish white privilege). Though the "black" Griffin attempts to "lose" himself in passing, the observing Griffin never suspends his disbelief, never completely loses himself in the illusion of having "become" the other.

"JOURNEY INTO SHAME"

So far my reading of *Black Like Me* has stayed within the terms of Griffin's explicit narrative of his intentions, as articulated in the previously cited passage from the book's first journal entry. Now I would like to propose another narrative, one that supplements and perhaps contradicts Griffin's consciously constructed account. Although he claims to be appropriating passing as a political strategy and a way of understanding others, I want to suggest that Griffin also appropriates passing as a form of introspection and personal freedom: freedom to explore the contours of his own (racial) identity. To say that such self-referentiality is the repressed subtext of Griffin's experiment is not to say that it cannot also be governed by humanitarian impulses but merely to point out that these impulses are never free of self-interest. Griffin's compassion for the plight of black people under Jim Crow is inseparable, in other words, from a corresponding concern for his own spiritual well-being. Racial passing thus affords Griffin a way of discovering his own links (by virtue of a white racial identity) to the very system of segregation that he is attacking.

The dependency of white self-scrutiny on various concepts of "blackness" is a theme played out in the history of Western colonialism, in which African cultures are used to "revitalize" fallen white Western cultures, as well as in much of the fiction of white American authors in the nineteenth and twentieth centuries. In her examination of the "Africanist presence" in American literature, Toni Morrison has demonstrated how writers from Herman Melville and Ernest Hemingway to Willa Cather and Gertrude Stein have incorporated images of blackness into their fiction as a backdrop against which to stage dramas of white identity. Often these fictions invert the conventional symbolism of white

and black, so that whiteness, usually associated with moral purity, signifies spiritual depravity and corporeal corruption in contrast to black
moral rectitude and physical beauty. In his novels William Faulkner, for
example, obsessively recycled the notion that African Americans were
the conscience of the South, that they "endured" (in the words of *Absalom, Absalom* and other works) precisely through the "nobility" of black
suffering. The "unspoken" presence of Africanist peoples in American
fiction has often served, in Morrison's account, not only to repress the
intersubjectivity of cultures and races but also to reduce black humanity
to a prop for white conscience and white selfhood.[25]

Karen McCarthy Brown, a white feminist anthropologist who studies
Haitian voodoo, provides another angle on the white intellectual's use
of the racial "other" for her own self-enrichment. In an essay about her
initiation into voodoo, she describes the process through which she exploits not only a concept of "otherness" but also a concept of "difference" for the purposes of self-discovery: "The subtext goes something
like this: I am fascinated by the 'other.' I feel most alive in her presence. I
have my best insights into myself, other people and life in general when
I am in relation to her. More precisely, the clarity and energy come in
the moment when I pull back from the primacy of experience and stand
in the current of fresh air that pulses gently through the crack between
our worlds."[26] Griffin's project is less suited to authenticating "black experience" than it is to the task of self-exploration that Brown describes,
in part because Griffin's donning of racial disguise requires him to acknowledge the ways his own white masculinity is mediated through, and
constructed by, a corresponding imagination of black masculinity.[27] As
McCarthy Brown argues that proximity to the "other" affords her an
opportunity for self-discovery, so Griffin's ethnojournalistic enterprise
authorizes him to undertake a pointed—albeit perhaps not intended—
inquiry into his own self as raced. To return to my own earlier formulation, Griffin's experiment requires him simultaneously to see and be
seen, to participate and observe, to theorize as well as apprehend "whiteness." His racial imposture thus serves less as a window into black experience, as he initially believes, than as a mirror that reflects back on
the sources of his own social construction as a white man, including the
complicity of white supremacy in white subject-formation. That Griffin was interested not only in the observation of others but also in self-
observation can be inferred from the two questions he poses in the first

journal entry: "If a white man became a Negro in the Deep South, what adjustments would he have to make? What is it like to experience discrimination based on skin color, something over which one has no control?" (2). Griffin's language in the second of these questions bespeaks a desire temporarily to relinquish mastery, to forgo the social authority of white masculinity.

"Journey into Shame," the rather curious title of Griffin's journals as they were serialized in *Sepia* magazine, picks up on these themes of self-mirroring. The "shame" into which Griffin journeys is ostensibly born of the indignity of his experiences, as a black man, of chronic unemployment and persistent objectification. Yet the more salient, if unexplored, shame in Griffin's text is his mortification at his complicity with racial hierarchy. Significantly, Griffin's experiences of shame (for example, when he witnesses the racism of white southerners) dovetail with his loss of mastery over the stability of the racialized looking relations that would seemingly guarantee his theoretical distance from the subjects of his observation. This second type of shame suggests Griffin's projection onto himself of his revulsion at such blatant display of racial hatred, and thus his enduring sense of racial identification (across lines of class and gender) with those white men and women from whom he would prefer to distinguish himself.[28]

Although the project of white self-examination may not in and of itself seem reprehensible, much of the apprehension around white appropriations of qualities romantically ascribed to blacks descends from the fact that white people (especially white men) traditionally have enjoyed a greater liberty than others to play with racial identities and to do so in safety, without permanent loss or costs. White sanction to "pass" inevitably hinges on the structure of race itself, that is, on a system in which some racial identifications are more rigidly organized and maintained than are others. In an important essay on the social construction of whiteness, Richard Dyer has written that whiteness accrues power precisely through its ability to "pass" as universal and invisible, as at once "everything and nothing."[29] The "depth" of white male identity, which retains its social value despite conscious efforts to depreciate it, contrasts in this narrative with the "surface" of black identity, which can be put on or taken off at will. Griffin's experiment evokes anxiety because it takes for granted these conditions of freedom; his passing ensues from a sovereignty over identity rather than from the exigencies of economic necessity or personal safety. It is precisely because of the social construction of race, in other words, that Griffin can equate "becoming a Negro" with losing control. Indeed, it is by claiming a right to such "white" agency that Griffin authorizes his own experiment.

Despite these structural links to the preservation of white male privilege, however, passing has been identified with white countercultural resistance and rebellion. In the tradition of white hipsterism exemplified by Mailer's "White Negro" essay, passing for black has served as a mode through which white men in particular have symbolized their alienation from cultural norms and their pleasurable embrace of marginality and radicalism. By adopting black radical chic as a mode of self-conscious unorthodoxy, white liberals have attempted to indicate their solidarity with the struggles of marginalized African Americans, as well as their belief in basic principles of racial equality. Yet even these self-conscious attempts to stylize a self "outside" the dominant social order are fraught by white privilege. It is precisely the prerogative of white people to "try on" black identities that paradoxically weakens their ability thus to assume an oppositional identity through cross-racial "identification." White experiments with "blackness" are drained of their subversive potentiality, in other words, because they will always be recognized as experiments. Here the marginality ascribed to black identity is associated not only with freedom and autonomy—precisely those qualities that would seem to be conferred by white status—but also with a disruptive power, an ability to interfere, shock, or terrorize, to play with ideas of centrality and marginality. White people who pass may be attracted to this disruptive power of marginality because they recognize and acknowledge its salience within their own experience.

Griffin's experiment in passing is informed by both tendencies that I have been describing: to use passing as a metaphor for self-examination and self-disclosure, and to use passing as a metaphor for rebellion and oppositionality. Because it is not the act of passing in and of itself but Griffin's own fantasies of passing that are important to his transformation, it doesn't matter whether his cosmetic disguise fools black people or even whether readers believe in the verisimilitude of his experiment. Because Griffin's own illusions of what it means to be black are ultimately the driving force behind his narrative, the most important drama is that which plays itself out in Griffin's own mind—and hence in his choices, actions, and behaviors.

A whole series of such productive tensions are at work in *Black Like Me:* those that materialize in the gap between illusion and reality; black mask and white skin; conscious, philanthropic intentions and subconscious, self-referential desires; as well as those between expectations and outcome. Griffin "assumed he would find racism," writes Ernest Sharpe, "but he did not expect to find it everywhere, least of all in himself."[30] Because Griffin fully expected to find racism in white people who (unlike himself) had neither the benefits of education nor the generosity of spirit that sometimes accompanies personal wealth and success, he was proportionately unprepared for his self-discovery; having assumed that he was outside white supremacist ideology, Griffin was shocked to realize that his own "invisible" racism was merely the alter ego of a more visible and externalized racism that he associated with "inferior" white people. To the degree that Griffin had placed responsibility for racism on the shoulders of white "others," he had in effect merely displaced his own racist beliefs and emotions.

PASSING AND THE MIRRORING OF WHITENESS

[T]he ultimate test of a person's repudiation of racism is not what she can contemplate doing for or on behalf of black people, but whether she herself can contemplate calmly the likelihood of being black. If racial hatred has not manifested itself in any other context, it will do so here if it exists, in hatred of self as identified with the other — that is, as self-hatred projected on the other.
—ADRIAN PIPER, "Passing for White, Passing for Black"[31]

In this section I want to examine in more depth several passages that trace the process of Griffin's self-transformation, from his initial confrontation with his "Negro face" in a traumatic and paradigmatic mirror scene to his eventual formulation of a theory of "passing for white." Griffin affronts what he calls his "Negro self" for the first time on November 7, 1959, just before midnight. After a week of preparation, he walks into a dark bathroom, closes the door, stands before a mirror, turns on the light, and stares at his reflection. The exaggerated theatricality of Griffin's representation of this scene underscores the histrionic, performative nature of racial identities and the psychic drama inherent in "passing over." Yet what I would like to focus on in this passage is Griffin's uncanny confrontation with and misrecognition of his own mirror image. Turning on the light, he stares at the reflection of "a fierce, bald, very dark Negro" who, he writes, "in no way resembled me" (11):

> The transformation was total and shocking. I had expected to see myself disguised, but this was something else. I was imprisoned in the flesh of an utter stranger, an unsympathetic one with whom I felt no kinship. All traces of the John Griffin I had been were wiped from existence. Even the senses underwent a change so profound it filled me with distress. I looked into the mirror and saw reflected nothing of the white John Griffin's past. No, the reflections led back to Africa, back to the shanty and the ghetto, back to the fruitless struggles against the mark of blackness. Suddenly, almost with no preparation, no advance hint, it became clear and it permeated my whole being. My inclination was to fight against it. I had gone too far. I knew now that there is no such thing as a disguised white man, when the black won't rub off. The black man is wholly a Negro, regardless of what he once may have been. I was a newly created Negro who must go out [the] door and live in a world unfamiliar to me.
>
> The completeness of this transformation appalled me. It was unlike anything I had imagined. I became two men, the observing one and the one who panicked, who felt Negroid even into the depths of his entrails. (11–12)

What is most remarkable about the passage, and what links it to Freud's "uncanny," is Griffin's visceral feeling of distress at and estrangement from the reflection of his "newly created" self in the mirror.[32] Or, rather, we might say that the anxiety symptomatic of uncanniness is here manifested in the radical disjunction of Griffin's "self" from his "wholly" Negro mirror-image. Most "shocking" to Griffin is the fact that he is unable to sustain a sense of controlling distance between his "self" as he conceives it and the "disguise" he has intentionally donned in order to investigate (among other things) the contours of that self. In effect, that is, the disguise wears Griffin more than he wears it; appropriating agency, *it* imprisons and transforms, annihilating the "traces" of John Griffin from existence. Most notably, the disguise undermines what confidence Griffin has in the realness and stability of his whiteness by collapsing the self/other distinction that is vital to the projection of "white" identities as pure. Blackness, by contrast, is represented as impenetrable as well as indelible, as something that "won't rub off" no matter how assiduously Griffin might work to erase it. Griffin gives expression to its power to define through his anxiety—even terror—that he will never again regain "white" identity but be forever constrained to living the life of "an utter stranger," one who moves in "a world unfamiliar to me."

As in the Freudian prototype, here Griffin's experience of the uncanny involves the surfacing or articulation of repressed feelings. In particular, Griffin's loss of the ability to wield skin color as a "separating strategy against difference" results in his projection, onto his mirror reflection, of heretofore disavowed or unspoken perceptions of blackness.[33] Referring back to Morrison's discussion of "whiteness and the literary imagination," we might say that Griffin becomes—to the point of embodying—the "Africanist presence" that simultaneously haunts and structures his narrative, enabling his notions of "white" self-concept. Indeed, the passage contains many of the tropes that Morrison identifies as recurring images in the literary construction of a "white" self. Echoing Marlowe's fear, in Conrad's *Heart of Darkness*, that the character Kurtz had "gone too far," Griffin produces a string of associative references that link blackness to chaos and upheaval, shadow and blemish, poverty and disgrace. Appearing at the end of the passage, the word "Negroid" marks the crescendo of vocabulary that seeks to "fix" difference—even as it produces it—through the evocation of culturally sanctioned fetishes of blood and purity, "flesh" and "entrails."

My point is that the passage does not merely rehearse or reflect racist imagery, but that the "Africanist presence," typically mediated through the subject who is seen to embody otherness, is here introjected as the uncanny self-as-other. Griffin not only becomes a stranger to himself in the passage, but he ironically produces, through the expression of an anxiety of otherness, a more accurate and "true" reflection of his "white" self. Just as, as Priscilla Wald explains, Freud's own notion of the uncanny encompasses the uneasiness produced in process of confronting a faulty image of the self,[34] so here in Griffin's text the mirror generates a "cracked" image of Griffin as a transcendent authorial presence within his own narrative. The moment of self-revelation that fills Griffin "with distress" because it engenders a "stranger" where the stable "self" is thought to be also reveals Griffin to be thoroughly imbricated in the racial discourse that he is preparing to investigate. Likewise, the pretense of disinterested observation falls away in this moment, to be replaced by the pathetic (in the sense of poignant and also deplorable) image of Griffin as he gazes, as if for the first time, at a deidealized self-reflection. In the rupture between Griffin's self as he (and perhaps the reader) previously imagined it and the self that the mirror reveals is the uncanny reflection of racism itself.

Such rupture exerts a formal pressure on the narrative to make up for the anxiety generated in this scene through the recuperation of a stable self/other distinction. This is evidenced most clearly at the end of the passage I have quoted, when Griffin opposes the agency of the "observing" self to the "self who panicked, who felt Negroid even into the depths of his entrails," in the process resecuring the racial binary through the implied association of the function of looking with whiteness. Yet because this attempted recentering of the self-as-observer can only succeed at the expense of Griffin's "Negro" self, it generates a tension between recognition and denial that will continue to haunt his text. I have suggested that in his experiment, Griffin internalizes something akin to Du Boisian double-consciousness. Yet whereas Du Bois describes a condition of "twoness," of internalized self-contradiction and self-striving that he attributes to a dominant social order that projects its own pathologies onto the raced subject,[35] Griffin, in an attempt to contain the anxiety about his self that is given expression in his contempt for the "Negroid" face, relates a more literalized splitting of the self in two. This internalization of an observer figure in turn facilitates the rest of the narrative, which consists primarily of Griffin's self-observation, enabling Griffin simultaneously to occupy positions of detachment from and engagement with his own experience.

By racially coding the functions of observer and observed, Griffin also internalizes the larger southern economy of spectatorship under the dominant social order. His experiment in passing proves instructive in these "invisible" laws of looking, under which spectatorship is a function of economic and social power and hence mediated through categories of identity. For example, he discovers that a black male passenger on a Jim Crow bus can signify his defiance of white male hegemony by meeting the gaze of the white driver, an act that recuperates the legitimacy of black masculinity. He learns that although black men are prohibited from meeting the gaze of white women, with whom eye contact is tantamount to physical contact and hence rape, white men and black men are socially sanctioned in their objectification of black women. He learns the role of spectatorship in policing, how observation is related to supervision, and how supervision is dependent on hierarchy.

Using the eyes of others as a yardstick, Griffin's observing self also notes how his "Negro self" is made into a spectacle. In the journal entry of November 7, for example, as Griffin awaits a bus to take him from New Orleans to Hattiesburg, Mississippi, he describes the "hate stare" of a white man whose hostility bears a strong resemblance to Griffin's own previous self-contempt: "[The hate stare] came from a middle-age, heavy-set, well-dressed white man. He sat a few yards away, fixing his eyes on me. Nothing can describe the withering horror of this. You feel lost, sick at heart before such unmasked hatred, not so much because it threatens you as because it shows humans in such an inhuman light. You see a kind of insanity, something so obscene the very obscenity of it (rather than its threat) terrifies you. It was so new I could not take my eyes from the man's face. I felt like saying: 'What in God's name are you doing to yourself?'" (4).

While the man fixes his eyes on Griffin, Griffin in turn feels himself fixed to the spot, paralyzed and transfixed by the Medusa-like horror of the spectacle of a stranger's malevolence. Instead of responding to the hate stare with anger, Griffin directs his outrage and disgust at the fact of the man's "unmasked hatred," at the sheer visibility of such malice. As opposed to the previous mirror scene, in which Griffin expresses no conscious compunction at his own visceral response to "the mark of blackness," here the nakedness of the stranger's reaction (itself a kind of mirror image) reflects clearly on Griffin himself. Whereas the previous mirror scene located "shame" in the identity of the "bald Negro," here the focus of Griffin's concern is the potential of "unmasked hatred" to shame and dishonor the white subject.

The depth of Griffin's simultaneous identification with and revulsion from the white stranger is reflected in the ambiguity of the pronoun "you." Whereas the stranger's hate stare is intended to provoke feelings of shame in the black (observed) Griffin, in the white (observing) Griffin the expression kindles both shame (at the obvious brutality of the act) and guilt (at his own complicity with the act). The narrator's use of the word "you," in phrases such as "You see a kind of insanity," reiterates this doubleness, at once depersonalizing and universalizing his response;

in such cases, "you" both includes and excludes the speaker's "I." Out of this sense of doubleness, Griffin is able to experience the withering effects of racism on black self-realization as well as the shattering effects of the realization of racism on his own self-esteem.

Griffin's encounter with the stranger in New Orleans portends his even more traumatic arrival in Hattiesburg on November 14. Just before departing New Orleans, Griffin had learned of a federal grand jury's failure to hand down any indictments in the April 25 lynching of Mack Parker, a twenty-three-year-old truck driver. At the time a mob attacked him, Parker was being held in a Poplarville, Mississippi, jail on trumped-up charges of rape. Though FBI agents, called in to assist with the investigation, had managed to obtain several admissions of guilt and had included these in a 378-page report on the lynching, the jury—composed of twenty white people and one black man—found no basis for prosecution.[36] When Griffin arrives in Hattiesburg, not far from the site of the lynching, the black population is reeling from rage and despair at the verdict. It is under these circumstances (and perhaps out of an unconscious desire to probe the limits of his own response to the lynching and jury verdict) that Griffin, now in a dilapidated Hattiesburg hotel room, decides to write a letter to his wife:

> The observing self saw the Negro surrounded by the sounds and smells of the ghetto, write "Darling" to a white woman. The chains of my blackness would not allow me to go on. Though I understood and could analyze what was happening, I could not break through.
> *Never look at a white woman—look down or the other way. What you mean, calling a white woman "darling" like that, boy?* (72)

In its staging this scene reveals both the sexualized aspects of racism (its mediation by, and expression through, sexual fear and sexual jealousy) and the attendant intractability of white taboos against the transgression of racialized sexual prohibitions. Here the observing self—now internalized as "conscience"—takes on the menacing voice of white lynchers, thereby recasting Griffin in the image of their victim, Mack Parker. The voice not only forbids look and address, it also castrates desire, ultimately forcing Griffin to lay down his pen. Whereas in previous scenes Griffin remains ambivalent, split by the terms of his double-identification, here—in a scene explicitly concerned with the punishment of black male sexuality (even where no rape has occurred)—an

"I" emerges that affiliates itself explicitly with white power. Unable to "break through" the imaginary "chains of blackness" that shackle him to a narrow conception of black subjectivity as wholly given over to shame and dishonor, Griffin succumbs to the authority of the observing self. The result is the banishment of a black "I," the eclipsing of black autonomy by the regulatory power of a masterful white other.

Black Like Me hinges on this first night in Hattiesburg, the nadir of Griffin's experiment in passing. Exhausted and frightened, he ultimately calls sympathetic white friends and spends two days recuperating in their home before returning (in the backseat of his friend's car) to New Orleans. From New Orleans, Griffin sets out on the second leg of his journey, first traveling by bus to Biloxi, Mississippi, and then hitchhiking to Mobile, Alabama. The journal entry for November 19 recounts Griffin's disgust as white man after white man stops to offer him a ride, coming on to him through a ritualized "curiosity" about black male sexuality. (Here Griffin reminds the reader of how his awareness of his body as an instrument of his "experiment" dovetails with the ways that he is seen *as* a body—how he is sexualized and spectacularized through the agency of the curious, compassionate, or fetishistic "looking" of others.) In these cases the observing (white) Griffin is able to distance himself from the white men, whose sexualized interests evoke Griffin's own homophobia. Yet Griffin is struck by the apparent kindness of one young man, even despite the man's desire to discuss Negroes' "lack of neuroses." "I knew," Griffin writes, "that he showed me a side of his nature that was special to the night and the situation, a side rarely brought to light in his everyday living" (95).

With this Jekyll/Hyde conceit, Griffin comes full circle from his first journal entry, which details the splitting (into night and day, spectacle and spectator, black and white) of his own subjectivity. Yet in distinction to the mirror scene, which associates the characteristics of Hyde with "the mark of blackness," here Griffin links depravity to the white subject. In so doing Griffin not only abdicates his prior belief in an essential white goodness (of intention, if not of character) but also deessentializes and reindividualizes black and white subject-positions (so that each is capable of becoming Hyde).

When Griffin finally arrives in Mobile, his perceptions of the city's white residents are radically changed. "The gracious Southerner, the wise Southerner, the kind Southerner was nowhere visible," he writes. "I knew that if I were white, I would find him easily, for his other face is there for whites to see. It is not a false face; it is simply different from the one the Negro sees" (107). Yet later Griffin recuperates the image of the gracious, wise, and kind southerner in a portrait of a black family who takes him in for the night while he is traveling through to Montgomery. Eight people—two adults and six young children—share an unpainted two-room shanty, "patched at the bottom with a rusting Dr Pepper sign." Together they eat a meal consisting of bread and yellow beans, to which Griffin contributes several Milky Way bars for dessert: "Closed into two rooms, with only the soft light of two kerosene lamps, the atmosphere changed. The outside world, outside standards disappeared. They were somewhere beyond in the vast darkness. In here, we had all we needed for gaiety. We had shelter, some food in our bellies, the bodies and eyes and affections of children who were not yet aware of how things were. And we had treats. We cut the Milky Way bars into thin slices for dessert" (115). Although intended to contrast his experiences of the antagonism of southern whites with those of the hospitality of southern blacks, this scene—with its pastoral overtones, its romanticization of suffering, its nostalgia for southern graciousness, and its idealization of the noble nuclear family—instead serves to domesticate blackness and a black family's poverty, reinscribing them within a protective rhetorical veil of home life and even (to invoke a phrase with more recent connotations) "family values." In portraying those within the shack as washed in "warm light," whereas the outside (white) world recedes as a space of "vast darkness," Griffin merely reverses the dominant symbolism of good and evil, white and black.

The domesticating gaze that Griffin directs upon his black informants is a product, as I have been arguing, of a white liberal political discourse that posits black subjects—here the "deserving," ennobled poor —as objects of ethnographic contemplation, a positioning that serves retroactively to justify the white researcher's presumed prerogative of masterful and disinterested observation. Even under the disciplinary conventions of modernist anthropology, Griffin's position would seem baldly exploitative; recall that he never announces his intentions to the family and that the Milky Way bar is his contribution to dinner. Although he provides a detailed description of the decrepitude of the family's home, down to the specifics of how the shanty has been pieced together with the abandoned remnants of commodity culture (the rusting Dr Pepper sign), Griffin does not allow any of his informants to speak, to join him in his privileged position as observer. According a voice to his informants at this point in the narrative not only would displace some of Griffin's authority as spokesman by situating his voice in critical relation to other voices, but it would also upset the whole economy of Griffin's sentimental portraiture, in which pathos depends upon passivity. If the dinner table symbolizes commonality as well as community—in its ideal political and social form, the "beloved community" imagined by Martin Luther King Jr.—then Griffin's staging of this scene in *Black Like Me* would seem to suggest that silence, or the denial of black political agency, is paradoxically the source of black political agency, insofar as it is the means by which blacks win concessions from white elites. Silent suffering and "making do"—the two dominant tropes in Griffin's description—are in this context both sources of sentimental appeal and the pretext of white liberal political alliance across the color line.

Although *Black Like Me*'s sentimental narrative reaches a climax with Griffin's description of his night with a poor southern family, it is also during his stay with this family that Griffin's growing distrust of whiteness enters his unconscious in the form of a nightmare about his own lynching: "White men and women, their faces stern and heartless, closed in on me. The hate stare burned through me. I pressed back against a wall. I could expect no pity, no mercy. They approached slowly and I could not escape them" (122). Griffin's imagination of his entrapment by a white mob would seem to symbolize his emerging consciousness of being bombarded by the sheer weight of evidence contradicting the lie of harmonious southern race relations. Moreover, the dream would seem to indicate that despite the deeply flawed foundation of Griffin's ethnojournalistic experiment, his experiences exert a transformative power over Griffin's self-conception.

Not surprisingly, in the process of shedding his illusions about the South, Griffin is left feeling somewhat naked himself. In a passage that describes his rather ignominious arrival in Georgia (shame now associated with the heart of whiteness, rather than of darkness), Griffin expresses this sense of bareness rhetorically, his normally straightforward, sometimes clunky prose slipping unsubtly into irony: "I was back in the land of my forefathers, Georgia. The town of Griffin was named for one of them. [I] . . . carried the name hated by all Negroes, for former

Governor Griffin (no kin that I would care to discover) devoted him-self heroically to the task of keeping Negroes 'in their place.' Thanks in part to his efforts, this John Griffin celebrated a triumphant return to the land from which his people had sprung by seeking sanctuary in a toi-let cubicle at the bus station" (140). In the passage that follows, Griffin, his supply of oxsoralen now depleted, removes the stain from his face with cleansing cream and scrubs the rest of his body with an undershirt, until he is satisfied that he can "pass for white." For the remainder of his experiment, Griffin switches back and forth between identities, re-moving the dye when he wants to be white and reapplying it when he wants to become black again. In contrast to the consternation and dis-comfort his disguise once inspired, these more rapid transformations do not seem to faze Griffin. A *Time* magazine article about his "Journey into Shame" series unintentionally puns on the shift in Griffin's sensi-bility in the caption below a photograph of him, which reads: "After four weeks as a Negro, Griffin harbors new doubts about his own race." [37] Whether "his own race" refers to Griffin as an individual or whites in general, in fact the experiment in passing has proved transformative. Although Atlanta—the "New South"—promises respite from the night-mare of Mississippi, Griffin no longer needs to shield himself from the damage such discoveries inflict on his white self-image. Feeling like shit, he seeks sanctuary in a toilet stall.

REFLECTING BACK

It is not easy to escape mentally from a concrete situation, to refuse its ideology while continuing to live with its actual relationships. From now on, [the colonizer] lives his life under the sign of contradiction which looms at every step, depriving him of all coherence and all tranquility.
—ALBERT MEMMI, *The Colonizer and the Colonized* [38]

In his 1973 follow-up articles to the original *Sepia* series that became *Black Like Me*, Griffin draws on the historical lessons of the preceding decade to reexamine the status of *Black Like Me* as a work of civil rights advocacy and to rethink his role as a civil rights advocate. In particu-lar, "What's Happened since *Black Like Me*" (the name given to the epi-logue of the second edition) reflects the generational shift in tactics and goals that accompanied the transition from a politics of rights in the late 1950s, which emphasized integration and interracialism, to politics of power in the mid-1960s, which emphasized black pride, nationalism, and economic empowerment. The shift in civil rights heralded a period of rift—what Griffin calls a new "area of unknowing"—between black activists and white liberals, one with enduring repercussions. Godfrey Hodgson argues that the 1965 Watts riots are a watershed in this history, marking "the beginning of a period when the same events took on utterly different meanings for white people and for blacks."[39] The breakdown of an alliance between black and white liberals, which previously had been exemplified by moderate groups such as the NAACP, resulted in changes in the membership and the philosophy of black political organizations. In 1966 the Student Nonviolent Coordinating Committee (SNCC) became the first major black group to vote to exclude whites from membership; a year later, in their nationalist manifesto *Black Power*, Stokely Carmichael and Charles Hamilton outlined their determination to "take care of business" by "whatever means necessary."[40] The shift in mood can be measured in terms of the shifts in Griffin's ongoing narrative: in 1961 he published *Black Like Me* as a treatise against segregation, using the knowledge gained by racial passing to expound a liberal critique of white supremacy; yet in 1973 he critiqued white liberalism and argued that whites needed to remove themselves from the spotlight, if not the margins, of the movement.

In a brief aside to an essay on the interventions of white critics into the study of African American literary history, Michael Awkward calls *Black Like Me* "a generally selfless response to white liberal guilt" (597). Apt as Awkward's pat response might seem, it nevertheless overlooks Griffin's ultimate skepticism about guilt as a useful tool for fostering white racist political consciousness. Perhaps because he had come to recognize its inadequacy in the course of examining his own racism, Griffin disparaged guilt as a screen for covert or unacknowledged intolerance. "There is not necessarily any guilt attached to *having* the prejudices," he wrote, "since most of us are no more guilty of acquiring our prejudices than we are of acquiring a disfiguring pockmark from some childhood illness."[41] If guilt was to have any relevance in the struggle against racism, it had to be reconceived along ethical lines—not in terms of blame and liability but in terms of responsibility. James Baldwin once wrote that black skin "operate[s] as a most disagreeable mirror" for white people, an intolerable reminder of their part in black persecution.⁴² Having discovered in himself what Baldwin had all along discerned in white people generally, Griffin fully advocated facing this reflection, not merely assuaging the anxiety associated with it. Guilt thus transformed could become a force in relations not only between blacks and whites but—as in the trope of whites confronting their mirror images—between whites and whites.

In later years Griffin would come to reevaluate his recruitment as a spokesman for the experiences of African Americans. In the epilogue to *Black Like Me*, he writes that in the years following the book's publication, "it was my embarrassing task to sit in on meetings of whites and blacks, to serve one ridiculous but necessary function. I knew, and every black man there knew, that I, as a man now white again, could say the things that needed saying but would be rejected if black men said them" (190–91). He adds: "Often in the presence of local black men whites would ask me questions that should have been addressed to the black men present. They knew the community, I didn't. Always this was an affront to black men, one of the many affronts that white men apparently could not perceive" (194). Paradoxically and retrospectively, Griffin illustrates the refusal of whites to recognize black people as reliable witnesses to their own experience. Paradoxically, because it was Griffin's own failure to recognize such a possibility that served as the original motivation for his own ethnojournalistic enterprise. In this, his belated disavowal of white entitlement to "speak for," Griffin has in some sense come full circle, his "journey into shame" transformed into an exploration of the shameful face of "white" selfhood.

Having said this, I want to turn in conclusion to the questions and possibilities that *Black Like Me* raises for thinking about difference and its relation to political alliance, especially alliances that link the interests of individuals across boundaries of race. In its failure to transcend the domesticating gaze of ethnography, as well as its attempt to construct an authoritative white voice that would occupy the positions of "seer" as well as "seen," *Black Like Me* illustrates some of the pitfalls associated with Griffin's discourse of white liberalism. In a deft reading of *Black Like Me* that regards Griffin's project as continuous with that of blackface minstrelsy, Eric Lott argues that Griffin's "disguise" is nothing more—and nothing less—than an "externalization" of the "sexualized racial unconscious of American whiteness," or white masculinity's repressed libidinal investment in black masculinity.⁴³ I would add to Lott's account a related observation: namely, that Griffin's fidelity to a liberal thesis of "sameness under the skin" interferes with his ability to elaborate, much less come to terms with, the difference between playing and being "Negro"—or for that matter playing and being "white"—without reinscribing race in the very essentialist terms that he seeks to redress. The black separatist rejection of white liberal voices such as Griffin's in the late 1960s is precisely a response to the sort of mimetic desire that *Black Like Me* embodies: one that wants to appropriate black "experience" without compromising a presumed white entitlement to speak for this experience, one that wants to lose itself in the "other" without losing control. To be sure, a certain degree of self-referentiality may be inevitable in the practical "deconstruction" of whiteness, and yet it is crucial, as the shortcomings of Griffin's enterprise indicate, that white self-examination not turn into an occasion for the display of white self-interest masquerading as empathy.

Griffin's own ultimate response to the problem of confronting racism was to step aside. In the epilogue to *Black Like Me*, Griffin broadens his definition of passing so that it includes not only the contrivances of disguise but also the conditions of white identity. Dismayed after hearing the 1967 State of the Union address by Lyndon Johnson, whose appeal to save the California redwoods drew more applause than the appeal for civil rights, Griffin wires the president: AM TIRED OF BEING A LOSER. FROM NOW ON I'M GOING TO FORGET HUMANITY AND WORK FOR THE TREES (196). In his frustration Griffin could not see that working for "the trees" and working for "humanity" might be complementary rather than mutually exclusive goals. Indeed, Griffin's wire to the president ironically draws attention to significant weaknesses in his personalistic approach to racism, which privileges the agency of the rational, individual subject in his triumphs over stereotype, significantly downplaying the agency of those depersonalized, and yet more powerful, social and cultural narratives that mediate race and racial identities. Ironically, that is, that part of his narrative that is supposed to express Griffin's loss of hope in the ability of his fellow "humans" to recognize their self-interest in supporting the burgeoning civil rights movement also expresses his text's abiding faith in an individualism that can carry the day. So focused was Griffin on racism as an individual pathology and a violation of individual rights that he failed to see how "resistance" might take the form of working to produce alternative narratives of humanity and coalition, including those that might include trees. It is thus fitting, perhaps, that having already spoken on behalf of "others," Griffin takes recourse in self-silencing. By the late 1960s, though still serving as a white "observer," he had finished giving voice to what he observed. "I hardly ever opened my mouth," he writes. "The day was past when black people wanted any advice from white men" (196).

EPILOGUE

Passing, Color

Blindness, and

Contemporary

Discourses of Race

and Identity

The rules may be colorblind, but people are not. The question remains, therefore, whether the law can truly exist apart from the color-conscious society in which it exists, as a skeleton devoid of flesh; or whether law is the embodiment of society, the reflection of a particular citizenry's arranged complexity of relations.
—PATRICIA J. WILLIAMS, *The Alchemy of Race and Rights* [1]

The mystery of the world is the visible, not the invisible.
—MICHELLE CLIFF, *Claiming an Identity They Taught Me to Despise* [2]

A long time ago I disappeared. One day I was here, the next I was gone. It happened as quickly as all that. One day I was playing schoolgirl games with my sister and our friends in a Roxbury playground. The next I was a nobody, just a body without a name or a history, sitting beside my mother in the front seat of our car, moving forward on the highway, not stopping. (And when I stopped being nobody, I would become white—white as my skin, hair, bones allowed. My body would fill in the blanks, tell me who I should become, and I would let it speak for me.)
—DANZY SENNA, *Caucasia* [3]

In ending with *Black Like Me*, we are left squarely in the middle of the problem of contemporary U.S. liberal discourse, with its commitment to ideals of universality and equal rights and its concomitant ambivalence regarding how much the socially produced "fact" of racial difference ought to matter in confronting or combating racial injustice.[4] *Black Like Me*'s notion of "sameness under the skin" additionally brings the historical trajectory of this study full circle, recalling Justice John Harlan's famous lone dissenting opinion in *Plessy v. Ferguson*, in which Harlan articulated the now widely embraced principle of a "color blind" U.S. Constitution.[5] Indeed, Griffin's discourse of racelessness resonates with contemporary "color blind" critiques, which argue that the social effectuality of race is best remedied through policies that enforce the formal racelessness of all citizens, no matter their racial ascription or their self-recognition within or across prescribed racial categories. Today's proponents of color-blind social policy do not universally embrace the conservative notion that the United States has *achieved* such formal racial equality—a notion both reflected and forwarded, for example, by the policies of the Reagan administration—yet it is now commonly held, by liberals and conservatives alike, that a purposeful indifference to race and a corresponding elevation of the "individual" as a social agent is an effective strategy of achieving the end of a just, democratic society.[6] According to such color-blind arguments, a concerted "blindness" to race presents the most promising alternative to a society in which racialization—however unstable, shifting, or unenforceable—historically has played a role in governing social opportunity and status.

In recent years one of the most interesting developments in this regard has been the emergence of a certain discourse of passing within discussions of social policy designed to advance the goals of a color-blind society. For example, within the highly charged political battles waged in the late 1990s over affirmative action in the admissions processes of public universities in racially and ethnically diverse states such as California and Texas, it was not unusual to hear proponents of so-called "race blind" admissions policies asserting that the middle-class status of certain racial-ethnic minority applicants made them inappropriate targets of affirmative action. Subsuming race under the sign of class, opponents of affirmative action in the California and Texas debates in effect implied that the class positionality of these students rendered them symbolically "white," and that they therefore should have been able to "compete" on the basis of individual merit (as measured by test scores, grade-point averages, and the like).[7] At the same time, anti-affirmative-action activists were able to mobilize voter support for their cause by raising the specter of "reverse discrimination," a strategy that has proved effective in drumming up fears that the gains of "minorities" must come at the expense of those who have enjoyed access to public resources on the basis of their race and gender. Appealing to the authority of SAT scores in order to symbolically position Asian American students on the "white" side of the color line, these tactics proved particularly effective in stirring up antagonisms among differently racialized "minority" populations.

Ironically, given their stated ends of improving opportunities for the social mobility and educational access of racial-ethnic students, the most telling result of such "color blind" critiques has been the racialization of affirmative action itself. For example, by framing affirmative action as a struggle over public resources waged between symbolically "white" Asian Americans and "others" positioned on the "black" side of the color line, opponents of affirmative action not only pitted the interests of differently racialized groups against one another in the name of universalism, but they have enabled the interests of those unmarked by race and/or gender to "pass" out of the picture. Perhaps most insidiously, the racialization of affirmative action (as "race-based preferences") has quietly eroded fragile political alliances between feminists and anti-racism advocates by abetting historical amnesia of affirmative action as a loosely confederated series of public policies and private initiatives that primarily have assisted white women. In racializing affirmative action, its critics thus paradoxically have enabled the erasure of critical questions of profit and gain that cannot be subsumed under the sign of race, all the while threatening to turn the principal beneficiaries of affirmative action into its newest detractors.[8]

Similarly, in a curious reversal of the traditional discourse of racial passing, which has emphasized the relation between social privilege and freedom from racial definition, "race blind" critiques of affirmative action have often exploited the notion that in a post-civil-rights world, it "pays" to be a member of a racial-ethnic minority group. Such is the explicit premise of a 1972 *Sepia* article, "How Passing Passed Out," which argues that in light of fair employment requirements imposed on corporations and government bodies, the only passing in the post-civil-rights era will be "passing for black."[9] More recently, the notion of "blackness" as a means of social mobility has been simultaneously recuperated and lampooned in the 1986 movie *Soul Man*, an equivocally pro-affirmative-action film structured around an explicitly classed and gendered narrative of racial passing. In *Soul Man* the eponymous protagonist, a self-absorbed, wealthy white male college graduate, procures a scholarship to Harvard Law School by passing for black. Although he initially gives little thought to the ethical implications of his actions, through his encounters with racial discrimination at Harvard and his romance with a fellow law student, a black woman who also happens to be a struggling single mother, the "soul man" gradually acquires empathy for black suffering and comes to realize that black students are deserving of law school scholarships. Yet though this moral and political turnaround rehabilitates the soul man as an object of positive audience identification, meanwhile impelling recognition of his girlfriend as more deserving of the scholarship, such narrative closure comes at the expense of a more profound and critical inquiry into race in its interactions with class and gender. The film never seriously asks what makes the soul man "white," or interrogates the social and cultural presumptions that elevate his quest for "identity" as a subject of narrative representation. Hence though *Soul Man* suggests—without exemplifying—a progressive critique of the protagonist's gendered and classed racial advantage, it ironically reinscribes the soul man's ability to mediate the definitions of race from which he profits. In contrast to his girlfriend, the soul man benefits from blackness without having to sacrifice the certainty or stability of his "own" identity.

As represented by their proponents, color-blind social policies present an alluring alternative to the "problem of the color line" (to recall the phrase of W. E. B. Du Bois that I cited at the outset of this study), emphasizing the agency of the individual over her inscription within collectivizing categories based in inherently multiple, unstable and acategorical conceptions of race. Yet the arguments I have developed around the representation of racial passing in the foregoing chapters alert us to potential pitfalls of such a predetermined "blindness" to collective identities that are at once sites of self-recognition and self-identification and also regulated and enforced by racial ideology, and whose production is dialectically linked to the management of national narratives of the (abstract) "individual" as the preeminent social agent.

These arguments, which have emphasized the production of racial difference through socially manufactured categories of the visible, lead us
to question the metaphor of "blindness," a term that implies that race is
inherently seeable, thereby presuming a stable relation between identity
and that which is knowable through the "evidence" of the body.[10] Such
inquiry might additionally alert us to the difficulty of choosing "blindness" as a political strategy, given that our racial identities are ascribed
rather than elected, our ability to "see" race—or to (mis)perceive its
ever-present absence—itself shaped by collectivizing scripts not of our
own design. Finally, this interrogation of racial passing has prompted an
exploration of the relation between the agency of individual subjects and
the narratives in and through which their mobility is managed. What if,
instead of staking a response to racial injustice on the concept of individual negotiations of social "lines," we grounded our critique in an interrogation of how narratives of individual mobility themselves function
to secure the lines of collective identification?

Through my readings of various passing narratives, this book has
offered the argument that race *mediates* identity, even in those instances
when it fails to *represent* it according to convention. Whereas the metaphor of "blindness" assumes a stable distinction between what is "actually" visible and what is seen, passing narratives reveal that categories
of race (in combination with the various categories that intercut and
complicate race) are also radically contingent on a certain interpretive
(and yet also socially mandated) performance of visibility. Sometimes
this performance may contradict or otherwise exceed the socially produced "text" of the body, as demonstrated by the "case history" of Mezz
Mezzrow, who passed for black although (in *Ebony* magazine's words)
"his skin [was] too white." On the other hand, in representing the transgression of the categories through which subjects are socially compelled
to "see" themselves, passing narratives render visible the contradictions
of race as a locus of identification, even in cases when the subject's self-
recognition conforms to that identity that is ascribed by racial discourse.
I have shown this to be the case, for example, in representations in which
the condition of narrative closure is the return of the passer to an apparently stable racial order based on the exclusivity of categories of black
and white. In these narratives, however, embracing one's "proper" racial
identity is no less complex or potentially less fraught an act than choosing to pass, although the subject's refusal to "cross the line" may be con-

stitutive of a different set of political possibilities, or of different opportunities for the construction of agency.

The issue of agency inexorably leads to the question of social struggle, raising once again Du Bois's notion of race as a means of regulating the circulation of social power. In each of the chapters of this study, I have demonstrated how racial passing confronts us with the circumscription of our strategies of resistance by race itself. Passing narratives remind us, through their very contradictions, that it is the nature of any "strategy" that we do not get to choose either it or the circumstances in which its desirability is manifested.[11] Hence even when racial passing is predicated on conscious choice—as opposed to instances in which subjects are "passed," or pass involuntarily, through the (mis)recognitions of others—such choice occurs within the context of a negotiation of categories that are authorized by racial ideology and quite literally mandated by the state.[12] The durability of the black/white paradigm may in certain cases be abetted rather than undermined by its instability, insofar as this quality lends it a discursive mobility and flexibility. In short, whereas passing is conditioned on the radical instability of the racial sign, the fluidity of race that it appropriates is a function of its (socially produced) stability in marking out the binary possibilities of the national narrative. As my readings of various passing narratives have demonstrated, representation is the means by which race establishes social power—hence the metaphor of a dividing "line" between black and white identities; yet it is through representation that we are able to envision challenges to the color line's authority.

Above all, this study has emphasized that although race is a fiction, racial identities are both substantive and "real"; indeed, as my readings of passing narratives have demonstrated, their consequence is a function of race's nonexistence and immateriality. Identities are sites of contradiction through which subjects make known and express their desire, even as their desire is a function of who they "are"; they may be arbitrarily produced without the subject's conscious consent and may link her to other subjects with whom she shares no prior relation, but they are also the grounds upon which self-recognition is subsequently produced and negotiated. The intimate link between identity and agency explains why subjects who are the bearers of marginalized identities have often fought hardest to preserve a notion of "identity" in the face of attempts to declare it moot or obsolete. Not by coincidence is the moment of the "passing of racial passing" also the era that witnessed the inception of the modern civil rights movement—and with it, new attempts on the parts of African Americans to appropriate the discourses of identity itself for new kinds of political expression. Moreover, such political stakes of identity do not simply disappear at that moment when the dominant culture begins to cast off its previous and strategic "blindness" to the fictitiousness of race. What today is often disparagingly referred to as "identity politics"—a term that misleadingly suggests that identities are "political" only when they designate "marked" subjects—often entails struggles over the agency to dictate such blindness.

The issues of race, agency, and the politics of identity that this book has raised are no less relevant in an era in which, increasingly, the binary model is being subjected to interrogation, criticism, and outright challenge—not only by people who find their identities rendered marginal or invisible by this binary, but increasingly by the state itself.[13] Such issues are taken up by the writer Danzy Senna in her recent novel *Caucasia*, in which the authority of the color line is imagined in its capacity to mediate the most intimate bonds of "blood" relations, disrupting ties between parent and child, sister and sister, that are ordinarily thought to be sequestered from the public sphere of race politics.[14] Set initially in Boston in the early 1970s, *Caucasia* explores the effects of the racial binary as it penetrates the private, domestic sphere, literally dividing a nuclear family in two. When their parents suddenly decide to separate, the two sisters in the novel, Birdie and Cole, enter into the custody of separate parents, the "cinnamon-skinned, curly-haired" Cole accompanying Deck, their black father, an intellectual and a "race man," to Brazil; Birdie, straight-haired and lighter-skinned than her older sister, remaining with Sandra, their white mother, a political activist who moves them from place to place to elude her enemies (real or imagined). Having struggled to fit in at the all-black Boston school that she and Cole previously attended, Birdie thus finds herself living as Jesse Goldman in small-town New Hampshire, acting out the Jewish-girl identity that she and her mother have concocted.

Narrated from Birdie's point of view, *Caucasia* explores themes of love and longing, particularly Birdie's longing for Cole. "Before I ever saw myself, I saw my sister," she recalls in the first chapter titled "Face." "When I was still too small for mirrors, I saw her as the reflection that proved my own existence" (5). Yet the novel denies Birdie and the reader this fantasy of boundarylessness. When at the end of the novel Birdie, now in her twenties, relates her story to her father, who has spent the intervening years producing his magnum opus—a seven-hundred-page manuscript titled *The Petrified Monkey: Race, Blood, and the Origins of Hypocrisy*—he assures her that "there's no such thing as passing." "We're all just pretending," he tells her. "Race is a complete illusion, make-believe. It's a costume. We all wear one. You just switched yours at some point. That's just the absurdity of the whole race game" (334). Birdie shares Deck's belief that race is a social construct, and yet her experience also contradicts his assurances of a racially transcendent universalism. "If race is so make-believe," she asks him, "why did I go with Mum? You gave me to Mum 'cause I looked white. You don't think that's real? Those are the facts" (336). Later, when she and Cole are reunited, Birdie explains how passing felt like becoming "somebody I didn't like. Somebody who had no voice or color or conviction" (349). The novel ends with the sisters making plans to live together, and together confronting both the necessity and the consequences of "choosing." [15]

This study, too, has sought to explore the dialectics of race and identity. In examining stories that refute and recuperate, complicate and transgress, the "line" that has shaped this century's national narrative of race, I have explored possibilities for defying and subverting racial ascription; yet I have also stayed alert to the hazards of constructing "transcendence" without equality, "universality" without justice. Using the notion of "crossing the line" as a means of drawing together diverse representations, I have demonstrated how "identity" has been imagined simultaneously as a locus of social denomination and a locus of agency, a space from which subjects may engage in practices of self-naming and self-identification, even if these violate the conventions of the dominant racial discourse. I have likewise shown that although passing is problematic as a paradigm of "resistance," it nevertheless renders visible the conditions that produce identities as sites of struggle.

It is with this in mind that I refer, in conclusion, to a passage from Williams's *The Alchemy of Race and Rights*, in which she names resistance to white supremacy as a distinctive type of border-crossing, one that recalls Gloria Anzaldúa's definition of "borderlands" as "vague and undetermined" places that may also be spaces of creativity, tolerance, and hope.[16] Having described an incident in which she was made an unwitting accomplice to anti-Semitism, Williams reflects on the means of attempting to redraw the real and symbolic lines that make "wilderness of . . . others": "I think that the hard work of a nonracist sensibility is the boundary crossing, from safe circle into wilderness: the testing of boundary, the consecration of sacrilege. It is the willingness to spoil a good party and break an encompassing circle, to travel from the safe to the unsafe. This transgression is dizzyingly intense, a reminder of what it is to be alive. It is a sinful pleasure, this willing transgression of a line, which takes one into new awareness, a secret, lonely and tabooed world—to survive the transgression is terrifying and addictive" (129).

It is in the spirit of Williams's recuperation of border-crossing as a transgression of a certain "etiquette" of racial discourse that I close *Crossing the Line*. Passing narratives reveal that the ongoing legacy of race may require what Williams describes as a commitment to "sacrilege": to a project of "boundary-crossing" that entails the vigilant and energetic challenging of seemingly permanent boundaries. The stakes of the color line, in its historical capacity simultaneously to affiliate and to divide, demand nothing less.

NOTES

PREFACE

1 Daniel Zalewski, "Cloning the Classics," *Lingua Franca* 7, no. 9 (November 1997): 28.

INTRODUCTION

1 Gloria Anzaldúa, *Borderlands/La Frontera: The New Mestiza* (San Francisco: Aunt Lute Books, 1987), 3.
2 Charles W. Chesnutt, *The House behind the Cedars* (1900; reprint, New York: Penguin, 1993), 24.
3 Adrian Piper, "Passing for White, Passing for Black," *Transition* 58 (1992): 25.
4 Originally performed on the December 5, 1984, episode of *Saturday Night*

Live, "White Like Me" is available on the videotape *The Best of "Saturday Night Live" Hosted by Eddie Murphy* (Paramount, 1989).

5 Michael Omi and Howard Winant discuss the genealogy of "color-blind" thinking in the years of the Reagan presidency in *Racial Formation in the United States: From the 1960s to the 1990s*, 2d ed. (New York: Routledge, 1994), esp. 132–36. For a useful discussion of the figurations of "race" in social policy, see Cornel West, "Race and Social Theory: Towards a Genealogical and Materialist Analysis," in *The Year Left: An American Socialist Yearbook*, vol. 2, ed. Mike David et al. (London: Verso, 1987), 74–85.

6 See George Lipsitz, *The Possessive Investment in Whiteness: How White People Profit from Identity Politics* (Philadelphia: Temple University Press, 1998), esp. 1–23.

7 Cheryl I. Harris, "Whiteness as Property," in *Critical Race Theory: The Key Writings That Formed the Movement*, ed. Kimberlé Crenshaw, Neil Gotanda, Gary Peller, and Kendall Thomas (New York: New Press, 1995), 277.

8 My source for the text of Piper's "calling cards" is Peggy Phelan, *Unmarked: The Politics of Performance* (New York: Routledge, 1993). Phelan, in turn, quotes from Darcy Grimaldo Grigsby, "Dilemmas of Visibility: Contemporary Women Artists' Representations of Female Bodies," *Michigan Quarterly Review* (fall 1990): 584–619. Phelan's book (especially 97–99) contains a compelling discussion of Piper's performance.

9 Du Bois's 1900 address appears in *W. E. B. DuBois: A Reader*, ed. David Levering Lewis (New York: Henry Holt, 1995), 639, where it is reprinted from *Report of the Pan-African Conference, held on the 23rd, 24th and 25th July, 1900, at Westminster Town Hall, Westminster, S.W.* [London] (Headquarters 61 and 62, Chancery Lane, W.C., London [1900]), 1–12. See also Du Bois, *The Souls of Black Folk* (1903; reprint, New York: Penguin, 1989).

10 For more on the "territorializing" function of race, see Aldon Lynn Nielson, *Reading Race: The White American Poet and the Racial Discourse in the Twentieth Century* (Athens, Ga.: University of Georgia Press, 1988), which argues that "[r]ace serves simultaneously as the means by which hegemonic discourse organizes its policing functions, erecting boundaries that define and oppress an other, *and* as the ever-shifting strategic locus from which others assault and reterritorialize American identity" (3). The notion of racial territories is also productively explored by Anzaldúa in *Borderlands/La Frontera*, and by Samira Kawash in *Dislocating the Color Line: Identity, Hybridity, and Singularity in African-American Narrative* (Stanford: Stanford University Press, 1997), esp. chaps. 4 and 5, where she explores the failure of the racial "order" to sustain the social order, which erupts into violence around issues of race.

11 Here I am in agreement with Amy Robinson, who similarly claims that "The 'problem' of identity, a problem to which passing owes the very possibility of

its practice, is predicated on the false promise of the visible as an epistemological guarantee." See her essay "It Takes One To Know One: Passing and Communities of Common Interest," *Critical Inquiry* 20 (summer 1994): 716. I would only add that the visual dimension of race must operate in conjunction with the ideologies of social privilege that it also enables in order for "race" — and for that matter, "passing" — to have significance.

12 Whereas the phrase "crossing the line" conveys my sense of passing as transgression of white supremacy, it also enables my interpretation of representations of "white" passing. In *Neither Black Nor White Yet Both: Thematic Explorations of Interracial Literature* (New York: Oxford University Press, 1997), Werner Sollors usefully traces the etymology of the term "passing" and its many and varied citations in American literature of the nineteenth and twentieth centuries. As Sollors notes, the word "passing" "is used most frequently . . . as if it were short for 'passing for white,' in the sense of 'crossing over' the color line in the United States from the black to the white side" (247). In using the phrase "crossing the line" to define passing, I am therefore also interrogating the presumption of the desirability of "white" identity that informs such a construction, as well as the varied histories and cultural representations of "passing for black."

13 The question of passing as resistance is discussed in Carole-Ann Tyler's essay "Passing: Narcissism, Identity, and Difference," *differences: A Journal of Feminist Cultural Studies* 6, nos. 2/3 (1994): 212–48. Tyler's framing of passing as "not quite not resistance" is persuasive, although I disagree with her definition of passing as "the uncanny experience of the *lack* of an identity" (213).

14 My discussion of race draws upon a number of influences. Works that have been especially helpful include Angela Y. Davis, *Women, Race and Class* (New York: Random House, 1981); David Theo Goldberg, *Racist Culture: Philosophy and the Politics of Meaning* (Oxford: Blackwell, 1993); Stuart Hall, "Gramsci's Relevance for the Study of Race and Ethnicity," *Journal of Communication Inquiry* 10, no. 2 (1986): 5–27; UNESCO, "Race, Articulation, and Societies Structured in Dominance," in *Sociological Theories: Race and Colonialism* (Paris: UNESCO, 1980); Michael Omi and Howard Winant, *Racial Formation in the United States: From the 1960s to the 1990s*, 2d ed. (New York: Routledge, 1994); Coco Fusco; *English Is Broken Here: Notes on Cultural Fusion in the Americas* (New York: New Press, 1995).

15 Robyn Wiegman, *American Anatomies: Theorizing Race and Gender* (Durham, N.C.: Duke University Press, 1995), 46.

16 The idea of the "social effectuality" of race is cited by Stuart Hall in his essay "For Allon White: Metaphors of Transformation," in *Stuart Hall: Critical Dialogues in Cultural Studies*, ed. David Morley and Kuan-Hsing Chen (London: Routledge, 1996), 302. I additionally have found useful to my conceptualization of racial metaphor Linda Martin Alcoff's notion of the "produced

obviousness" of race in "Philosophy and Racial Identity," *Radical Philosophy* 75 (January/February 1996): 6.

17 Here I am adopting a phrase of Gayatri Chakravorty Spivak made in the context of a discussion of history and (national) identities. See her *Outside in the Teaching Machine* (New York: Routledge, 1993), 53.

18 See Hortense J. Spillers, "Mama's Baby, Papa's Maybe: An American Grammar Book," *diacritics* 17, no. 2 (1987): 65–81; Dana Nelson, *The Word in Black and White: Reading 'Race' in American Literature, 1638–1867* (New York: Oxford University Press, 1993); and Patricia J. Williams, *The Alchemy of Race and Rights: Diary of a Law Professor* (Cambridge: Harvard University Press, 1991).

19 Langston Hughes, "Passing," in *The Ways of White Folks* (New York: Alfred A. Knopf, 1934), 49–53.

20 The phrase "fiction of identity" is from Elaine Ginsberg, ed., *Passing and the Fictions of Identity* (Durham, N.C.: Duke University Press, 1996).

21 Signithia Fordham demonstrated this point in her talk "The Discourse Around 'Multiracial' Identity," delivered at the annual meeting of the American Studies Association/Canadian Association for American Studies, Washington, D.C., October 31, 1997. Here my conceptualization of passing resembles that proposed by Samira Kawash in her essay *"The Autobiography of an Ex-Coloured Man:* (Passing for) Black Passing for White," which appears in Ginsberg's volume. There Kawash writes, "In the cultural logic of passing, race functions as a form of embodied identity" (69). Later she concludes that "at the heart of racial identity" lies the problem of the " 'that which one cannot be' . . . Perhaps it is the case, then, that my identity is not what I am but what I am passing for" (73). Yet although these arguments are persuasive, they downplay the nonvolunteerism of race, potentially conflating causes with effects. It is not merely under the "cultural logic of passing" that race "functions as a form of embodied identity," in other words; rather, the fantasy of embodiment is part of the cultural logic of race itself. Kawash develops these arguments in *Dislocating the Color Line.*

22 Langston Hughes, "Why Not Fool Our White Folks?" *Chicago Defender* (January 4, 1958): 10. An expanded version of the column appears as "Fooling Our White Folks" in *Negro Digest* (April 1950): 38–41.

23 Walter Benn Michaels, "Autobiography of an Ex-White Man," *Transition* 73 (1998): 122–43. Michaels's article expands an argument previously developed in his book *Our America: Nativism, Modernism, and Pluralism* (Durham, N.C.: Duke University Press, 1995).

24 K. Anthony Appiah makes a similar argument about the necessity of constructing identity within a limited universe of choice in "Race, Culture, Identity: Misunderstood Connections," in *Color Conscious: The Political Morality of Race*, ed. K. Anthony Appiah and Amy Gutmann (Princeton, N.J.: Princeton University Press, 1996) and in a brief essay, "Identity, Authenticity, Survival:

Multicultural Societies and Social Reproduction," in Charles Taylor, *Multi-culturalism: Examining the Politics of Recognition*, ed. Amy Gutmann (Princeton, N.J.: Princeton University Press, 1994). Yet this leads Appiah, like Michaels, to downplay possibilities that race can serve other than an imperial function in ascribing identity. For example, in "Race, Culture, Identity," he invokes the specter of colonial authority in warning of the tendency of collective—especially racial—identities to "go imperial," dominating the other, disparate identities "whose shape is exactly what makes each of us what we individually and distinctively are" (103). Although Appiah does not go so far as Michaels in prescribing individualism as an alterantive to "race," he nevertheless ends up resorting to vague exhortations of contingency, irony and intentional "identity play" (104)—what he himself concedes to be "the proposals of a banal 'postmodernism,'"—as solutions to what he perceives to be the inevitable pitfalls of "identity."

25 For more on the one-drop rule and other means of extralegal racial classification or ascription, see F. James Davis, *Who Is Black? One Nation's Definition* (University Park, Pa.: Pennsylvania State University Press, 1991). See also Theodore W. Allen, *The Invention of the White Race*, vol. 1 (London: Verso, 1994). For an overview of contemporary implications of racial classification in the U.S. census, see Lawrence Wright, "One Drop of Blood," *New Yorker*, July 25, 1994, 46–55.

26 Donald B. Gibson, introduction to *The House behind the Cedars* (1900; reprint, New York: Penguin, 1993), ix.

27 According to Allen in *The Invention of the White Race*, the legacy of the one-drop rule is unique to the United States, where the undifferentiated social status of racially "mixed" people is, in effect, the hallmark of their racial oppression (32).

28 As Michael Omi and Howard Winant explain, "From the very inception of the Republic to the present moment [the 1990s], race has been a profound determinant of one's political rights, one's location in the labor market, and indeed one's sense of 'identity.' The hallmark of this history has been *racism*, not the abstract ethos of equality, and while racial minority groups have been treated differently, all can bear witness to the tragic consequences of racial oppression." See Omi and Winant, *Racial Formation in the United States: From the 1960s to the 1990s*, 2d ed. (New York: Routledge, 1994), 1.

29 *Plessy v. Ferguson*, 160 U.S. 537 (1896): 538, 539–40. Ultimately, because Plessy's attorney's did not contest the Court's determination of race, the Court was free to focus on the issue of the constitutionality of separate rail facilities. For more on *Plessy*, see Richard Kluger, *Simple Justice: The History of "Brown v. Board of Education" and Black America's Struggle for Equality* (New York: Vintage, 1975). For a discussion of the *Plessy* case in the context of issues of identity and performance, see Amy Robinson, "Forms of Appearance of

Value: Homer Plessy and the Politics of Privacy," in *Performance and Cultural Politics*, ed. Elin Diamond (New York: Routledge, 1996), 239-61.

30 *Plessy v. Ferguson*, 160 U.S. 537 (1896): 548.

31 C. Vann Woodward, *The Strange History of Jim Crow* (New York: Oxford University Press, 1955), 68.

32 The number of scholars who have critiqued the notion of universal, abstract citizenship is too great for me to list all of them here. The works that have most influenced my own thinking include: Lisa Lowe, *Immigrant Acts: On Asian American Cultural Politics* (Durham, N.C.: Duke University Press, 1996), esp. 1-36; The Black Public Sphere Collective, ed., *The Black Public Sphere* (Chicago: University of Chicago Press, 1995), especially the essay by Michael Hanchard, "Black Cinderella? Race and the Public Sphere in Brazil"; Nancy Fraser, *Unruly Practices: Power, Discourse and Gender in Contemporary Social Theory* (Minneapolis: University of Minnesota Press, 1989), esp. 113-43; Etienne Balibar and Immanuel Wallerstein, *Race, Nation, Class: Ambiguous Identities* (London: Verso, 1991), esp. 29-36; Etienne Balibar, *Masses, Classes, Ideas: Studies on Politics and Philosophy before and after Marx*, trans. James Swenson (New York: Routledge, 1994), esp. 191-204; Lauren Berlant, *The Queen of America Goes to Washington City: Essays on Sex and Citizenship* (Durham, N.C.: Duke University Press, 1997), esp. 175-246; Gayatri Spivak, *Outside in the Teaching Machine* (New York: Routledge, 1993), esp. 1-24, 53-76.

33 Henry Louis Gates Jr. suggests that Toomer places "negroness" under erasure in *Figures in Black: Words, Signs and the "Racial" Self* (New York: Oxford University Press, 1987), 202.

34 Here I would call the reader's attention to a growing body of scholarship on "whiteness." In addition to Lipsitz's book *The Possessive Investment in Whiteness*, the most salient works in this regard include David Roediger, *The Wages of Whiteness: Race and the Making of the American Working Class* (London: Verso, 1991); Ruth Frankenberg, *White Women, Race Matters: The Social Construction of Whiteness* (Minneapolis: University of Minnesota Press, 1993); Theodore W. Allen, *The Invention of the White Race*, vol. 1 (London: Verso, 1994); Noel Ignatiev, *How the Irish Became White* (New York: Routledge, 1995). *Transition* 73 (1998): "The White Issue" and *Whiteness: A Critical Reader*, ed. Mike Hill (New York: New York University Press, 1997) also contain engaging recent scholarship. See Daniel Boyarin and Jonathan Boyarin, eds., *The New Jewish Cultural Studies* (Minneapolis: University of Minnesota Press, 1997) and Ann Pelligrini, *Performance Anxieties: Staging Psychoanalysis, Staging Race* (New York: Routledge, 1997) for recent work that specifically interrogates whiteness in the context of Jewish identities.

35 For an important discussion of the embodied (hyper)visibility of the so-called mulatta citizen/subject, see Lauren Berlant, "National Brands/Na-

tional Body: *Imitation of Life*," in *The Phantom Public Sphere*, ed. Bruce Robbins (Minneapolis: University of Minnesota Press, 1993), 173–208.

36 The idea that white people live "racially structured lives" is explored in Ruth Frankenberg, *White Women, Race Matters*, 1.

37 Quoted in James Ledbetter, "Imitations of Life," *Vibe* 1, no. 1 (September 1993).

38 As Phelan observes, "The focus on skin as the visible marker of race is itself a form of feminizing those races which are not white. Reading the body as the sign of identity is the way men regulate the bodies of women" (10).

39 See Phillip Brian Harper, *Are We Not Men? Masculine Anxiety and the Problem of African-American Identity* (New York: Oxford University Press, 1996), esp. 103–26.

40 Patricia Hill Collins, *Black Feminist Thought: Knowledge, Consciousness, and the Politics of Empowerment* (London: Unwin Hyman, 1990), 77.

41 Doris Black, "How Passing Passed Out," *Sepia* (December 1972): 66–69.

42 I am thinking here of such examples as the now famous fall 1993 *Time* magazine cover heralding "The New Face of America" (recently echoed in a September 7, 1999 feature article of the same name in *USA Today*) and, more recently, the book *Liberal Racism* (New York: Penguin, 1977), by journalist and essayist Jim Sleeper. These differ, as I see it, from the so-called new abolitionist writing—primarily associated with the journal *Race Traitor*—which proposes the eradication of race through conscious strategies of dis-identification on the parts of those who are the beneficiaries of racial discourse. For more on *Race Traitor*, see Cornel West, "I'm Ofay, You're Ofay: A Conversation with Noel Ignatiev and William 'Upski' Wimsatt," *Transition* 73 (1998): 176–98. Similar to my own critique, Eric Lott has recently written about "The New Cosmopolitanism," which he describes as an emerging post-liberal consensus that "repudiate[s] the entailments of ethnic descent" while "welcom[ing] polyethnic identities, so long as they can be transcended by some national form of cultural cohesion." Lott calls the new cosmopolitanism a "new liberal commonsense in studies of race and culture." See his "The New Cosmopolitanism," *Transition* 72 (1996): 108–35.

43 For example, in *Liberal Racism* Sleeper argues that "fascination with racial differences"—a fascination he attributes to liberalism—begets "policies and programs that reinforce nineteenth-century assumptions about race that are patently racist" (4). In pitting the interests of racial equality against "identity politics," Sleeper thus conflates racial discourse with efforts to resist and/or refashion its authority. My thinking on this issue is influenced by the work of Etienne Balibar, especially his persuasive argument for "racism without races" in "Is There a Neo-Racism?" in Balibar and Immanuel Wallerstein, *Race, Nation, Class: Ambiguous Identities* (London: Verso, 1991), 17–28.

44 According to Coco Fusco, "Cultural identity and values are politically and

historically charged issues of peoples in this country whose access to exercis-ing political power and controlling their symbolic representations has been limited within mainstream culture. While some might look upon the current wave of multiculturalism as inherently empowering and/or new, others look upon the present in relation to a long tradition of 'celebrating' (or rather, ob-jectifying) difference as light but exotic entertainment for the dominant cul-ture." See Fusco, *English Is Broken Here: Notes on Cultural Fusion in the Ameri-cas* (New York: New Press, 1995).

45 Du Bois, *Souls*, 34.

46 This quotation is from Twain's novel *Pudd'nhead Wilson* (1894; reprint, New York: Penguin, 1987), 224. Robyn Wiegman makes a similar argument in her review of Michaels's *Our America* in *American Literature* 69, no. 2 (June 1977): 432–33. In the epilogue, I return to Wiegman's question, "What use is it to say that identity makes no sense without engaging how and why identity has been mobilized in the first place?"

CHAPTER 1 HOME AGAIN

1 Quoted in Carolyn Wedin Sylvander, "Jessie Redmon Fauset," in *Dictionary of Literary Biography, Vol. 51: Afro-American Writers from the Harlem Renaissance to 1940*, ed. Trudier Harris and Thadious M. Davis (Detroit: Gale Research, 1987), 78–79.

2 Deborah E. McDowell, "Regulating Midwives," in Jessie Redmon Fauset, *Plum Bun* (Boston: Beacon Press, 1990), xiv.

3 In *The Big Sea* Langston Hughes acknowledges Fauset as one of the three people who "midwifed" the Harlem Renaissance into being, but as McDowell observes, the designation carries particular irony for Fauset. In this particu-lar instance, she observes, Fauset "played the now deprecated role of one who assists at a birth but is otherwise considered inessential to it" (cited in McDowell, "Regulating Midwives," ix). See Langston Hughes, *The Big Sea* (New York: Hill and Wang, 1940).

4 See Robert Bone, *The Negro Novel in America* (1958; reprint, New Haven, Conn.: Yale University Press, 1976), in which he calls Fauset "prim" and argues that her novels are "uniformly sophomoric, trivial, and dull" (101). These judgments echo those of Sterling Brown, who finds Fauset to be "sen-timental" and a class "apologist." See Brown, *The Negro in American Fiction* (Washington, D.C.: Associates in Negro Folk Education, 1937), 142.

5 On the domestic labor of black women, see Angela Y. Davis, *Women, Race and Class* (New York: Vintage, 1983), 237–38.

6 Such an interpretation would also resonate with recent feminist revaluations of Fauset's own work, as I discuss in the following section.

7 Hazel Carby, *Reconstructing Womanhood: The Emergence of the Afro-American*

Woman Novelist (New York: Oxford University Press, 1987), 88. Carby's use of the term "mulatto" incorporates a critique of the dominant racial discourse that must invent such a category (and subsequently project onto the subjectivity of the "mulatto" the assumptions that animate such categorization) to protect the stability of the color line. For a persuasive critique of "mulatto" as a term that manifests cultural anxiety about "white" purity, see Hortense Spillers, "Notes on an Alternative Model—Neither/Nor," in *The Difference Within: Feminism and Critical Theory*, ed. Elizabeth Meese and Alice Parker (Philadelphia: John Benjamins, 1989). Also see Jennifer DeVere Brody, *Impossible Purities: Blackness, Femininity, and Victorian Culture* (Durham, N.C.: Duke University Press, 1998), esp. the chapter "Miscegenating Mulattaroons," 14–58.

8 Deborah McDowell, "Introduction," in Nella Larsen, *Quicksand and Passing* (New Brunswick, N.J.: Rutgers University Press, 1986). A version of McDowell's essay appears as "The 'Nameless . . . Shameful Impulse': Sexuality in Nella Larsen's *Quicksand* and *Passing*" in McDowell, *"The Changing Same": Black Women's Literature, Criticism, and Theory* (Bloomington: University of Indiana Press, 1995) and again in *The Lesbian and Gay Studies Reader*, ed. Henry Abelove, Michèle Aina Barale, and David M. Halperin (New York: Routledge, 1993).

9 McDowell, "Introduction," xxxi. In persuasive reading, Jennifer DeVere Brody refutes McDowell's emphasis on sublimated homoerotic desire by "insisting on the importance of race and class in *Passing*." In particular, Brody inverts the traditional reading of the relation between Larsen's two protagonists by arguing that although the character Irene "remains at least superficially a part of the Black world," it is she, not Clare, "who harbors a secret desire to be white." See Jennifer DeVere Brody, "Clare Kendry's 'True' Colors: Race and Class Conflict in Nella Larsen's *Passing*," *Callaloo* 15, no. 4 (1992), especially 1053–55.

10 Ibid., xxx. McDowell never explicitly uses the word "lesbian" to describe the relationship between Larsen's female protagonists, although in the version of the essay that appears in her 1995 book *"The Changing Same,"* McDowell explicitly references "lesbian desire" (97), suggesting a distinction between lesbian desire and homoerotic longing introjected as "nameless" and "shameful" impulses. McDowell's essay has proved particularly enabling for scholarship in lesbian and gay studies, assisting in the process whereby Larsen's novel has itself successfully "crossed over" disciplinary boundaries separating African American and gay and lesbian studies within the academy.

11 Deborah McDowell, "Regulating Midwives," in Jessie Redmon Fauset, *Plum Bun: A Novel without a Moral* (1929; reprint, Boston: Beacon Press, 1990), xxi.

12 See also Carby, *Reconstructing Womanhood*, 158: " 'Passing' involved the conscious decision to use a white appearance to hide a black heritage for social

advancement; disguise was used by the author as a narrative mechanism, not a narrative subject." Carby makes this claim in the context of a discussion of Hopkins's short story "The Test of Manhood."

13 McDowell, "Regulating Midwives," xv.

14 Ann duCille, *The Coupling Convention: Sex, Text, and Tradition in Black Women's Fiction* (New York: Oxford University Press, 1993), 93. DuCille's judgment of Fauset echoes that of Alice Dunbar-Nelson, who in a review of *Passing* argues: "The real situation [of the book] is not that Clare 'passed.' It is that she came back into the life of Irene and that she loved Brian. She did not have to be a near-white woman to do this, nor did the others have to be colored. It is a situation that is so universal that race, color, country, time, place have nothing to do with it. Of course, the author was wise in hanging the situation onto a color complex: the public must have that now. But the book would have been just as intriguing, just as provocative, just as interesting if no mention had been made of color or race. Clare might have been any woman hungry for childhood friends; Irene and her brown-skinned friends any group out of the class of the socially elite." In admiring the universality of Larsen's text, Dunbar-Nelson (who frequently portrayed the crossing of racial boundaries in her own fiction) effects a recuperation of the racial passing plot in terms of its fundamental "racelessness." In so doing, she not only glosses over the centrality of racial passing to Larsen's text (for example, it is hard to imagine that Irene would feel so ambivalent about Clare's behavior were Clare simply trying to initiate an affair with Brian) but she additionally downplays the specificity of the literature of passing as a site of textual negotiation with race. See *The Works of Alice Dunbar-Nelson*, vol. 2, ed. Gloria T. Hull (New York: Oxford University Press, 1988), 262.

15 Valerie Smith, "Reading the Intersection of Race and Gender in Narratives of Passing," *diacritics* 24, nos. 2–3 (summer/fall 1994): 43–45; Phillip Brian Harper, "Gender Politics and the Passing Fancy," in *Are We Not Men? Masculine Anxiety and the Problem of African American Identity* (New York: Oxford University Press, 1996).

16 Smith, "Reading the Intersection of Race and Gender," 43. Smith goes on to argue that contemporary cinematic narratives are less determined by the one-drop rule in their racial representation. "Unlike modernist literary works, she writes, "[t]hese newer texts presuppose to some degree the intersectionality of race and gender," and thereby construct passing as a "potentially subversive activity" (43).

17 Ibid., 44.

18 Harper, "Gender Politics and the Passing Fancy," 112.

19 James Weldon Johnson, *The Autobiography of an Ex-Colored Man* (1912; reprint, New York: Penguin, 1990).

20 This is a point made by Claudia Tate in "Allegories of Black Female Desire;

or, Rereading Nineteenth-Century Sentimental Narratives of Black Female Authority," in *Changing Our Own Words: Essays on Criticism, Theory, and Writing by Black Women*, ed. Cheryl A. Wall (New Brunswick, N.J.: Rutgers University Press, 1989), 104–5.

21 See Gaines's analysis of racial uplift ideology in *Uplifting the Race: Black Leadership, Politics, and Culture in the Twentieth Century* (Chapel Hill, N.C.: University of North Carolina Press, 1996).

22 Frederick Douglass, *The Narrative of Frederick Douglass* (1945; reprint, New York: Penguin, 1982), 107.

23 Walter White, *A Man Called White: The Autobiography of Walter White* (Bloomington: Indiana University Press, 1948), 11.

24 Washington pronounced, "In all things purely social we can be as separate as the five fingers, and yet one as the hand in all things essential to material progress." See James Weldon Johnson, *Along This Way* (1933; reprint, New York: Penguin, 1990), 311–12.

25 Jessie Redmon Fauset, "The Sleeper Wakes," in *The Sleeper Wakes: Harlem Renaissance Stories by Women*, ed. Marcy Knopf (New Brunswick, N.J.: Rutgers University Press, 1993), 1–25. Fauset's short story anticipates characters and themes developed at more length in *Plum Bun* (Boston: Beacon Press, 1990).

26 This is not to argue that such earlier texts are any less sophisticated in their critiques, only that they frame these within the political context of Reconstruction.

27 Harriet Jacobs, *Incidents in the Life of a Slave Girl* (1865; reprint, New York: Oxford University Press, 1988), 302.

28 Nella Larsen, *Quicksand and Passing* (1929; reprint, New Brunswick, N.J.: Rutgers University Press, 1986).

29 Barbara Smith, "Introduction," *Home Girls: A Black Feminist Anthology*, ed. Barbara Smith (New York: Kitchen Table—Women of Color Press, 1983), xx.

30 For related explorations of home, see Biddy Martin and Chandra Talpade Mohanty, "Feminist Politics: What's Home Got to Do with It?" in *Feminist Studies/Critical Studies*, ed. Teresa de Lauretis (Bloomington: Indiana University Press, 1986), 191–212. "Home" as contingency, as site of terror, pleasure, and desire, is a constant theme in the work of Toni Morrison. See especially her novels *Beloved* (New York: Knopf, 1987) and *Paradise* (New York: Knopf, 1998).

CHAPTER 2   MEZZ MEZZROW AND THE VOLUNTARY NEGRO BLUES

1 Mezz Mezzrow and Bernard Wolfe, *Really the Blues* (1946; reprint, New York: Citadel Underground, 1990), 14. Long out of print, *Really the Blues* was reissued in 1990 by Citadel Underground. Though all page references are to

the recent Citadel edition (the only edition that contains Bernard Wolfe's undated afterword), they are identical to those from the 1946 Random House
edition.

2 In the appended glossary to *Really the Blues*, Mezzrow defines "The Mezz"
(also known as "the mighty mezz") as "the best brand of marihuana; anything
unusually good." Along the same lines he defines "Mezzroll" as "fat sticks of
marihuana, hand-rolled, with the ends tucked in" (376).

3 Mezzrow's recorded music is not readily available on compact disc, although
his collaboration with Bechet on the song "Really the Blues" (Mezzrow's own
composition) can be found on *The Legendary Sidney Bechet* (RCA, 1988).

4 By his own account Mezzrow drafted *Really the Blues* in longhand and then
submitted the manuscript to Wolfe for editing and revising. See Mike Hennessey, "Mezz Mezzrow: Alive and Well in Paris," *Down Beat*, May 30, 1968,
p. 25. Mezzrow also claimed that 365,000 words were cut from the original
manuscript, but, he said, the material was later lost.

5 The phrase is from George Lipsitz, *Dangerous Crossroads: Popular Music, Postmodernism, and the Poetics of Place* (London: Verso, 1994), 54.

6 In an influential essay on the representation of Jewish assimilation into the
American "melting pot," Michael Rogin argues that blackface minstrelsy
provided immigrant Jewish men with a secular medium in which to fashion themselves as more fully "American." Attaining their rebirth through
the very mass-entertainment industries that would eventually come to be
powerful purveyors of American cultural and national identities, not only
within the context of the United States but globally speaking, Jewish male
jazz singers such as Al Jolson constructed a means of speaking in the accents of their adoptive country and "from [their] own authentically felt interior[s]." See Rogin, "Blackface, White Noise: The Jewish Jazz Singer Finds
His Voice," *Critical Inquiry* 18 (spring 1992), 421. Ann Pellegrini's work on
the performances of Sandra Bernhard complicates these models by explicitly foregrounding gender as a category of analysis. See "You Make Me Feel
(Mighty Real): Sandra Bernhard's Whiteface," in *Performance Anxieties: Staging Psychoanalysis, Staging Race* (New York: Routledge, 1997), 49–64.

7 Bernard Wolfe, "Ecstatic in Blackface: The Negro as a Song-and-Dance
Man," in Mezz Mezzrow and Bernard Wolfe, *Really the Blues* (New York:
Citadel Underground, 1990), 389.

8 "Case History of an Ex-White Man," *Ebony* (December 1946): 11. The pun
on James Weldon Johnson's *The Autobiography of an Ex-Colored Man* was apparently first suggested by Richard Wright.

9 As Antonio Gramsci reminds us, what is subjectively perceived as voluntary is
also liable to be hegemonic. See Gramsci, *Selections from the Prison Notebooks*,
ed. and trans. Quintin Hoare and Geoffrey Nowell Smith (New York: Inter-

national Publishers, 1971), esp. the essay "On Education," which interrogates the relation between coercion, hegemony, and the subject's "freely" offered consent.

10 For a brief but insightful reading of Mezzrow's text that emphasizes its racial essentialism, see William Howland Kenney, *Chicago Jazz: A Cultural History, 1904–1930* (New York: Oxford University Press, 1993), 111–14.

11 See Richard B. Gehman, "Poppa Mezz," *Saturday Review*, November 16, 1946, p. 26; and Bucklin Moon, "The Real Thing," *The New Republic*, November 4, 1946, p. 605.

12 "Vipers, Tea and Jazz," *Newsweek*, October 28, 1946, p. 88.

13 In her essay " 'Experience,' " Joan W. Scott writes that in order to write about identity without essentializing it, scholars must first take "the emergence of concepts and identities as historical events in need of explanation." See Scott, " 'Experience,' " in *Feminists Theorize the Political*, ed. Judith Butler and Joan W. Scott (New York: Routledge, 1992), 33.

14 Quoted in Winthrop Sargeant, *Jazz, Hot and Hybrid*, 3d ed. (1938; reprint, New York: Da Capo, 1975), 265.

15 See Eric Lott, *Love and Theft: Blackface Minstrelsy and the American Working Class* (New York: Oxford University Press, 1993) and " 'The Seeming Counterfeit': Racial Politics and Early Blackface Minstrelsy," *American Quarterly* 43 (June 1991): 223–54. Another useful discussion of minstrelsy may be found in David Roediger, *The Wages of Whiteness: Race and the Making of the American Working Class* (New York: Verso, 1991).

16 Susan Gubar calls this process of identification "racechange," a term that potentially reinscribes the stability of racial categories. I prefer the phrase "identification across the color line," even if more unwieldy, because it inscribes the notion of "crossing," reminding us that race is organized in and through the fiction of a color "line." Gubar's book contains a discussion of Mezzrow's text that focuses on his verbal play and its relation to modernist aesthetics. My intention here is to place Mezzrow's linguistic performance alongside the other modes of performance and/or theatricality that his text variously enacts or refers to. See Gubar, *Racechanges: White Skin, Black Face in American Culture* (New York: Oxford University Press, 1997), esp. 158–59.

17 George Lipsitz, who describes this process as one of "discursive transcoding" (after the work of film theorists), suggests that for subjects who may be cut off from other sources of oppositional practice, such self-fashioning is a potential means of mobilizing a certain notion of disguise to "articulate desires and subject positions" that they cannot express in their own voices. See Lipsitz, *Dangerous Crossroads*, 53.

18 Andrew Ross, *No Respect: Intellectuals and Popular Culture* (New York: Routledge, 1989), 67.

19 Quoted on the back cover of the Citadel edition of *Really the Blues.*

20 See Norman Mailer, *The White Negro* (San Francisco: City Lights Books, 1957).

21 Frantz Fanon, *Black Skin, White Masks,* trans. Charles Lam Markmann (New York: Grove Weidenfeld, 1967), esp. 49–50, 173–77. Wolfe's article appears in English translation as "Uncle Remus and the Malevolent Rabbit," *Commentary* 8, no. 1 (July 1949): 31–41.

22 Bob Wilber with Derek Webster, *Music Was Not Enough* (London: Macmillan, 1987), 15.

23 I return to Becher's assessments of Mezzrow at the end of the chapter. Others' evaluations of Mezzrow's significance to the development of jazz music vary. For those who shared his cultural aesthetic, Mezzrow was jazz's "greatest white musician," a traveling "jazz ambassador." To champions of the avant-garde, he symbolized traditionalist incompetence, while to many black musicians of the 1930s he was a competent clarinetist tolerated, at least in part, because he was a dependable source of marijuana. Occasionally Mezzrow was lambasted as an amateur who got by on theatrics rather than musical talent; *Down Beat* writer Nat Hentoff, for example, once sardonically dubbed Mezzrow the "Baron Munchausen" of jazz, accusing him of being "so consistently out of tune that he may have invented a new scale system" (see Hentoff, "Counterpoint," *Down Beat,* February 11, 1953, p. 5). Undoubtedly Mezzrow's greatest public booster was the French jazz critic Hughes Panassié, who wrote frequently about Mezzrow for the *Bulletin de Hot Club de France* and authored a monograph titled *Quand Mezzrow enregistre* (*When Mezzrow Records*).

24 A number of cultural histories of jazz offer critical readings of Whiteman's role as a jazz popularizer. See, in particular, LeRoi Jones, *Blues People: Negro Music in White America* (New York: Morrow Quill, 1963).

25 Ken Palmer, "Mezzrow at Sixty-five," *Jazz Monthly* 10, no. 9 (1964): 5.

26 There is also a second boy in the photograph, standing behind Milton Mesirow Jr., but he is unidentified in the caption. Like the article, the photograph is unattributed, and I have to date been unsuccessful in discovering its authorship.

27 The image of a crossroads also evokes the idea of having come from the "other side of the tracks," a late-nineteenth-century colloquialism that defines intersecting race and class identities; for as Paul Oliver once noted, "the poorest sectors [of the major American cities] were those that back on to the railroad tracks, where the great locomotives as they gathered speed on leaving the immense railroad terminals of Chicago, Kansas City, or St. Louis caused the poor frame houses to shudder to their inadequate foundations, blackening their walls with grime and smoke, cracking the ceilings and killing the vegetation. When Jack Ranger sang of seeing his woman pass his door as the Texas-Pacific train took her away, he was speaking literally, not metaphori-

cally." See Oliver, *Blues Fell This Morning* (1960; reprint, London: Cambridge University Press, 1990), 67.

28 One example is the oral tradition concerning Robert Johnson, said to have sold his soul to the devil at a crossroads in exchange for the secret of playing blues guitar. For a reading of the legend of Johnson that relates closely to my own reading of Mezzrow, see George Lipsitz, "White Desire: Remembering Robert Johnson," in *The Possessive Investment in Whiteness: How White People Profit from Identity Politics* (Philadelphia: Temple University Press, 1998).

29 Jones, *Blues People*, 100.

30 On the modernist framing of the non-European "other" as "primitive," see Marianna Torgovnick, *Gone Primitive: Savage Intellects, Modern Lives* (Chicago: University of Chicago Press, 1990). See also Gubar, *Racechanges*, 178.

31 Gubar, *Racechanges*, 136.

32 Gary Giddins, *Riding on a Blue Note: Jazz and American Pop* (New York: Oxford University Press, 1981), 254.

33 Here I am in agreement with Homi Bhabha, who in his essay "The Other Question: Stereotype, Discrimination, and the Discourse of Colonialism," observes that "the point of intervention should shift from the ready recognition of images as positive or negative, to an understanding of the *processes of subjectification* made possible (and plausible) through stereotypical discourse." See Bhabha, *The Location of Culture* (New York: Routledge, 1994), 67.

34 In a related vein, Kobena Mercer defines such "negrophilia" as "an aesthetic idealization and eroticized investment in the racial other that inverts and reverses the binary axis of the fears and anxieties invested in or projected onto the other in 'negrophobia.'" Both positions, he argues, "inhabit the representational space of what Bhabha calls colonial fantasy." See Mercer, "Skin Head Sex Thing," in *How Do I Look? Queer Film and Video*, ed. Bad Object-Choices (Seattle: Bay Press, 1991), 175. Also see Wolfe's discussion in the afterword, especially 390–94.

35 Several historical factors belie Mezzrow's characterization of leaving home as a way of entering "Bessie Smith's world." For one thing, and like most of his fellow "Chicagoans," Mezzrow would spend most of his career playing and recording with white artists, in part because segregation precluded the viability of "mixed" touring bands well after the 1937 Disciples of Swing experiment. Likewise, Jim Crow laws and racism discouraged many "white" outlets from booking African American performers, with the result that white musicians more often than not played for white audiences, often touring such "hincty" venues as could be found along the Ivy League college circuit from Providence to Princeton.

36 In her essay, "Jazz, Jews, Jive, and Gender: The Ethnic Politics of Jazz Argot," (in *Jews and Other Differences: The New Jewish Cultural Studies*, ed. Jonathan Boyarin and Daniel Boyarin [Minneapolis: University of Minnesota Press,

1997], 150–75), Maria Damon argues that for Mezzrow and other Jewish men, "blackness becomes a way to be 'more Jewish' by providing a New World context for social critique, community, and an understanding of suffering and the 'human condition' both social and metaphysical" (157). Yet in making this claim, Damon (who is responding to Michael Rogin, *op. cit.*) risks recuperating Jewishness in essentialist terms, since her essay doesn't specify what being "more Jewish" would mean for Mezzrow. Several essays in the Boyarin and Boyarin collection are relevant in this context. See in particular Ann Pelligrini, "Whiteface Performances: 'Race,' Gender, and Jewish Bodies" (108–49) and Daniel Itzkovitz, "Secret Temples" (176–202).

37 In fact, not soon after Mezzrow leaves his parents' home, he manages to assemble his first band, Milton Mezzrow and His Perolatin' Fools, and to get the group booking at a Chicago burlesque house.

38 Although Mezzrow once told an interviewer that he believed that *Really the Blues* "was a success because I wrote in plain, simple language that anybody could understand," in fact his decision to include an extensive "glossary of terms" as an appendix to the narrative proper underscores his desire to use jive talk as a means of signifying difference. See Bruynoghe, "Mezzrow Talks about the Old Jim Crow," *The Melody Maker and Rhythm*, November 17, 1951, p. 9.

39 In addition to the Jive Section and its translation, *Really the Blues* has, as an appendix, an extensive "glossary of terms" that recalls Cab Calloway's 1938 *Hepsters Dictionary*.

40 White musicians apparently found occasion to make fun of Mezzrow's "black talk." Eddie Condon nicknamed Mezzrow "Southmouth," while Bob Wilber wrote that it was "ridiculous to hear this Jewish guy from Chicago coming out with a rich southern drawl." See Bob Wilber with Derek Webster, *Music Was Not Enough* (London: Macmillan, 1987), 40.

41 Kobena Mercer, "Skin Head Sex Thing," in *How Do I Look? Queer Film and Video*, ed. Bad Object-Choices (Seattle: Bay Press, 1991), 207–8.

42 James Baldwin, "The Black Boy Looks at the White Boy," in *Nobody Knows My Name: More Notes of a Native Son* (New York: Dell, 1961), 182.

43 I find helpful here Michel Foucault's definition of discourse in *The History of Sexuality: An Introduction*. There he writes, "Discourses are not one and for all subservient to power or raised up against it. . . . We must make allowance for the complex and unstable process whereby a discourse can be both an instrument and an effect of power, but also a hindrance, a stumbling-block, a point of resistance and starting point for an opposing strategy." Quoted in Lora Romero, *Home Fronts: Domesticity and Its Critics in the Antebellum United States* (Durham, N.C.: Duke University Press, 1997), 109.

44 In *How Do I Look?* Mercer's essay is followed by a question-and-answer ses-

sion, which was edited and revised for inclusion in the volume. I here count as part of Mercer's essay his responses to the questions of his audience.

45 bell hooks, "Eating the Other: Desire and Resistance," in *Black Looks: Race and Representation* (Boston: South End Press, 1992), 23. For a discussion of such racial appropriations in historical context, see David Roediger, "Guineas, Wiggers, and the Dramas of Racialized Culture," *American Literary History* 7, no. 4 (1995): 654–68.

46 In contemporary popular culture, nowhere is this dynamic more obviously displayed than in the realm of men's professional sports, a context that both enables and encourages a particular kind of commercially and televisually mediated "intimacy" with the bodies of African American male athletes such as Michael Jordan, the basketball icon who is often said to have "transcended" race.

47 Lipsitz's discussion of "strategic anti-essentialism" in *Dangerous Crossroads* contains a similar argument for the political potentiality of racially transgressive desire. See esp. 62–63. For an interesting take on the question of critical transcendence, see William "Upski" Wimsatt's defense of the "wigger" in his self-published book *Bomb the Suburbs*, rev. 2d ed. (Chicago: Subway and Elevated Press, 1994), 22. Upski's writings on "wiggers" and contemporary white hip-hop fans have earned him a certain celebrity within the fields of hip-hop journalism as well as cultural studies of "whiteness." "The White Issue" of *Transition* 7, no. 1 contains an excerpt from Upski's "In Defense of Wiggers" as well as an interview of Upski and cultural critic Noel Ignatiev with Cornel West. See "I'm Ofay, You're Ofay," 176–203.

48 See in this regard Robyn Wiegman, "Fiedler and Sons," in *Race and the Subject of Masculinities*, ed. Harry Stecopoulos and Michael Uebel (Durham, N.C.: Duke University Press, 1997), 45–68. I have written at more length about the question as it pertains to white female rock musicians in "One of the Boys? Whiteness, Gender, and Popular Music Studies," in *Whiteness: A Critical Reader*, ed. Mike Hill (New York: New York University Press, 1997), 151–67.

49 My reading here is influenced by Lora Romero's analysis of domestic ideology as a "a rich and pliable symbolism for representing power and resistance" in her study *Home Fronts: Domesticity and Its Critics in the Antebellum United States* (Durham, N.C.: Duke University Press, 1997), 109. In particular, I am persuaded by Romero's critique of the notion that "any progressive form of cultural expression must take the form of transcendent authorial critique of the status quo" (108).

50 Sidney Bechet, *Treat It Gentle* (New York: Hill and Wang, 1960), 168–69.

CHAPTER 3 BOUNDARIES LOST AND FOUND

Thanks to the staff at the Archive Center of the Historical Society of Cheshire County, New Hampshire (in Keene, New Hampshire), for providing me access to documents regarding *Lost Boundaries*. Thanks also to the staff of the Museum of Modern Arts film studies center for their help in researching and screening both *Pinky* and *Lost Boundaries*.

1 Lisa Jones, "Tragedy Becomes Her," *Village Voice*, June 29, 1993, p. 24.

2 My account of Roxborough's life summarizes Kathleen A. Hauke's article, "The 'Passing' of Elsie Roxborough," *Michigan Quarterly Review* 23, no. 12 (1984): 155–70.

3 Quoted in ibid., 163.

4 Ibid., 167. Hauke speculates that it was partly the limitations imposed by Jim Crow and partly Roxborough's ambivalence about how to express herself racially that led her to pass. In the end, Hauke muses, Roxborough's life resembled that of one of Jean Toomer's "desperate women"—always seeking a way out of oppressive conditions, and yet finally succumbing to suicide (168). See also Langston Hughes, *I Wonder as I Wander* (1956; reprint, New York: Hill and Wang, 1964), 328–39.

5 The notion of "wages" of white identity is from W. E. B. Du Bois, *Black Reconstruction in America* (1935; reprint, New York: Russell and Russell, 1966). David Roediger develops Du Bois's notion of "wages" in *The Wages of Whiteness: Race and the Making of the American Working Class* (London: Verso, 1991), esp. 11–13.

6 See, for example, Nella Larsen's novella *Quicksand* in *Quicksand and Passing* (New Brunswick, N.J.: Rutgers University Press, 1986).

7 Douglas McClelland, "Jeanne Crain," *Films in Review*, June–July 1969, 358.

8 Interestingly, Kazan's most recent project had been the 1948 "message" film *Gentleman's Agreement*, in which Gregory Peck stars as a Jewish protagonist who is the victim of anti-Semitism. *Pinky* is based loosely on Cid Ricketts Sumner's novel *Quality* (Indianapolis: Bobbs-Merrill, 1946), parts of which were originally serialized in *Ladies' Home Journal*. See Thomas Cripps, *Making Movies Black: The Hollywood Message Movie from World War II to the Civil Rights Era* (New York: Oxford University Press, 1993), esp. 233–35, for a detailed account of the process of negotiation among writers and outside consultants in putting the script of the film together.

9 *Lost Boundaries* was more or less the personal project of Louis de Rochemont, best known for his documentary *March of Time* newsreels. While on a visit to his hometown in New Hampshire, de Rochemont met Albert Johnston Jr., a student who told de Rochemont about his recent discovery that his parents had passed for white. De Rochemont, sensing that he could sell the story, took it to writer William White, who made the Johnstons the subject of a

1947 *Reader's Digest* article, which was later republished in book form. Once the "Lost Boundaries" family had achieved a degree of notoriety, de Rochemont took his idea for a screen version of their story to MGM, but when the studio turned down the idea, apparently fearful that the subject was too risky (Cripps, *Making Movies Black*, 227–28), he decided to finance the movie by mortgaging his house and soliciting another $300,000 from colleagues. *Lost Boundaries*, released before *Pinky* in the spring of 1949, did almost as well at the box office, although it never had the studio support, feature-film budget, or big-name cast of the latter.

10 Like the term "mulatto," the term "miscegenation" is problematically linked to racial essentialism and to notions of black racial inferiority. In brief, the term presumes a stable distinction between separate and opposed black and white identities, thereby reinscribing notions of racial purity that inevitably are invoked to the detriment of raced subjects (whereas "white" identities are the beneficiaries of such a discourse of "purity"). Like "mulatto," too, the term itself has a racist etymology implying the "mixing" of different "races."

11 Lisa Jones, "Passages," *Village Voice*, February 19, 1991, p. 72.

12 My argument highlights the liberal political convictions that shape the representation of race in *Pinky* and *Lost Boundaries*, although these were not the sole factors influencing the trajectory of the 1949 message films. Other contributing factors included the need for the studios to downsize film budgets in light of antitrust suits handed down in May of 1948, the extension into peacetime of the wartime desire for national unity, and the encroachment of television on movie-industry profits.

13 The discourse of movies as "entertainment" had also served the interests of film industry executives, shielding them from Congressional red-baiting throughout the early 1950s. See David A. Cook, *A History of Narrative Film* (New York: W. W. Norton, 1981), 407–10.

14 From the viewpoint of Hollywood executives, the attraction of a film like *Pinky* lay in its ability to call upon liberal interests without sacrificing widespread commercial appeal. In fact, *Pinky* and *Lost Boundaries* propelled Twentieth Century-Fox and Film Classics respectively to their biggest profits of 1949, and *Pinky*, which grossed four million dollars by year's end and received three Academy Award nominations (one each for its female leads), was the second-highest grossing film of the year, lagging only behind Columbia's *Jolsen Sings Again* (see Russel Campbell, "The Ideology of the Social Consciousness Movie: Three Films of Darryl F. Zanuck," *Quarterly Review of Film Studies* [winter 1978]: 56). In November 1949, *Variety* reported that together with *Home of the Brave*, a movie about the psychological recuperation of a black war veteran, *Pinky* and *Lost Boundaries* collectively had grossed twenty million dollars (quoted in Jacqueline Bobo, " 'The Subject is Money': Recon-

sidering the Black Film Audience as Theoretical Paradigm," *Black American Literature Forum* 25, no. 2 [summer 1991]: 424), much of which, according to Cripps, came from tickets sold to black moviegoers "who had broken family rules against sitting in Jim Crow [movie] houses" (*Making Movies Black*, 239). *Pinky*, the first movie about southern racism to play below the Mason-Dixon line, took in $3,000 in its first day at the Roxy, an Atlanta movie theater that opened its entire balcony to black patrons who had formerly been limited to gallery seats (Campbell, "Ideology of the Social Consciousness Movie," 56). Contrary to the fears of investors and film industry executives, the objections of southern censors to *Lost Boundaries*, which delayed the film's opening in southern theaters by several months, may have contributed to higher receipts and bigger-than-anticipated audiences for de Rochemont's otherwise B-budgeted movie. According to Ferrer, who played the lead in *Lost Boundaries*, the film was made for $600,000 and grossed approximately $2.5 million.

15 Cripps, *Making Movies Black*, 220.

16 Campbell, "Ideology of the Social Consciousness Movie," 51.

17 With *Pinky*, *Lost Boundaries* and the other message films, Hollywood came to direct creative energies that only four years earlier had gone into producing racist propaganda about an alien and enemy "other" to a seemingly contrary endeavor—commercial films that championed increasingly liberal attitudes toward an internal or domestic "other." The swiftness with which the industry switched from propagating one set of stereotypes to deploring another is striking, but equally so are the similarities between the orientalism of the wartime films and the racist imagery of Hollywood cinema, particularly in the case of people of apparently "mixed" racial heritage. *Know Your Enemy, Japan* (1945), made by the War Department, provides a telling case in point. Shown to enlisted men preparing to fight in the war in the Pacific, the film casts general aspersions on Shintoism and other aspects of Japanese culture. Yet its most virulent attacks are those that profess the enemy's racial degeneracy, comparing Japanese people to monkeys and vermin. The racial inferiority of the Japanese, according to *Know Your Enemy*, stems from a legacy of "mixed" Asian lineage, which combines "distinct" bloodlines into one degenerate race of "plasma cocktails." Homogenous in their heterogeneity, the Japanese are also, from the point of view of the white Western ethnographic gaze, virtually indistinguishable, identical "prints from the same negative." Of equal note is the reticence of Hollywood filmmakers to link racisms, or to acknowledge the European Holocaust and the Pacific War as race wars, fought with arsenals of images as well as atom bombs. The grotesque spectacle of European genocide—brought home in pictures and films from the concentration camps—had been an important factor in spurring Hollywood to confront American racism and anti-Semitism in commercial films. More-

over, as Hollywood liberals were painfully aware, the image of nearly half a million black soldiers returning from service in foreign battlefields to lynchings and rampant Jim Crowism (including segregated movie houses) made U.S. outrage at Nazi atrocities seem dangerously hypocritical.

18 From Philip Dunne, "An Approach to Racism," date and publication unknown. From the vertical file on *Pinky* at the Museum of Modern Art's Film Study Center.

19 NAACP leaders such as Walter White had long been pressing the Motion Picture Association of America for more humanistic and historically accurate depictions of African Americans, making film a site of cultural struggle over racial representation. When D. W. Griffith's *Birth of a Nation* was revived in 1947 by the Dixie Film Exchange, the NAACP picketed New York's Republic Theater, and fourteen thousand Philadelphians, including city mayor Bernard Samuel, sent an eight-block-long petition protesting the rerelease of the film to Eric Johnston, then MPAA president. For more on White and the NAACP's struggles regarding cinematic representations, see Donald Bogle, *Toms, Coons, Mulattoes, Mammies, Bucks* (New York: Viking, 1973), 19, and V. J. Jerome, *The Negro in Hollywood Films* (New York: Masses and Mainstream, 1950), 6.

20 As Cripps notes, *Pinky* was particularly noteworthy for having "direct black intervention on the lot, an outcome prayed for by [NAACP executive secretary] Walter White ever since 1942." See Cripps, *Making Movies Black*, 232.

21 Ibid., 227.

22 Rudy Behlmer, ed., *Memo from Darryl F. Zanuck: The Golden Years at Twentieth Century-Fox* (New York: Grove Press, 1993), 162.

23 As V. J. Jerome noted, "In 1948 the county medical societies of 17 states, in addition to the District of Columbia, prohibited Negro physicians from joining [the American Medical Association]." See Jerome, *The Negro in Hollywood Films*, 31.

24 Ibid., 23.

25 The scene in the southern hospital departed from the story of Albert Johnston.

26 Ralph Ellison, *Shadow and Act* (New York: Vintage, 1972), 280.

27 In a letter from Thyra Johnston (Albert Johnston's wife) to Louis de Rochemont, Johnston writes, "I do wish we could get some copies of the colored write ups this week for we are very interested in their reaction. Colored folks are very touchy, as you no doubt recall from the luncheon. I say, one thing at a time, and the risk of getting *Lost Boundaries* filmed at all was quite an undertaking. Had you known of its guaranteed success, no doubt you could have used colored actors, and yet I do think the impact would not have been half so forceful. The public might be reticent to accept everything at one throw,

and for that reason I think your judgment was sound. We think you made a great stride. Some day you show them what you have accomplished, and film another picture using colored actors, and then you will be their sт. Louis DE ROCHEMONT." Letter dated July 11, 1948, from the Cheshire County Historical Society.

28 There is some evidence that the producers of *Lost Boundaries* sought black actors for the roles. De Rochemont told the (New York) *Afro-American* that "efforts had been made" but that, "in competing with other racial films, time had not permitted a thorough canvass of the country for talent to play the lead roles." The same article quotes Beatrice Pearson, who played the role of Mrs. Carter, saying that she was "proud to play the role of the colored girl and explained that she understood the efforts made by the producer to find a colored woman suitable for the role." See " 'Never Again,' Says Man Who 'Passed' Twenty Years," *Afro-American*, July 16, 1949, p. 8.

29 Al Weisman, "He Passed as Negro," *Negro Digest*, October 1951, 18. Ferrer's self-description ironically recalls the U.S. Supreme Court's description of Homer Plessy, plaintiff in *Plessy v. Ferguson*. See my discussion in the introduction, 12–13.

30 Weisman, 20. Meanwhile, the scarcity of desirable roles for black film actors in the thirties and forties encouraged racial passing as a means of professional advancement for those light-skinned enough to take advantage of the more abundant opportunities for so-called Mediterranean or Latin performers such as Ferrer (no relation to Jose Ferrer), who also had Spanish ancestry.

31 Jerome, *The Negro in Hollywood Films*, 35.

32 Howard Barnes, "Stage Techniques Improve a Film," *New York Herald Tribune*, October 2, 1949; Alton Cook, " 'Pinky' Is Inspired Study of Race Bias," *New York Telegram*, September 30, 1949.

33 Mary Ann Doane makes a similar point, arguing that the cinematic embodiment of the subject who passes for white "produces a dilemma which is absent in its literary incarnation, for film requires an actual embodiment of the figure of the tragic mulatta—and hence a choice of the racial identity (defined genealogically) of the actress who represents the figure." Doane, *Femmes Fatales: Feminism, Film Theory, Psychoanalysis* (New York: Routledge, 1989), 235.

34 Frantz Fanon, *Black Skin, White Masks*, trans. Charles Lam Markmann (New York: Grove Weidenfeld, 1967), especially the chapter titled "The Fact of Blackness." In a similar vein, and drawing heavily from Fanon, Homi Bhabha discusses the "fixity" of the colonial stereotype in "The Other Question: Stereotype, Discrimination, and the Discourse of Colonialism," in *The Location of Culture* (New York: Routledge, 1994).

35 As Doane notes, passing lent to issues of race and racial subject-formation "a certain narratability," as well as a focus on questions of "knowledge, identity

and concealment" (see Doane, *Femmes Fatales*, 234), which the cinema, as a primarily visual medium, intuitively and enthusiastically embraced.

36 James Baldwin, *Notes of a Native Son* (1955; reprint, Boston: Beacon Press, 1984), 19.

37 Film historian Thomas Cripps has argued that this spotlighting of "the lone Negro" in 1949 carried "the central metaphor of integrationism into the civil rights movement" uncannily predicting "the shape that racial integration would actually take" in the following years. Cripps, *Making Movies Black*, 220, 250.

38 Fanon, *Black Skin, White Masks*, 112.

39 *Webster's New World Dictionary of the American Language* (New York: Warner Books, 1983), 185.

40 Fanon, *Black Skin, White Masks*, 112.

41 The double-take also complicates narrative point of view as it has been constructed within the tradition of women's film, which depends upon strong viewer identification with the female film star and the difficult choice she inevitably will face.

42 Kazan was "worried because people might think we're saying Negroes and whites shouldn't marry. We solve this story in personal terms. This particular boy and girl shouldn't get married. . . . we don't mean this story to be true of all people with colored and white skins." At one point, the film introduces the character of a black doctor—clearly imagined as a more suitable choice for Pinky—but it forecloses this possibility with the image of the doctor's wedding band. Such romantic coupling would have introduced its own problems in terms of the film's ability to elude censors (that is, it would have introduced an "actual" mixed couple on screen). See *Ebony*, September 1949, p. 25.

43 At the same time, in establishing a pleasurable, conspiratorial relation between the two women, the scene paves the way for Pinky's ultimate acquiescence to Miss Em's appeals to "truth," not Dicey's more old-fashioned appeals to "place."

44 Bogle, *Toms, Coons, Mulattoes*, 213.

45 Pinky's decision at the conclusion of the film to reject the rather stultifying option of becoming "Mrs. Thomas Adams" and of giving up her job as a nurse represents a significant divergence from the tradition of woman's films, in which the heroine typically sacrifices not marriage for career, but career for marriage. It is significant, too, that Pinky decides to fight it out within the white justice system for the right to retain ownership of the very property that once symbolized her own exclusion from white society. Reclaiming the house as her own becomes Pinky's way of revising the traumatic memory of once being turned away from its front gate. Pinky not only gains title to the estate, but she redecorates and repopulates it, transforming the space

from which she herself was once prohibited into one literally filled with black children. Pinky's decision to turn the house into a hospital allows the film to imagine a southern black solution to the "problem" of passing. As Cripps notes, it was rare at any time in Hollywood history for a movie to end with the celebration of autonomous black community, let alone a successful black hospital (*Making Movies Black*, 237–38).

46 In addition to depicting a white woman as the key to Pinky's self-discovery, Kazan's film uses Ethel Waters's character to pass on a conservative idea of "Negro service" that envisions work and struggle within financially dependent, segregated institutions as the natural and appropriate means of black survival.

47 In the final scene Reverend Robert Dunn, the rector of Portsmouth's St. John's Episcopal Church, plays himself.

48 Etienne Balibar, *Masses, Classes, Ideas: Studies on Politics and Philosophy before and after Marx*, trans. James Swenson (New York: Routledge, 1994), 196–97.

49 David Wilkins, "Introduction: The Context of Race," in *Color Conscious: The Political Morality of Race*, ed. K. Anthony Appiah and Amy Gutmann (Princeton: Princeton University Press, 1996), 21.

50 Balibar, *Masses, Classes, Ideas*, 241. Balibar's specific example here is gender identity.

51 Quoted in August Meier, Elliot Rudwick, and Francis L. Broderick, eds., *Black Protest Thought in the Twentieth Century*, 2d ed. (New York: Macmillan, 1971), 280.

52 Jerome, *The Negro in Hollywood Films*, 24.

CHAPTER 4 "I'M THROUGH WITH PASSING"

1 Stuart Hall, "What Is This 'Black' in Black Popular Culture?" in *Stuart Hall: Critical Dialogues in Cultural Studies*, ed. David Morley and Kuan-Hsing Chen (New York: Routledge, 1996), 474.

2 Janice Kingslow, "I Refuse to Pass," *Negro Digest*, May 1950, p. 30.

3 For a discussion of postwar "abundance" that pays attention to the material conditions of African Americans in the 1940s and 1950s and that resists the temptation to idealize, see Godfrey Hodgson, *America in Our Time* (New York: Vintage, 1990). For contemporary accounts that indulge in nationalist narratives of progress, see "How Negroes Are Gaining in the U.S.," *U.S. News and World Report*, June 28, 1957, pp. 105–6 and "Negroes: Big Advances in Jobs, Wealth, Status," *U.S. News and World Report*, November 28, 1958, pp. 90–92.

4 "Why 'Passing' Is Passing Out," *Jet*, July 17, 1952, pp. 12–13. The acronym FEPC usually refers to the Fair Employment Practices Committee, although it can also refer to the Fair Employment Practices Code. The former were com-

mittees established by executive order beginning in 1941 and charged with prohibiting discrimination in the defense industries and in government.

5 Hall, "What Is This 'Black' in Black Popular Culture?" 472. Hall uses this phrase when referring to contemporary struggles over naming black British identities as both black *and* British. Hall is referring to a moment in contemporary Britain when "old" essentializing strategies seem outdated or inadequate as responses to new social and cultural struggles. I use the phrase to name an earlier moment in the history of African American cultural practice, when material conditions of racial segregation give rise to similar strategies.

6 For this notion of resistance I am indebted to Rajeswari Sunder Rajan. In her introduction to *Real and Imagined Women: Gender, Culture, and Postcolonialism* (New York: Routledge, 1993), Sunder Rajan writes, "Resistance is not always a positivity; it may be no more than a negative agency, an absence of acquiescence in one's oppression" (12). Later in the same paragraph she cautions against the "romantic fiction of 'resistance'—however politically well-intentioned such a fiction may be," suggesting instead a redefinition of individual resistance "in terms of its social function rather than its performative intentionality" (12).

7 As I discuss in the next section, virtually all of the magazines that I consider here were owned by John Johnson, a black entrepreneur; yet ownership in this sense is not what I mean by the term "black" periodical. The question of ownership is additionally complicated by the fact that Johnson occasionally hired white editors, photographers, and writers, and that authorship of the contents of these periodicals is often not indicated. Ben Burns, the white editor of *Ebony* in its first decade, provides an interesting account of the magazine's production in its early years. See *Nitty Gritty: A White Editor in Black Journalism* (Jackson, Miss.: University of Mississippi Press, 1996).

8 My assumptions regarding the constant interplay between magazines' construction and interpellation of an "ideal audience" and actual readers' active constructions of the contents of these magazines are derived from the work of Hall, especially his work on media and communication, as well as from feminist scholars of popular literary and media culture in the United States. Especially relevant in this regard are Janice A. Radway, *Reading the Romance: Women, Patriarchy, and Popular Literature* (Chapel Hill, N.C.: University of North Carolina Press, 1984), and Tania Modleski, *Loving with a Vengeance: Mass-Produced Fantasies for Women* (New York: Methuen, 1984). See also Stuart Hall, "Encoding/decoding," in *Media Texts, Authors and Readers: A Reader*, ed. David Graddol and Oliver Boyd-Barrett (Clevedon, England: Open University, 1994).

9 This is already evident in "I Refuse to Pass," particularly in the classed terms in which the narrator imagines "freedom" from the bounds of racial definition.

10 See, for example, Richard Ohmann's "Advertising and the New Discourse of Mass Culture," in *Politics of Letters* (Middletown, Conn.: Wesleyan University Press, 1987), 152–70.

11 As the 1952 *Jet* article draws upon the examples of a successful male architect and doctor—as well as Janice Kingslow herself—as the "new faces" of an increasingly prosperous era in which passing was passé, so these magazines likewise imagined their "new Negro" readers as prosperous and educated subjects whose appearances conformed to a beauty ideal based upon the standard of light skin, thin noses, and straight hair.

12 Fredric Jameson, "Reification and Utopia in Mass Culture," in *Signatures of the Visible* (New York: Routledge, 1990), 30. Originally published in *Social Text* 1 (winter 1979): 130–48.

13 John H. Johnson with Lerone Bennett Jr., *Succeeding against the Odds* (New York: Warner Books, 1989), 156–57.

14 Thomas Holt, "Afterword: Mapping the Black Public Sphere," in *The Black Public Sphere*, ed. The Black Public Sphere Collective (Chicago: University of Chicago Press, 1995), 327.

15 See on this issue Ohmann, "Advertising and the New Discourse of Mass Culture," 152–69. See also Susan Willis, *A Primer for Daily Life* (New York: Routledge, 1991).

16 Much has been written on this problem as it relates to the reception and interpretation of rap music, particularly the variety of "hard" and aggressive music called gangsta rap. See, on these and other issues, Robin D. G. Kelley, *Yo' Mama's Disfunktional!: Fighting the Culture Ways in Urban America* (Boston: Beacon Press, 1997).

17 E. Franklin Frazier, *Black Bourgeoisie* (1957; reprint, New York: Macmillan, 1962). Frazier was also including black newspapers in his discussion, but for my purposes here I cite his arguments as they pertain to commercial magazines. See especially chapter 8, "The Negro Press and Wish-Fulfillment," 146–61.

18 Quoted in Johnson, *Succeeding against the Odds*, 160. The first issue of *Ebony* was distributed to newsstands in October 1945, where it sold for twenty-five cents a copy (Burns, *Nitty Gritty*, 85–86). The first issue readily sold out; by 1954, less than a decade later, circulation had swelled to half a million.

19 On the names of African American newspapers, see Burns, *Nitty Gritty*, 88. Of course, there is the additional issue of whether and how consumption may signify as an exercise of social power. As Regina Austin points out, within a context in which consumption itself is highly regulated (that is, through the criminalization or demonization of activities of consumption), demands that producers and/or sales agents respect or otherwise recognize black consumers can amount to a kind of political resistance. See Austin, " 'A Nation of Thieves': Consumption, Commerce, and the Black Public Sphere," in *The*

Black Public Sphere, ed. The Black Public Sphere Collective (Chicago: University of Chicago Press, 1995), 229–52.

20 Burns, *Nitty Gritty*, 94.

21 The language of Johnson's editorial anticipates Janice Kingslow's narrative, which similarly emphasizes the centrality of consumption in its imagination of national citizenship.

22 Indeed, it is a measure of black Americans' invisibility to white publishers that the producers of these magazines were flattered rather than threatened by Johnson's strategy.

23 James Baldwin, "The Harlem Ghetto," in *Notes of a Native Son* (1955; reprint, Boston: Beacon Press, 1984), 62.

24 The phrase is from Burns, *Nitty Gritty*, 90.

25 Here we might recall Jameson's argument (from "Reification and Utopia in Mass Culture") that "anxiety and hope are the two faces of the same collective consciousness, so that the works of mass culture, even if their function lies in the legitimation of the existing order—or some worse one—cannot do their job without deflecting in the latter's service the deepened and most fundamental hopes and fantasies of the collectivity, to which they can therefore, no matter in how distorted a fashion, be found to have given hope" (30).

26 "I'm Through with Passing," *Ebony* 6, March 1951, pp. 22–27.

27 It was not unusual in the early years of the popular black press for a majority of articles and photographs to go unattributed as magazines developed regular staffs. In the case of confessional stories such as "I'm Through with Passing," such anonymity may have contributed to the impression of the authenticity of the narrator's voice.

28 Fair Employment Practices laws were enacted in eleven states and twenty-five cities, according to Frazier (*Black Bourgeoisie*, 47).

29 Julianne Malveaux, "The Political Economy of Black Women," in *The Year Left, 2: An American Socialist Yearbook*, ed. Mike Davis et al. (London: Verso, 1987), 63.

30 On this point see Amy Robinson, "It Takes One to Know One: Passing and Communities of Common Interest," *Critical Inquiry* 20 (summer 1994): 715–36.

31 There are other instances of such photographic quizzes of racial identity that appear in various magazines throughout the decade. See, for example, "What Color Will Your Baby Be?" *Ebony*, May 1951, pp. 54–57, as well as the illustrations to Masco L. Young, "Is Passing for White a Dying Fad?" *Color*, April 1957, pp. 46–49.

32 Hortense Spillers, "Notes on an Alternative Model: Neither/Nor," in *The Difference Within: Feminism and Critical Theory* (Amsterdam: John Benjamins, 1989), 165.

33 "I Passed for Love," *Tan*, March 1953, pp. 33–34, 61–68. The contrivances of

the narrative of "I Passed for Love" suggest that it is a fictionalized "true" confession. In any case, it is the article's conveyance of a certain *impression* of verisimilitude that is crucial to the reader's ability to derive pleasure and meaning from it. For more detailed analyses of methodologies for interpreting formulaic popular texts, particularly those that construct women readers as ideal audiences, see Radway, *Reading the Romance*, and Modeleski, *Loving with a Vengeance.*

34 A daughter's self-sacrifice for her mother is a conventional premise of women's confessional stories and usually serves as a means by which maternal desire is elicited in the daughter.

35 Langston Hughes, "Fooling Our White Folks," *Negro Digest*, April 1950, pp. 38–41.

36 "Why I Never Want to Pass," *Ebony*, June 1959, pp. 49–52, 54.

37 Richard Dyer discusses whiteness as a "terrorizing imposition, a power that wounds, hurts, tortures" in his essay "White." See Dyer, "White," *Screen* 29, no. 4 (autumn 1998): 44–64. See also bell hooks's discussion of Dyer's essay in her essay "Representations of Whiteness in the Black Imagination," in *Black Looks: Race and Representation* (Boston: South End Press, 1992), 169.

38 This point is similar to one that hooks makes in "Representations of Whiteness," 168.

39 "Have Negroes Stopped Passing?" *Jet*, September 13, 1956, pp. 10–12, and Masco L. Young, "Is Passing for White a Dying Fad?" *Color*, April 1957, pp. 46–49. The *Jet* article contains no byline. The *Color* article is essentially a revision and expansion of the earlier piece.

40 The *Jet* article doesn't specify whether Saunders asked her new employer the same rhetorical question, although it implies that she was not passing—or being passed—when she found the new job.

CHAPTER 5 "A MOST DISAGREEABLE MIRROR"

1 On "looking relations" and race, see Jane Gaines, "White Privilege and Looking Relations: Race and Gender in Feminist Film Theory," *Screen* 29, no. 4 (autumn 1988): 12–27; bell hooks, *Black Looks: Race and Representation* (Boston: South End Press, 1992); and Deborah McDowell, "Pecs and Reps: Muscling in on Race and the Subject of Masculinities," in *Race and the Subject of Masculinities*, ed. Harry Stecopoulos and Michael Uebel (Durham, N.C.: Duke University Press, 1997), esp. 365–66.

2 W. E. B. Du Bois, *The Souls of Black Folk* (1903; reprint, New York: Penguin, 1989), 5.

3 The journal entries of which *Black Like Me* is composed originally appeared as the series "Journey into Shame" in *Sepia*, a now defunct black monthly

whose white publisher funded Griffin's experiment, in monthly installments between April and October 1960. Modeled after *Look* and *Ebony*, the latter its closest competitor, *Sepia* probably never attained circulation over seventy-five thousand.

4 For a trenchant discussion of this failure, as well as the visibility politics of passing more generally speaking, see Peggy Phelan's discussion of Adrian Piper's "calling card" performances and Jennie Livingston's 1991 film *Paris Is Burning* in *Unmarked: The Politics of Performance* (New York: Routledge, 1993), 93–111. Phelan's discussion on pp. 96–99 is particularly relevant to my argument about Griffin's narrative.

5 Foucault's arguments about the agency of panoptics in the subjectification of the modern "self" are well-known. I refer the reader to his *Discipline and Punish: The Birth of the Prison* (New York: Vintage, 1979). For a critique of Foucault's work in the context of a larger discussion of race, gender, and modernity, see Robyn Wiegman, *American Anatomies: Theorizing Race and Gender* (Durham, N.C.: Duke University Press, 1995), 36–42.

6 Wiegman, *American Anatomies*, 40.

7 I insert the term "cross-racial" in scare quotes here to draw attention to the complicity of language in the enforcement of the racial binary. To the degree that "cross-racial" refers to opposing "spheres" of racial "being," the phrase has much the same inadequacy as the term "biracial," which is typically used only to refer to subjects who are already ethnoracially marked. David Theo Goldberg makes a related point in a discussion of the notion of "hyphenated" Americans in his essay "Multicultural Conditions," in *Multiculturalism: A Critical Reader*, ed. David Theo Goldberg (Oxford: Basil Blackwell, 1994), 37 n. 20.

8 Julie Ellison, "A Short History of Liberal Guilt," *Critical Inquiry* 22 (winter 1996): 352.

9 Ibid., 348.

10 I analyze this irony in greater detail later in this chapter in my discussion of passing's mirroring effect in Griffin's narrative.

11 Since its publication in book form in 1961, *Black Like Me* has sold more than twelve million copies, been translated into fourteen languages, and appeared in numerous English-language editions, including one in South Africa. By 1971, it had become enough of a staple in junior high and high school classrooms to merit its own *Cliffs Notes*, which are still in print. Even today, despite the ready availability of a range of more eloquent portrayals of racism and segregation by African American authors, from Richard Wright's "The Ethics of Living Jim Crow" to Anne Moody's *Coming of Age in Mississippi*, *Black Like Me* remains popular for teaching white students about their country's legacy of racial oppression. At my local bookstore newly minted copies

share a shelf crowded by recent titles in African American cultural studies, an arrangement that would have been unimaginable when *Black Like Me* first appeared.

12 See Grace Halsell, *Soul Sister* (Greenwich, Conn.: Fawcett, 1969). In 1968, on an impulse inspired by a single reading of *Black Like Me*, Halsell resigned from her job as a staff writer for Lyndon Johnson, flew (on Air Force One) to Texas to meet Griffin, and began drug and sun treatments to darken her skin. In her narrative Halsell represents her experiences in Harlem, where she works as a secretary in Harlem Hospital, and later her work as a domestic for a wealthy white family in Jackson, Mississippi. Her experiment abruptly ends when her employer attempts to rape her. For recent related discussions of Halsell, see hooks, *Black Looks*, 171, and Phillip Brian Harper, *Are We Not Men? Masculine Anxiety and the Problem of African-American Identity* (New York: Oxford University Press, 1996).

More recently Joshua Solomon, a white male college student, was inspired to reenact Griffin's experiment for much the same reason as Griffin (that is, because he wanted to verify black peers' accounts of racism)—a venture that landed him a feature article in the *Washington Post* and a brief spot on *The Oprah Winfrey Show*. See "Skin Deep: Reliving 'Black Like Me': My Own Journey into the Heart of Race-Conscious America," *Washington Post*, October 30, 1994, C1.

13 Although the original *Sepia* magazine serialization of Griffin's journals had prompted outrage in his hometown of Mansfield, Texas, where Griffin's neighbors burned him in effigy, response to *Black Like Me* was overwhelmingly positive. Reviewers generally greeted the book with widespread, if sometimes stiff, applause. In a diplomatic review for the *Saturday Review*, African American commentator Louis Lomax wrote that "it was a joy to see a white man become black for a while and then re-enter his own world screaming in the tones of Richard Wright and James Baldwin." See Louis E. Lomax, "It's Like This," *Saturday Review*, December 1961, p. 53. While Lomax's analogy seems far-fetched, his comment suggests that he understood *Black Like Me*'s central achievement to be Griffin's emergent sense of the theatricality of his own racial identity, a point missed by most white critics. Anxiously emphasizing the stability and purity of whiteness, the reviewer for *Commonweal*, for example, commended the book's liberal social critique but complained about Griffin's unconventional methodology, writing that "it seems perverse to tamper with one's identity in this way, no matter what the motive." See Bruce A. Cook, "What Is It Like to Be a Negro?" *Commonweal*, October 1961, p. 129.

14 There is no evidence to support these contentions, although the drugs Griffin took to darken his skin apparently can cause kidney problems and other ail-

ments. See Griffin's obituaries in *Jet*, September 25, 1980, p. 59 and the *New York Times*, September 10, 1980.

15 Donna J. Haraway, "Situated Knowledges: The Science Question in Feminism and the Privilege of Partial Perspective," in *Simians, Cyborgs, and Women: The Reinvention of Nature* (New York: Routledge, 1991), 191.

16 Quoted in hooks, *Black Looks*, 13.

17 From Bronislaw Malinowski, *Argonauts of the Western Pacific* (New York: Dutton, 1922), 25. Cited in George E. Marcus and Michael M. J. Fischer, *Anthropology as Cultural Critique* (Chicago: University of Chicago Press, 1986), 25.

18 On the politics of ethnography, see the essays collected in James Clifford and George E. Marcus, eds., *Writing Culture: The Poetics and Politics of Ethnography* (Berkeley: University of California Press, 1986). On the uses of anthropology as social and cultural critique, see Marcus and Fischer. The success of Griffin's disguise—no one, according to Griffin, ever doubted his identity—prompts additional ethical problems that are less typical within mainstream modernist anthropology, in which the relationship between ethnographer and informant is often made explicit through commodity exchange. Although Griffin stayed in black peoples' homes, broke bread with them, and sought out their companionship and advice, he never disclosed that he was on assignment for *Sepia*. The one exception is Sterling Brown, a shoeshine and *Black Like Me*'s only named "native informant," who knowingly serves as Griffin's intermediary when Griffin first crosses the line in New Orleans. Eric Lott's "White Like Me: Racial Cross-Dressing and the Construction of American Whiteness" discusses Griffin's representation of Brown at greater length. See Lott's article in *Cultures of United States Imperialism*, ed. Amy Kaplan and Donald Pease (Durham, N.C.: Duke University Press, 1993), esp. 474–75.

19 John Howard Griffin, *A Time to Be Human* (New York: Macmillan, 1977), 24.

20 Ernest Sharpe Jr., "The Man Who Changed His Skin," *American Heritage* 40, no. 1 (February 1989) 46.

21 Ellison references the conceptual quality of pain in her account of "liberal guilt" narratives. See "A Short History of Liberal Guilt," 352.

22 See James Clifford, "Partial Truths," in *Writing Culture: The Poetics and Politics of Ethnography* (Berkeley: University of California Press, 1986), 13.

23 Du Bois, *Souls of Black Folk*, 5.

24 Frederick Douglass, *Narrative of the Life of Frederick Douglass* (1845; reprint, New York: Penguin, 1982), 51.

25 Toni Morrison, *Playing in the Dark: Whiteness and the Literary Imagination* (New York: Vintage, 1993).

26 Karen McCarthy Brown, "Plenty Confidence in Myself: The Initiation of a White Woman Scholar into Haitian Voodoo," *Journal of Feminist Studies of Religion* 3 (1987): 67.

27   This is an argument elaborated at greater length by Lott in "White Like Me: Racial Cross-Dressing and the Construction of American Whiteness."

28   "Pure shame," according to Jean-Paul Sartre, "is not a feeling of being this or that guilty object but in general of being *an* object; that is, of *recognizing myself* in this degraded, fixed, and dependent being which I am for the Other. Shame is the feeling of an *original fall*, not because of the fact that I may have committed this or that particular fault but simply that I have "fallen" into the world . . . and . . . I need the mediation of the Other in order to be what I am." Quoted in Ellison, "A Short History of Liberal Guilt," 357.

29   Richard Dyer, "White," *Screen* 29, no. 3 (1988): 45.

30   Sharpe, "The Man Who Changed His Skin," 54.

31   Adrian Piper, "Passing for White, Passing for Black," *Transition* 2, no. 4 (1992): 19.

32   As Freud defined it, the uncanny, or *unheimlich*, designates an anxiety triggered when the familiar is radically defamiliarized and made frightening, an effect (or an affect) produced through a resurfacing of repressed feelings. See Sigmund Freud, "The Uncanny," in *The Standard Edition of the Complete Psychological Works of Sigmund Freud, vol. 17 (1917–1919)*, trans. James Strachey (London: Hogarth Press, 1955): 217–56. It is worth remarking that in a footnote to his essay "The Uncanny," Freud describes an experience much like Griffin's. On entering a train compartment at night, Freud mistakes his own reflection for that of an elderly "intruder": "Jumping up with the intention of putting him right, I at once realized to my dismay that the intruder was nothing but my own reflection in the looking-glass on the open door. I can still recollect that I thoroughly disliked his appearance. Instead, therefore, of being frightened by [my double] . . . I simply failed to recognize [it] as such" (248, n. 1). For a discussion of this footnote and a helpful analysis of the uncanny as it relates to the construction of narratives of the nation/national self, see Priscilla Wald, *Constituting Americans: Cultural Anxiety and Narrative Form* (Durham, N.C.: Duke University Press, 1995), 5–7. My reading of this scene in *Black Like Me* owes much to her example. For a slightly different, but equally important, reading of mirror scenes and the trope of mirroring in African American fiction (one that has influenced my reading of Griffin), see Kimberly W. Benston, "Facing Tradition: Revisionary Scenes in African American Literature," *PMLA* 105 (1990): 98–109.

33   The quote is from Toni Morrison, *Playing in the Dark*, 67.

34   Wald, *Constituting Americans*, 6.

35   See Wald's discussion of Du Bois, ibid., 176–77.

36   On the Parker lynching, see "Mack C. Parker of Lumberton, Miss., Kidnaped and Lynched: The Story behind the Lynching," *Jet*, May 14, 1959, pp. 12–15, as well as articles published during May 1959 in the *Chicago Defender*, the *Pittsburgh Courier* and the *Norfolk Journal and Guide*.

37 "Black Like Me," *Time*, March 28, 1960, p. 90.

38 Albert Memmi, *The Colonizer and the Colonized* (1957; reprint, Boston: Beacon, 1991), 20.

39 Godfrey Hodgson, *America in Our Time* (New York: Vintage, 1976), 266.

40 Stokely Carmichael and Charles V. Hamilton, *Black Power: The Politics of Liberation in America* (New York: Random House, 1967), 184–85.

41 "Black Like Me," 32.

42 James Baldwin, "Unnameable Objects, Unspeakable Crimes," in *The White Problem in America*, edited by the editors of *Ebony* (Chicago: Johnson, 1966), 173.

43 Lott, "White Like Me," 487.

EPILOGUE

1 Patricia J. Williams, *The Alchemy of Race and Rights: Diary of a Law Professor* (Cambridge, Mass.: Harvard University Press, 1991), 120.

2 Michelle Cliff, *Claiming an Identity They Taught Me to Despise* (Watertown, Mass.: Persephone Press, 1980), 19.

3 Danzy Senna, *Caucasia* (New York: Riverhead, 1998), 1.

4 In *Race, Nation, Class: Ambiguous Identities* (London: Verso, 1991), Etienne Balibar and Immanuel Wallerstein argue forcefully that universalism and particularism are connected in such a way that they are also sometimes mutually securing, not merely opposite tendencies, as liberal discourses would have us believe. For the purposes of this project, I have also found useful discussions of the liberal "quandary" in Cornel West, "Race and Social Theory: Towards a Genealogical Materialist Analysis," in *The Year Left: An American Socialist Yearbook*, vol. 2, ed. Mike Davis, Manning Marable, Fred Pfeil, and Michael Sprinker (London: Verso, 1987), 74–90, and Amy Gutmann, "Responding to Racial Injustice," in *Color Conscious: The Political Morality of Race*, ed. K. Anthony Appiah and Amy Gutmann (Princeton, N.J.: Princeton University Press, 1996), 106–78.

5 Harlan's dissent underscores the barely concealed purposes of the 1890 Louisiana statute at issue in *Plessy*. "Every one knows," he wrote, "that the statute in question had its origins in the purpose, not so much to exclude white persons from railroad cars occupied by blacks, as to exclude colored people from coaches occupied by or assigned to white persons." *Plessy v. Ferguson* 160 U.S. 537 (1896) 557. It is worth noting in this context that although the Constitution, as originally ratified, makes no direct references either to slavery or to black people, such silence is itself a strategy of evasion that predicates the freedoms of those it performatively constitutes as "citizens" upon the exclusion (rhetorical as well as actual) of others. The notion of "We the people" is thus neither as self-evident nor as inclusive as might be presupposed.

6 For a useful discussion of the rise to hegemony of the notion of a "color blind" society, see Michael Omi and Howard Winant, *Racial Formation in the United States: From the 1960s to the 1990s*, 2d ed. (New York: Routledge, 1994).

7 I use the term "color conscious" following Gutmann in "Responding to Racial Injustice." In *The Alchemy of Race and Rights*, Williams argues that "[s]tandards are nothing more than structured preferences (103), asserting that in the rhetoric of "color blindness," "neutrality" is the equivalent of "racism in drag" (116).

8 On the racialization of affirmative action and its relation to "women" as a political category, see Cathy Davidson, "Preface," *American Literature* 70, no. 3 (September 1998): 454.

9 Doris Black, "How Passing Passed Out," *Sepia*, December 1972, pp. 66–69.

10 For more on metaphors of blindness, see Georgina Kleege, "Call It Blindness," *The Yale Review* 82, no. 2 (April 1994): 46–69, and "Here's Looking at You," *Southwest Review* (spring/summer 1995): 285–96. Thanks to Rosemarie Garland Thomson for bringing these articles to my attention.

11 My argument here is informed by Gayatri Chakravorty Spivak's useful clarification of her widely circulated notion of "strategic essentialism" in "In a Word," an interview with Ellen Rooney. There she observes that in certain situations when "strategic essentialism" is invoked, "[t]he emphasis then inevitably falls on being able to speak from one's own ground, rather than matching the trick to the situation, that the word strategy implies." I take Spivak's comment as a reminder that strategies are themselves socially constructed. See Gayatri Chakravorty Spivak, *Outside in the Teaching Machine* (New York: Routledge, 1993), 4.

12 I derive the notion of "misrecognition" here from Louis Althusser, who argues that ideology compels "misrecognition" as the condition of any apparent truth. Likewise, I have argued throughout this book that racial (self-)recognition constitutes a *mis*recognition, insofar as "seeing" race depends on a process of perceiving the self and others through the lens of racial ideology. See Louis Althusser, "Ideology and Ideological State Apparatuses," in *Lenin and Philosophy*, trans. Ben Brewster (New York: Monthly Review Press, 1971), 170–83.

13 On attempts by the state to officially introduce new categories of race and ethnicity, see Lawrence Wright, "One Drop of Blood," *New Yorker*, July 25, 1994, pp. 46–55. See also Mike Hill's unpublished paper, "Whiteness Redux: 'Race,' Recognition, and the State," presented at the South Atlantic Modern Language Association annual meeting, Atlanta, Ga., November 1997.

14 Other recent texts that explore similar issues through the lens of "passing" include Shirley Taylor Haizlip, *The Sweeter the Juice: A Family Memoir in Black and White* (New York: Simon and Schuster, 1994); Judy Scales-Trent, *Notes of a White Black Woman: Race, Color, Community* (University Park, Pa.: Penn-

sylvania State University Press, 1995); Gregory Howard Williams, *Life on the Color Line: The True Story of a White Boy Who Discovered He Was Black* (New York: Dutton, 1995); and Toi Derricotte's remarkable *The Black Notebooks: An Interior Journey* (New York: Norton, 1997). I review Scales-Trent's and Williams's books in "Along the Color Line: Memory, Community, Identity," *Minnesota Review* 47 (May 1997): 191–97.

15 For an essay that offers a similar reading of *Caucasia*, see Margo Jefferson, "Seeing Race as a Costume That Everyone Wears," *New York Times*, May 4, 1998.

16 Describing the process of forging a "new" "mestiza" consciousness, Anzaldúa writes, "At some point, on our way . . . we will have to leave the opposite bank, the split between the two mortal combatants somehow healed so that we are on both shores at once and, at once, see through serpent and eagle eyes" (78–79). She continues: "The new *mestiza* copes [with the crossing of borders] by developing a tolerance for contradictions, a tolerance for ambiguity. . . . Not only does she sustain contradictions, she turns the ambivalence into something else" (79). See Gloria Anzaldúa, *Borderlands/La Frontera: The New Mestiza* (San Francisco: Aunt Lute Books, 1987).

Abelove, Henry, Michèle Aina Barale, and David M. Halperin, eds. *The Lesbian and Gay Studies Reader*. New York: Routledge, 1993.

Alcoff, Linda Martin. "Philosophy and Racial Identity." *Radical Philosophy* 75 (January/February 1996): 5–14.

Allen, Theodore W. *The Invention of the White Race*, vol. 1. London: Verso, 1994.

Althusser, Louis. "Ideology and Ideological State Apparatuses." In *Lenin and Philosophy*. Trans. Ben Brewster. New York: Monthly Review Press, 1971.

Andrews, William L. "Introduction." In *The Autobiography of an Ex-Colored Man*, by James Weldon Johnson. New York: Penguin, 1990.

Anzaldúa, Gloria. *Borderlands/La Frontera: The New Mestiza*. San Francisco: Aunt Lute Books, 1987.

Appiah, K. Anthony. "Identity, Authenticity, Survival: Multicultural Societies

And Social Reproduction." In Charles Taylor, *Multiculturalism: Examining the Politics of Recognition*. Ed. Amy Gutmann. Princeton, N.J.: Princeton University Press, 1994.

Appiah, K. Anthony, and Amy Gutmann. *Color Conscious: The Political Morality of Race*. Princeton: Princeton University Press, 1996.

Austin, Regina. "'A Nation of Thieves': Consumption, Commerce, and the Black Public Sphere." In *The Black Public Sphere*. Ed. Black Public Sphere Collective. Chicago: University of Chicago Press, 1995.

Awkward, Michael. "Negotiations of Power: White Critics, Black Texts, and the Self-Referential Impulse." *American Literary History* 2, no. 4 (1990): 581–606.

Bad Object-Choices, ed. *How Do I Look? Queer Film and Video*. Seattle: Bay Press, 1991.

Baldwin, James. *Nobody Knows My Name: More Notes of a Native Son*. New York: Dell, 1961.

———. *Notes of a Native Son*. 1955. Reprint, Boston: Beacon Press, 1984.

———. "Unnameable Objects, Unspeakable Crimes." In *The White Problem in America*. Ed. the editors of *Ebony*. Chicago: Johnson Publishing, 1966.

Balibar, Etienne. *Masses, Classes, Ideas: Studies on Politics and Philosophy before and after Marx*. Trans. James Swenson. New York: Routledge, 1994.

———. "Is There a Neo-Racism?" In *Race, Nation, Class: Ambiguous Identities*. Ed. Balibar and Wallerstein. London: Verso, 1991.

Balibar, Etienne, and Immanuel Wallerstein. *Race, Nation, Class: Ambiguous Identities*. London: Verso, 1991.

Barnes, Howard. "Stage Techniques Improve a Film." *New York Herald Tribune*, October 2, 1949.

Bechet, Sidney. *The Legendary Sidney Bechet*. RCA, 1988.

———. *Treat It Gentle*. New York: Hill and Wang, 1960.

Behlmer, Rudy, ed. *Memo from Darryl F. Zanuck: The Golden Years at Twentieth Century-Fox*. New York: Grove Press, 1993.

Benston, Kimberly W. "Facing Tradition: Revisionary Scenes in African American Literature." *PMLA* 105, no. 1 (1990): 98–109.

Berlant, Lauren. "National Brands/National Body: *Imitation of Life*." In *The Phantom Public Sphere*. Ed. Bruce Robbins. Minneapolis: University of Minnesota Press, 1993.

———. *The Queen of America Goes to Washington City: Essays on Sex and Citizenship*. Durham, N.C.: Duke University Press, 1997.

Bhabha, Homi. *The Location of Culture*. New York: Routledge, 1994.

Black, Doris. "How Passing Passed Out." *Sepia*, December 1972, pp. 66–69.

"Black Like Me." *Time*, March 28, 1960, p. 90.

Black Public Sphere Collective, ed. *The Black Public Sphere*. Chicago: University of Chicago Press, 1995.

Bobo, Jacqueline. "'The Subject is Money': Reconsidering the Black Film Audience as Theoretical Paradigm." *Black American Literature Forum* 25, no. 2 (summer 1991): 421–32.

Bogle, Donald. *Toms, Coons, Mulattoes, Mammies, Bucks: An Interpretive History of Blacks in American Films.* New York: Viking, 1973.

Bone, Robert. *The Negro Novel in America.* 1958. Reprint, New Haven, Conn.: Yale University Press, 1976.

Boyarin, Jonathan, and Daniel Boyarin, eds. *Jews and Other Differences: The New Jewish Cultural Studies.* Minneapolis: University of Minnesota Press, 1997.

Brody, Jennifer DeVere. "Clare Kendry's 'True' Colors: Race and Class Conflict in Nella Larsen's *Passing*." *Callaloo* 15, no. 4 (1992): 1053–65.

———. *Impossible Purities: Blackness, Femininity, and Victorian Culture.* Durham, N.C.: Duke University Press, 1998.

Brown, Sterling. *The Negro in American Fiction.* Washington: Associates in Negro Folk Education, 1937.

Bruynoghe. "Mezzrow Talks about the Old Jim Crow." *The Melody Maker and Rhythm,* November 17, 1951, p. 9.

Burns, Ben. *Nitty Gritty: A White Editor in Black Journalism.* Jackson, Miss.: University Press of Mississippi, 1996.

Butler, Judith. *Bodies That Matter: On the Discursive Limits of "Sex".* New York: Routledge, 1993.

———. "Performative Acts and Gender Constitution: An Essay in Phenomenology and Feminist Theory." In *Performing Feminisms: Feminist Critical Theory and Theatre.* Ed. Sue-Ellen Case. Baltimore: Johns Hopkins University Press, 1990.

Butler, Judith, and Joan W. Scott, eds. *Feminists Theorize the Political.* New York: Routledge, 1992.

Campbell, Russel. "The Ideology of the Social Consciousness Movie: Three Films of Darryl F. Zanuck." *Quarterly Review of Film Studies* (winter 1978): 49–71.

Carby, Hazel. *Reconstructing Womanhood: The Emergence of the Afro-American Woman Novelist.* New York: Oxford University Press, 1987.

Carmichael, Stokely, and Charles V. Hamilton. *Black Power: The Politics of Liberation in America.* New York: Random House, 1967.

Case, Sue-Ellen, ed. *Performing Feminisms: Feminist Critical Theory and Theatre.* Baltimore: Johns Hopkins University Press, 1990.

"Case History of an Ex-White Man." *Ebony,* December 1946, pp. 11–16.

Chesnutt, Charles. *The House behind the Cedars.* 1900. Reprint, New York: Penguin, 1993.

Christian, Barbara. *Black Women Novelists: The Development of a Tradition, 1892–1976.* Westport, Conn.: Greenwood Press, 1980.

Cliff, Michelle. *Claiming an Identity They Taught Me to Despise.* Watertown, Mass.: Persephone Press, 1980.

Clifford, James and George E. Marcus, eds. *Writing Culture: The Poetics and Politics of Ethnography*. Berkeley: University of California Press, 1986.

Collins, Patricia Hill. *Black Feminist Thought: Knowledge, Consciousness, and the Politics of Empowerment*. London: Unwin Hyman, 1990.

Cook, Alton. "'Pinky' Is Inspired Study of Race Bias." *New York Telegram*, September 30, 1949.

Cook, Bruce A. "What Is It Like to Be a Negro?" *Commonweal*, October 1961, 129.

Cook, David A. *A History of Narrative Film*. New York: W. W. Norton, 1981.

Cooke, Michael. *Afro-American Literature in the Twentieth Century: The Achievement of Intimacy*. New Haven, Conn.: Yale University Press, 1984.

Crenshaw, Kimberlé, Neil Gotanda, Gary Peller, and Kendall Thomas, eds. *Critical Race Theory: The Key Writings That Formed the Movement*. New York: New Press, 1995.

Cripps, Thomas. *Making Movies Black: The Hollywood Message Movie from World War II to the Civil Rights Era*. New York: Oxford University Press, 1993.

"The Curse of Passing." *Ebony*, December 1955, pp. 50–56.

Damon, Maria. "Jazz, Jews, Jive, and Gender: The Ethnic Politics of Jazz Argot." In *Jews and Other Differences: The New Jewish Cultural Studies*. Eds. Jonathan Boyarin and Daniel Boyarin. Minneapolis: University of Minnesota Press, 1997.

Davidson, Cathy. "Preface." *American Literature* 70, no. 3 (September 1998): 443–63.

Davis, Angela Y. *Women, Race and Class*. New York: Random House, 1981.

Davis, F. James. *Who Is Black? One Nation's Definition*. University Park, Pa.: Pennsylvania State University Press, 1991.

Davis, Mike, et al., eds. *The Year Left: An American Socialist Yearbook*, vol. 2. London: Verso, 1987.

Derricotte, Toi. *The Black Notebooks: An Interior Journey*. New York: Norton, 1997.

Diamond, Elin. *Performance and Cultural Politics*. New York: Routledge, 1996.

Doane, Mary Ann. *Femmes Fatales: Feminism, Film Theory, Psychoanalysis*. New York: Routledge, 1991.

Douglass, Frederick. *Narrative of the Life of Frederick Douglass*. 1845. Reprint, New York: Penguin, 1982.

Du Bois, W. E. B. *Black Reconstruction in America*. 1935. Reprint, New York: Russell and Russell, 1966.

———. *The Souls of Black Folk*. 1903. Reprint, New York: Penguin, 1989.

duCille, Ann. *The Coupling Convention: Sex, Text, and Tradition in Black Women's Fiction*. New York: Oxford University Press, 1993.

Dunbar-Nelson, Alice. *The Works of Alice Dunbar-Nelson*. Vol. 2. Ed. Gloria T. Hull. New York: Oxford University Press, 1988.

Dunne, Philip. "An Approach to Racism." Undated article. *Pinky* vertical file, Film Study Center of the Museum of Modern Art, New York.

Duke, Lynne. "S. African 'Coloreds' End Race Charade: People of Mixed Ancestry Reclaim Black Identity Hidden under Apartheid." *Washington Post*, July 16, 1998.

Dyer, Richard. "White." *Screen* 29, no. 4 (autumn 1998): 44–64.

Ellison, Julie. "A Short History of Liberal Guilt." *Critical Inquiry* 22 (winter 1996): 344–71.

Ellison, Ralph. *Shadow and Act.* New York: Vintage, 1972.

Fanon, Frantz. *Black Skin, White Masks.* Trans. Charles Lam Markmann. 1952. Reprint, New York: Grove Press, 1967.

Fauset, Jessie. *Plum Bun.* 1928. Reprint, Boston: Beacon Press, 1990.

———. "The Sleeper Wakes." In *The Sleeper Wakes: Harlem Renaissance Stories by Women.* Ed. Marcy Knopf. New Brunswick, N.J.: Rutgers University Press, 1993.

Feinstein, Elaine. *Bessie Smith: Empress of the Blues.* London: Penguin, 1985.

Fordham, Signithia. "The Discourse around 'Multiracial' Identity." Unpublished paper presented at the annual meeting of the American Studies Association/ Canadian Association for American Studies, Washington, D.C., October 31, 1997.

Foucault, Michel. *Discipline and Punish: The Birth of the Prison.* Trans. Alan Sheridan. New York: Vintage, 1979.

———. *Foucault Reader.* Ed. Paul Rabinow. New York: Pantheon, 1984.

Frankenberg, Ruth. *White Women, Race Matters: The Social Construction of Whiteness.* Minneapolis: University of Minnesota Press, 1993.

Fraser, Nancy. *Unruly Practices: Power, Discourse, and Gender in Contemporary Social Theory.* Minneapolis: University of Minnesota Press, 1989.

Frazier, E. Franklin. *Black Bourgeoisie.* 1957. Reprint, New York: Collier Books, 1962.

Freud, Sigmund. *The Standard Edition of the Complete Psychological Works of Sigmund Freud, Vol. 17 (1917–1919).* Trans. James Strachey. London: Hogarth Press, 1955.

Fusco, Coco. *English Is Broken Here: Notes on Cultural Fusion in the Americas.* New York: New Press, 1995.

Gaines, Jane. "White Privilege and Looking Relations: Race and Gender in Feminist Film Theory." *Screen* 29 (1988): 12–27.

Gaines, Kevin K. *Uplifting the Race: Black Leadership, Politics, and Culture in the Twentieth Century.* Chapel Hill, N.C.: University of North Carolina Press, 1996.

Gates, Henry Louis, Jr. *Figures in Black: Words, Signs, and the "Racial" Self.* New York: Oxford University Press, 1987.

————. "Introduction." In *The Autobiography of an Ex-Colored Man*. By James Weldon Johnson. New York: Vintage, 1990.

————, ed. *"Race," Writing, and Difference*. Chicago: University of Chicago Press, 1986.

Gehman, Richard B. "Poppa Mezz." *Saturday Review*, November 16, 1946, p. 26.

Giddins, Gary. *Riding on a Blue Note: Jazz and American Pop*. New York: Oxford University Press, 1981.

Ginsberg, Elaine K., ed. *Passing and the Fictions of Identity*. Durham, N.C.: Duke University Press, 1996.

Goldberg, David Theo. "Multicultural Conditions." In *Multiculturalism: A Critical Reader*. Ed. David Theo Goldberg. Oxford: Basil Blackwell, 1994.

————. *Racist Culture: Philosophy and the Politics of Meaning*. Oxford: Blackwell, 1993.

Gramsci, Antonio. *Selections from the Prison Notebooks*. Ed. and trans. Quintin Hoare and Geoffrey Nowell Smith. New York: International Publishers, 1971.

Griffin, John Howard. *Black Like Me*. Boston: Houghton Mifflin, 1961.

————. *Nuni*. Boston: Houghton Mifflin, 1956.

————. *A Time to Be Human*. New York: Macmillan, 1977.

————. "What's Happened in America Since Black Like Me." *Sepia*, March 1973, pp. 16–20.

————. "Why Black Separatism." *Sepia*, April 1973, pp. 26–36.

Gubar, Susan. *Racechanges: White Skin, Black Face in American Culture*. New York: Oxford University Press, 1997.

Gutmann, Amy. "Responding to Racial Injustice." In *Color Conscious: The Political Morality of Race*. Ed. K. Anthony Appiah and Gutmann. Princeton: Princeton University Press, 1997.

Haizlip, Shirlee Taylor. *The Sweeter the Juice: A Family Memoir in Black and White*. New York: Simon and Schuster, 1994.

Hall, Stuart. "Encoding/decoding." In *The Cultural Studies Reader*. Ed. Simon During. New York: Routledge, 1993.

————. "For Allon White: Metaphors of Transformation." In *Stuart Hall: Critical Dialogues in Cultural Studies*. Ed. David Morley and Kuan-Hsing Chen. New York: Routledge, 1996.

————. "Gramsci's Relevance for the Study of Race and Ethnicity." *Journal of Communication Inquiry* 10, no. 2 (1986): 5–27.

————. "Race, Articulation and Societies Structured in Dominance." In *Sociological Theories: Race and Colonialism*. Paris: UNESCO, 1980.

————. "What Is This 'Black' in Black Popular Culture?" In *Stuart Hall: Critical Dialogues in Cultural Studies*. Ed. Morley and Chen. New York: Routledge, 1996.

Halsell, Grace. *Soul Sister*. Greenwich, Conn.: Fawcett, 1969.

Haraway, Donna J. "Situated Knowledges: The Science Question in Feminism and the Privilege of Partial Perspective." In *Simians, Cyborgs, and Women: The Reinvention of Nature*. New York: Routledge, 1991.

Harper, Francis E. W. *Iola Leroy, or Shadows Uplifted*. 1893. Reprint, New York: Oxford University Press, 1988.

Harper, Phillip Brian. *Are We Not Men? Masculine Anxiety and the Problem of African-American Identity*. New York: Oxford University Press, 1996.

Harris, Cheryl I. "Whiteness as Property." *Critical Race Theory: The Key Writings That Formed the Movement*. Ed. Kimberlé Crenshaw, Neil Gotanda, Gary Peller, and Kendall Thomas. New York: New Press, 1995.

Hauke, Kathleen A. "The 'Passing' of Elsie Roxborough." *Michigan Quarterly Review* 23, no. 12 (1984): 155–70.

"Have Negroes Stopped Passing?" *Jet*, September 13, 1956, pp. 10–12.

Hennessey, Mike. "Mezz Mezzrow: Alive and Well in Paris." *Down Beat*, May 30, 1968, pp. 24–25.

Hentoff, Nat. "Counterpoint." *Down Beat*, February 11, 1953, p. 5.

Hermann, Anne. " 'Passing' Women, Performing Men." In *The Female Body: Figures, Styles, Speculations*. Ed. Laurence Goldstein. Ann Arbor: University of Michigan Press, 1991.

Hill, Mike. "Whiteness Redux: 'Race,' Recognition, and the State." Unpublished paper presented at the South Atlantic Modern Language Association annual meeting, Atlanta, Ga., November 1997.

———, ed. *Whiteness: A Critical Reader*. New York: New York University Press, 1997.

Hirsch, Paul M. "An Analysis of *Ebony:* The Magazine and Its Readers." *Journalism Quarterly* 45, no. 2 (summer 1968): 261–70.

Hodgson, Godfrey. *America in Our Time*. New York: Vintage, 1976.

Holt, Thomas. "Afterword: Mapping the Black Public Sphere." In *The Black Public Sphere*. Ed. Black Public Sphere Collective. Chicago: University of Chicago Press, 1995.

hooks, bell. *Black Looks: Race and Representation*. Boston: South End Press, 1992.

"How Negroes Are Gaining in the U.S." *U.S. News and World Report*, June 28, 1957, pp. 105–6.

Hughes, Langston. "American Art or Negro Art?" *Nation* 123 (1926): 151.

———. *The Big Sea*. New York: Hill and Wang, 1940.

———. "Fooling Our White Folks." *Negro Digest*, April 1950, 38–41.

———. *I Wonder as I Wander*. 1956. Reprint, New York: Hill and Wang, 1964.

———. "The Negro Artist and the Racial Mountain." *Nation* 122 (1926): 692–94. Reprinted in *Voices of the Harlem Renaissance*. Ed. Nathan Huggins. New York: Oxford University Press, 1976.

———. "Passing." *The Ways of White Folks*. New York: Alfred A. Knopf, 1934.

———. "Why Not Fool Our White Folks?" *Chicago Defender*, January 5, 1958, p. 10.

Hutchinson, George. *The Harlem Renaissance in Black and White*. Cambridge, Mass.: Harvard University Press, 1995.

Ignatiev, Noel. *How the Irish Became White*. New York: Routledge, 1995.

"I Passed for Love." *Tan*, March 1953, p. 33.

"I'm Through with Passing." *Ebony*, March 1951, pp. 22–27.

"Is Passing for White a Dying Fad?" *Color*, April 1957, pp. 46–49.

Itzkovitz, Daniel. "Secret Temples." In *Jews and Other Differences: The New Jewish Cultural Studies*. Ed. Jonathan Boyarin and Daniel Boyarin. Minneapolis: University of Minnesota Press, 1997.

Jacobs, Harriet. *Incidents in the Life of a Slave Girl*. 1865. Reprint, New York: Oxford University Press, 1988.

Jameson, Fredric. "Reification and Utopia in Mass Culture." In *Signatures of the Visible*. New York: Routledge, 1990.

Jefferson, Margo. "Seeing Race as a Costume That Everyone Wears." *New York Times*, May 4, 1998.

Jerome, V. J. *The Negro in Hollywood Films*. New York: Masses and Mainstream, 1950.

Johnson, James Weldon. *The Autobiography of an Ex-Colored Man*. 1912. Reprint, New York: Penguin, 1990.

———. *Along This Way*. 1933. Reprint, New York: Penguin, 1990.

Johnson, John H. with Lerone Bennett Jr. *Succeeding against the Odds*. New York: Warner Books, 1989.

Jones, LeRoi. *Blues People: Negro Music in White America*. New York: Morris Quill, 1963.

Jones, Lisa. "Passages." *Village Voice*, February 19, 1991, p. 72.

———. "Tragedy Becomes Her." *Village Voice*, June 29, 1993, p. 24.

Kawash, Samira. "*The Autobiography of an Ex-Coloured Man*: (Passing for) Black Passing for White." In *Passing and the Fictions of Identity*. Ed. Elaine K. Ginsberg. Durham, N.C.: Duke University Press, 1996.

———. *Dislocating the Color Line: Identity, Hybridity, and Singularity in African-American Narrative*. Stanford, Calif.: Stanford University Press, 1997.

Kelley, Robin D. G. *Yo' Mama's Disfunktional!: Fighting the Culture Wars in Urban America*. Boston: Beacon Press, 1997.

Kenney, William Howland. *Chicago Jazz: A Cultural History, 1904–1930*. New York: Oxford University Press, 1993.

Kingslow, Janice. "I Refuse to Pass." *Negro Digest*, May 1950, pp. 22–31.

Kleege, Georgina. "Call It Blindness." *The Yale Review* 82, no. 2 (April 1994): 46–69.

———. "Here's Looking at You." *Southwest Review* (spring/summer 1995): 285–96.

Kluger, Richard. *Simple Justice: The History of "Brown v. Board of Education" and Black America's Struggle for Equality*. New York: Vintage, 1975.

Larsen, Nella. *Quicksand and Passing.* Ed. Deborah E. McDowell. 1928, 1929. Reprint, New Brunswick, N.J.: Rutgers University Press, 1986.

Ledbetter, James. "Imitations of Life." *Vibe,* November 1993, p. 112.

Lewis, David Levering. *W. E. B. DuBois: A Reader.* New York: Henry Holt, 1995.

Lipsitz, George. *Dangerous Crossroads: Popular Music, Postmodernism, and the Politics of Place.* London: Verso, 1994.

———. *The Possessive Investment in Whiteness: How White People Profit from Identity Politics.* Philadelphia: Temple University Press, 1998.

Lomax, Louis E. "It's Like This." *Saturday Review,* December 1961, p. 53.

Lost Boundaries. Film Classics, 1949.

Lowe, Lisa. *Immigrant Acts: On Asian American Cultural Politics.* Durham, N.C.: Duke University Press, 1996.

Lott, Eric. *Love and Theft: Blackface Minstrelsy and the American Working Class.* New York: Oxford University Press, 1993.

———. "The New Cosmopolitanism." *Transition* 72 (1996): 108–35.

———. " 'The Seeming Counterfeit': Racial Politics and Early Blackface Minstrelsy." *American Quarterly* 43 (June 1991): 223–54.

———. "White Like Me: Racial Cross-Dressing and the Construction of American Whiteness." In *Cultures of United States Imperialism.* Ed. Amy Kaplan and Donald Pease. Durham, N.C.: Duke University Press, 1993.

"Mack C. Parker of Lumberton, Miss., Kidnapped and Lynched: The Story behind the Lynching." *Jet,* May 14, 1959, pp. 12–15.

Mailer, Norman. *The White Negro.* San Francisco: City Lights Books, 1957.

Malveaux, Julianne. "The Political Economy of Black Women." In *The Year Left: An American Socialist Yearbook.* Vol. 2. Ed. Mike Davis et al. London: Verso, 1987.

Marcus, George E. and Michael M. J. Fischer. *Anthropology as Cultural Critique: An Experimental Moment in the Human Sciences.* Chicago: University of Chicago Press, 1986.

Martin, Biddy and Chandra Talpade Mohanty. "Feminist Politics: What's Home Got to Do With It?" In *Feminist Studies/Critical Studies.* Ed. Teresa de Lauretis. Bloomington: Indiana University Press, 1986.

McCarthy Brown, Karen. "Plenty Confidence in Myself: The Initiation of a White Woman Scholar into Haitian Voudou." *Journal of Feminist Studies of Religion* 3 (1987): 67–76.

McClelland, Douglas. "Jeanne Crain." *Films in Review,* June–July 1969, 357–67.

McDowell, Deborah E. "Introduction." In *Quicksand and Passing.* By Nella Larsen. New Brunswick, N.J.: Rutgers University Press, 1986.

———. "The 'Nameless . . . Shameful Impulse': Sexuality in Nella Larsen's *Quicksand* and *Passing.*" In *"The Changing Same": Black Women's Literature, Criticism, and Theory.* Bloomington: Indiana University Press, 1995.

———. "Pecs and Reps: Muscling in on Race and the Subject of Masculinities."

In *Race and the Subject of Masculinities.* Ed. Harry Stecopoulos and Michael Uebel. Durham, N.C.: Duke University Press, 1997.

———. "Regulating Midwives." In *Plum Bun.* By Jessie Redmon Fauset. Boston: Beacon Press, 1990.

Meier, August, Elliot Rudwick, and Francis L. Broderick. *Black Protest Thought in the Twentieth Century.* 2d ed. New York: Macmillan, 1971.

Memmi, Albert. *The Colonizer and the Colonized.* 1957. Reprint, Boston: Beacon, 1991.

Mercer, Kobena. "Skin Head Sex Thing." In *How Do I Look? Queer Film and Video.* Ed. Bad Object-Choices. Seattle: Bay Press, 1991.

Mezzrow, Mezz and Bernard Wolfe. *Really the Blues.* 1946. Reprint, New York: Citadel Underground, 1990.

Michaels, Walter Benn. "Autobiography of an Ex-White Man: Why Race Is Not a Social Construction." *Transition* 73 (1998): 122–43.

———. *Our America: Nativism, Modernism, and Pluralism.* Durham, N.C.: Duke University Press, 1995.

Modleski, Tania. *Loving with a Vengeance: Mass-Produced Fantasies for Women.* New York: Methuen, 1984.

Moon, Bucklin. "The Real Thing." *New Republic,* November 4, 1946, p. 605.

Morley, David, and Kuan-Hsing Chen, eds. *Stuart Hall: Critical Dialogues in Cultural Studies.* New York: Routledge, 1996.

Morrison, Toni. *Beloved.* New York: Knopf, 1987.

———. *Paradise.* New York: Knopf, 1998.

———. *Playing in the Dark: Whiteness and the Literary Imagination.* New York: Vintage, 1993.

"Negroes: Big Advances in Jobs, Wealth, Status." *U.S. News and World Report,* November 28, 1958, pp. 90–92.

Nelson, Dana D. *The Word in Black and White: Reading 'Race' in American Literature, 1638–1867.* New York: Oxford University Press, 1993.

" 'Never Again,' Says Man Who 'Passed' 20 Years." *Afro-American,* July 16, 1949, p. 8.

Nielson, Aldon Lynn. *Reading Race: The White American Poet and the Racial Discourse in the Twentieth Century.* Athens, Ga.: University of Georgia Press, 1988.

Ohmann, Richard. "Advertising and the New Discourse of Mass Culture." In *Politics of Letters.* Middletown, Conn.: Wesleyan University Press, 1987.

Oliver, Paul. *Blues Fell This Morning: Meaning in the Blues.* 1960. Reprint, London: Cambridge University Press, 1990.

Omi, Michael and Howard Winant. *Racial Formation in the United States: From the 1960s to the 1990s.* 2d ed. New York: Routledge, 1994.

Palmer, Ken. "Mezz Mezzrow at Sixty-five." *Jazz Monthly* 10, no. 9 (1964): 4–6.

Pellegrini, Ann. *Performance Anxieties: Staging Psychoanalysis, Staging Race.* New York: Routledge, 1997.

———. "Whiteface Performances: 'Race,' Gender, and Jewish Bodies." In *Jews and Other Differences: The New Jewish Cultural Studies*. Eds. Jonathan Boyarin and Daniel Boyarin. Minneapolis: University of Minnesota Press, 1997.

Phelan, Peggy. *Unmarked: The Politics of Performance*. New York: Routledge, 1993.

Pinky. Twentieth Century-Fox, 1949.

Piper, Adrian. "Passing for White, Passing for Black." *Transition* 58 (1992): 4–32.

Plessy v. Ferguson. 160 U.S. 537 (1896).

Radway, Janice A. *Reading the Romance: Women, Patriarchy, and Popular Literature*. Chapel Hill: University of North Carolina Press, 1984.

Report of the Pan-African Conference, held on the 23rd, 24th and 25th July, 1900, at Westminster Town Hall, Westminster, S.W. [London]. Headquarters 61 and 62, Chancery Lane, W.C., London, England [1900].

Robinson, Amy. "Forms of Appearance of Value: Homer Plessy and the Politics of Privacy." In *Performance and Cultural Politics*. Ed. Elin Diamond. New York: Routledge, 1996.

———. "It Takes One to Know One: Passing and Communities of Common Interest." *Critical Inquiry* 20 (summer 1994): 715–36.

Roediger, David. "Guineas, Wiggers, and the Dramas of Racialized Culture." *American Literary History* 7, no. 4 (1995): 654–68.

———. *The Wages of Whiteness: Race and the Making of the American Working Class*. London: Verso, 1991.

Rogin, Michael. "Blackface, White Noise: The Jewish Jazz Singer Finds His Voice." *Critical Inquiry* 18 (spring 1992): 417–53.

Romero, Lora. *Home Fronts: Domesticity and Its Critics in the Antebellum United States*. Durham, N.C.: Duke University Press, 1997.

Ross, Andrew. *No Respect: Intellectuals and Popular Culture*. New York: Routledge, 1989.

Sargeant, Winthrop. *Jazz, Hot and Hybrid*. 3d ed. 1938. Reprint, New York: Da Capo, 1975.

Scales-Trent, Judy. *Notes of a White Black Woman: Race, Color, Community*. University Park: Pennsylvania State University Press, 1995.

Schuyler, George. "The Negro Art Hokum." *Nation* 122 (1926): 662–63. Reprinted in *Voices of the Harlem Renaissance*. Ed. Nathan Irvin Huggins. New York: Oxford University Press, 1976.

Scott, Joan W. " 'Experience.' " *Feminists Theorize the Political*. Ed. Judith Butler and Joan Scott. New York: Routledge, 1992.

Senna, Danzy. *Caucasia*. New York: Riverhead, 1998.

Sharpe, Ernest, Jr. "The Man Who Changed His Skin." *American Heritage* 40, no. 1 (February 1989): 44–55.

Singh, Amritjit. *The Novels of the Harlem Renaissance: Twelve Black Writers, 1923–1933*. University Park: Pennsylvania State University Press, 1976.

Sleeper, Jim. *Liberal Racism*. New York: Vintage, 1997.

———. "Race and Folly." *Washington Post Book World*, August 24, 1997, p. 14.

Smith, Barbara, ed. *Home Girls: A Black Feminist Anthology*. New York: Kitchen Table-Women of Color Press, 1983.

Smith, Valerie. "Reading the Intersection of Race and Gender in Narratives of Passing." *diacritics* 24, no. 2–3 (summer/fall, 1994): 43–57.

———. *Self-Discovery and Authority in Afro-American Narrative*. Cambridge, Mass.: Harvard University Press, 1987.

Sollors, Werner. *Neither Black Nor White Yet Both: Thematic Explorations of Inter-racial Literature*. New York: Oxford University Press, 1997.

Solomon, Joshua. "Skin Deep: Reliving 'Black Like Me': My Own Journey into the Heart of Race-Conscious America." *Washington Post*, October 30, 1994.

Soul Man. New World, 1986.

Spillers, Hortense. "Mama's Baby, Papa's Maybe: An American Grammar Book." *diacritics* 17, no. 2 (1987): 65–81.

———. "Notes on an Alternative Model—Neither/Nor." In *The Difference Within: Feminism and Critical Theory*. Ed. Elizabeth Meese and Alice Parker. Philadelphia: John Benjamins, 1989.

Spivak, Gayatri Chakravorty. *Outside in the Teaching Machine*. New York: Routledge, 1993.

Stearns, Marshall. *The Story of Jazz*. New York: Oxford University Press, 1956.

Stecopoulos, Harry, and Michael Uebel, eds. *Race and the Subject of Masculinities*. Durham, N.C.: Duke University Press, 1997.

Sumner, Cid Ricketts. *Quality*. Indianapolis: Bobbs-Merrill, 1946.

Sunder Rajan, Rajeswari. *Real and Imagined Women: Gender, Culture and Postcolonialism*. New York: Routledge, 1993.

Sylvander, Carolyn Wedin. "Jessie Redmon Fauset." In *Dictionary of Literary Biography, Vol. 51: Afro-American Writers from the Harlem Renaissance to 1940*. Ed. Trudier Harris and Thadious M. Davis. Detroit: Gale Research, 1987.

Tate, Claudia. "Allegories of Black Female Desire; or, Rereading Nineteenth-Century Sentimental Narratives of Black Female Authority." In *Changing Our Own Words: Essays on Criticism, Theory, and Writing by Black Women*. Ed. Cheryl A. Wall. New Brunswick, N.J.: Rutgers University Press, 1989.

———. *Domestic Allegories of Political Desire: The Black Heroine's Text at the Turn of the Century*. New York: Oxford University Press, 1992.

Torgovnick, Marianna. *Gone Primitive: Savage Intellects, Modern Lives*. Chicago: University of Chicago Press, 1990.

Twain, Mark. *Pudd'nhead Wilson*. 1894. Reprint, New York: Penguin, 1987.

Tyler, Carole-Ann. "Passing: Narcissism, Identity, and Difference." *differences: A Journal of Feminist Cultural Studies* 6, no. 2/3 (1994): 212–48.

"Vipers, Tea, and Jazz." *Newsweek*, October 28, 1946, pp. 88–89.

Wald, Gayle. "Along the Color Line: Memory, Community, Identity." *Minnesota Review* 47 (May 1997): 191–97.

————. "One of the Boys? Whiteness, Gender, and Popular Music Studies." *Whiteness: A Critical Reader.* Ed. Mike Hill. New York: New York University Press, 1997.

Wald, Priscilla. *Constituting Americans: Cultural Anxiety and Narrative Form.* Durham, N.C.: Duke University Press, 1995.

Wall, Cheryl A. "Passing for What? Aspects of Identity in Nella Larsen's Novels." *Black American Literature Forum* 20 (1986): 97–111.

Weisman, Al. "He Passed as a Negro." *Negro Digest*, October 1951, pp. 16–20.

West, Cornel. "I'm Ofay, You're Ofay: A Conversation with Noel Ignatiev and William 'Upski' Wimsatt." *Transition* 73 (1998): 176–203.

————. "Race and Social Theory: Towards a Genealogical Materialist Analysis." In *The Year Left: An American Socialist Yearbook.* Vol. 2. Ed. Mike Davis et al. London: Verso, 1987.

"What Color Will Your Baby Be?" *Ebony*, May 1951, pp. 54–57.

White, Walter. *A Man Called White: The Autobiography of Walter White.* Bloomington: Indiana University Press, 1948.

White, W[illiam] L. *Lost Boundaries.* New York: Harcourt, Brace, 1948.

"White By Day . . . Negro By Night." *Ebony*, April 1952, p. 31.

"Why I Never Want to Pass." *Ebony*, June 1959, p. 49.

"Why 'Passing' Is Passing Out." *Jet*, July 17, 1952, pp. 12–16.

Wiegman, Robyn. *American Anatomies: Theorizing Race and Gender.* Durham, N.C.: Duke University Press, 1995.

————. "Fiedler and Sons." In *Race and the Subject of Masculinities.* Ed. Harry Stecopoulos and Michael Uebel. Durham, N.C.: Duke University Press, 1997.

————. Review of Michaels, *Our America. American Literature* 69, no. 2 (June 1977): 432–33.

Wilber, Bob, with Derek Webster. *Music Was Not Enough.* London: Macmillan, 1987.

Wilkins, David. "Introduction: The Context of Race." In *Color Conscious: The Political Morality of Race.* Ed. K. Anthony Appiah and Amy Gutmann. Princeton: Princeton University Press, 1996.

Williams, Gregory Howard. *Life on the Color Line: The True Story of a White Boy Who Discovered He Was Black.* New York: Dutton, 1995.

Williams, Patricia J. *The Alchemy of Race and Rights: Diary of a Law Professor.* Cambridge, Mass.: Harvard University Press, 1991.

Willis, Susan. *A Primer for Daily Life.* New York: Routledge, 1991.

Wimsat, William "Upski." *Bomb the Suburbs: Grafitti, Freight-Hopping, Race, and the Search for Hip Hop's Moral Center.* Rev. 2d ed. Chicago: Subway and Elevated Press, 1994.

Wolfe, Bernard. "Ecstatic in Blackface: The Negro as a Song-and-Dance Man." In *Really the Blues.* By Mezz Mezzrow. 1946. Reprint, New York: Citadel Underground, 1990.

———. "Uncle Remus and the Malevolent Rabbit." *Commentary* 8, no. 1 (July 1949): 31–41.

Woodward, C. Vann. *The Strange Career of Jim Crow*. New York: Oxford University Press, 1955.

Wright, Lawrence. "One Drop of Blood." *New Yorker*, July 35, 1994, 46–55.

Young, L. Masco. "Is Passing for White a Dying Fad?" *Color*, April 1957, pp. 46–49.

Zalewski, Daniel. "Cloning the Classics." *Lingua Franca* 7, no. 9 (November 1997): 27–29.

Gayle Wald is

Assistant Professor

of English at the

George Washington

University.

Library of Congress Cataloging-
in-Publication Data
Wald, Gayle Freda
Crossing the line : racial passing in
twentieth-century U.S. literature
and culture / Gayle Wald.
p.   cm. — (New Americanists)
Revision of the author's thesis (Ph. D)—
Princeton University, 1995.
Includes bibliographical references and index.
ISBN 0-8223-2479-2 (cloth : alk. paper)
— ISBN 0-8223-2515-2 (pbk. : alk. paper)
1. American prose literature—
20th century—History and criticism.
2. Passing (Identity)—United States—
History—20th century.
3. American prose literature—Afro-
American authors—History and criticism.
4. Passing (Identity) in literature.
5. Afro-Americans in literature.
6. Group identity in literature.
7. Race in literature.
I. Title.   II. Series.
PS366.P37 W35   2000
818'.509355—dc21   99-056662